# Believing

## REASON AND RELIGIOUS BELIEF

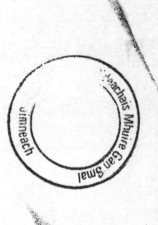

BY THE SAME AUTHOR

*The Nature of Moral Judgement*

# Believing in God

## REASON AND RELIGIOUS BELIEF

P.J. McGrath

MILLINGTON
in association with
WOLFHOUND PRESS

First published in Ireland 1995
by MILLINGTON BOOKS Ltd in association with
WOLFHOUND PRESS Ltd
68 Mountjoy Square
Dublin 1
Ireland

British Library Cataloguing-in-Publication Data
A catalogue record for this book is available from the British Library


ISBN 0 86327 510 9

Cover design: Slick Fish Design, Dublin. Cover photograph by Mike O'Toole
Typesetting & Origination by Wendy A. Cummins, The Curragh ?
Printing: Colour Books, Baldoyle Industrial Estate, Dublin

*For*
*K.P.C.*


οὐ μὲν γὰρ τοῦ γε κρεῖσσον καὶ ἄρειον
ἢ ὅθ᾽ ὁμοφρονέοντε νοήμασιν οἶκον ἔχητον
ανὴρ ἠδὲ γυνή· πολλ᾽ ἄλγεα δυσμενέεσσι,
χάρματα δ᾽ εὐμενετῃσι· μάλιστα δέ τ᾽ ἔκλυον αὐτοί.


*Odyssey*, VI, 182-5

# Acknowledgements

I am indebted to the following publishers and journals for permission to reprint copyright material: Gill and Macmillan, The Educational Company of Ireland, *The Irish Theological Quarterly*, *Philosophical Studies*, *The Furrow*, *Concilium*, *The Maynooth Review* and *The Philosophical Quarterly*. My thanks are due also to University College, Cork for a grant from its Arts Faculty Fund which covered part of the cost of publication. I am grateful to Dr Roddy Galvin and to my wife for their assistance with some of the medical details in the chapter on miracles. Ms Kathleen Murray of the Department of Philosophy, UCC gave me characteristically generous assistance in the preparation of the material for publication. Finally, I should like to thank the head of my department, Professor Brendan O'Mahony, for his support in good times and in bad. I have no doubt he would disagree with some of the opinions expressed here, but am equally certain that he would defend to the death my right to express them.

# Contents

The latter part of a wise man's life is taken up in curing the follies, prejudices and false opinions he had contracted in the former.

Jonathan Swift


Christmas Eve and twelve of the clock.
'Now they are all on their knees,'
An elder said as we sat in a flock
By the embers in hearthside ease.

We pictured the meek mild creatures where
They dwelt in their strawy pen,
Nor did it occur to one of us there
To doubt they were kneeling then.

So fair a fancy few would weave
In these years. Yet, I feel,
If someone said on Christmas Eve,
'Come; see the oxen kneel

'In the lonely barton by yonder coomb
Our childhood used to know,'
I should go with him in the gloom,
Hoping it might be so.

Thomas Hardy

# Introduction

This book contains a selection from the papers on the philosophy of religion which I wrote between 1969 and 1993. The first eight papers have already appeared in various books and journals. The final two, which between them contain almost half the entire text, are here published for the first time.

Twenty-four years is a significant part of one's life, so it is perhaps not wholly surprising that my religious beliefs have changed considerably during that period. Nevertheless there is comparatively little here that I would now wish to withdraw or amend. The first two essays are the furthest removed from my present outlook. In 'Faith and Reason' I try to defend the rationality of religious belief by arguing that the evidence in its favour is such that it can be properly appreciated only by one who already believes and in 'Believing in God' I argue that belief in God can be rational even though there is no satisfactory argument for God's existence. I now think that both these arguments are unsuccessful — the first for reasons that are given on pp 132-3, the second because it takes no account of the problem of evil, a topic that is discussed in detail in the final paper. But though both studies now appear to me to be defective, there are a number of reasons why I believe they are worth publishing in this collection. The first is that there is no philosophical issue so cut and dried that having a second opinion on it is pointless — even if both opinions come from the same person! The second is that the line of argument pursued in these two papers, though open to serious objection, still seems to me to represent the best way of defending the rationality of Christian and theistic belief. The third is that if these papers were omitted, the manner in which my thinking on religious issues has evolved between 1969 and 1992 would be seriously distorted.

The only other paper which I would wish to amend in any significant way is 'Reason and Authority'. This was written in the aftermath of *Humanae Vitae* and was an attempt to adjudicate between those who appealed simply to the authority of the Pope to show that contraception is immoral and those who put forward philosophical arguments to prove that the Pope's ruling was incorrect. I argued that there was a certain amount to be said for both points of view. I now think that this was a mistake. There is nothing to be said for an 'argument from authority' in morals, since there is no good reason for believing in a God-given authority to issue judgments on moral problems. The belief that there is such an authority needs to be supported by very strong evidence to be credible and, as we shall see in the essay on miracles, no evidence of any consequence is available. Furthermore, if we examine the history of those institutions which claim to have such authority, we find that their record on moral issues compares unfavourably with that of secular thinkers. Consider, for example, the moral teaching of the institution which makes the most emphatic claim to authority on moral questions — the Roman Catholic Church. The history of the Church's teaching on such topics as slavery, women's rights, justice in society, workers' rights, usury, freedom of expression, religious toleration, human sexuality, anti-semitism, colonialism and the treatment of animals amply demonstrates that this teaching emanated not from a divinely inspired institution, but from an all too fallible human one.

Two of the essays deal with the views of individual philosophers. Antony Flew is a prominent English philosopher whose book, *God and Philosophy*, is a trenchant, though perhaps unduly polemical, assault on all forms of theistic belief. One of the chief weapons employed in that assault is a principle which he calls the presumption of atheism or the Stratonician presumption. In 'Antony Flew and the Presumption of Atheism' I try to show that this weapon is ineffective and that Flew's use of it involves a considerable degree of confusion. Bernard Lonergan was a well known Jesuit philosopher and theologian who died in 1989. His book *Insight* was greeted enthusiastically by reviewers on its publication in 1957 and Lonergan became something of a cult figure in Catholic circles in the USA and Ireland. One reviewer, Professor E F O'Doherty, described it as 'one of the great philosophical treatises of the century' and compared it to Locke's *Essay* and Hume's *Inquiry*. Reasons for taking a less favourable view of Lonergan's importance as a thinker will be found in 'Knowledge, Understanding and Reality: Some Questions Concerning the Philosophy of Bernard Lonergan', where I argue that the basic tenet of Lonergan's thought is extremely vague and that any attempt to clarify it transforms it into something that is either trivial or palpably false. This paper is not directly concerned with issues in the philosophy of religion, but Lonergan's position in twentieth century Catholic thought would seem to warrant its inclusion in the present collection.

'The Concept of Infallibility' was written during the controversy that followed the publication of Hans Küng's book *Infallible? An Enquiry* in 1971. I contend that though Küng's basic argument against the doctrine of infallibility is unsound, the weakness of the case in favour of the Church's claim to possess infallibility renders the doctrine useless, since the exercise of infallibility could never produce certainty if the possession of infallibility is itself uncertain.

In 'The Catholic Church and Divorce' I argue that the Catholic stance on divorce is deeply inconsistent. The Church bases its position on Jesus' supposed absolute prohibition on divorce, yet it is prepared to permit divorce in certain circumstances. It teaches that marriage is intrinsically indissoluble, and at the same time claims the power to dissolve most of the marriages that take place throughout the world. And it rejects the right of the state to legislate for divorce while granting divorces itself.

'The Ontological Argument for God's Existence' is an examination of the most fascinating of all arguments in favour of theism. The ontological argument was devised by St Anselm in the eleventh century and it is still the subject of lively discussion to-day. Some may think it a topic that is of interest only to philosophers and that it has no relevance to religious belief. I believe that this is a mistake. The importance of the ontological argument for religious belief is that, if sound, it would outweigh the evidence against theism derived from the existence of evil in the universe, whereas if it is unsound, the evidence from evil would appear to outweigh whatever other evidence there may be for the existence of a theistic God. My conclusion is that there is no version of the ontological argument that possesses any probative force.

The final two studies have already been mentioned. 'Miracles' could be regarded as a critical response to a point once made by my New Testament teacher, Professor John O'Flynn. He wrote that 'the evidence for the miraculous in the life of Christ is just as good as the evidence for his historical existence and is inseparable from it; a radical distinction between the two could certainly not be justified on literary and historical grounds'.[1] What Fr Flynn seems to have overlooked is that a radical distinction between the two is justified on *logical* grounds, since the occurrence of a miracle is antecedently much more improbable than the historical existence of Jesus and therefore requires much stronger evidence in its favour if it is to be rationally acceptable. In 'Miracles' I defend the evidential use of miracles and consider a variety of miracle reports, including those contained in the New Testament, to see if any of them is supported by sufficient evidence to warrant acceptance.

'Evil and the Existence of God' is an examination of what is by far the most formidable obstacle to belief in a theistic God — the problem of evil. I examine there the various ways in which religious thinkers have attempted to dissolve or answer this problem and conclude that none of these attempts is successful.

All but one of these papers ought to be readily intelligible to readers with no training in philosophy. The exception is 'The Ontological Argument for God's Existence', which is more demanding technically than the others and, in one brief section, makes use of logical symbolism. However, this section may be skipped without losing the thread of the argument.

---

1  JA O'Flynn, 'The New Testament and Mythology', *The Irish Theological Quarterly*, Vol XXIII (1956), p 49.

Details of publication of the first eight studies are as follows. 'Faith and Reason' in *Faith: Its Nature and Meaning*, ed Paul Surlis, Dublin 1972, pp 133-49; 'Believing in God', *The Irish Theological Quarterly*, Vol XLV 1974, pp 87-96; 'Anthony Flew and the Presumption of Atheism' under the title 'Professor Flew and the Stratonician Presumption', *Philosophical Studies*, Vol XVIII 1969, pp 150-59; 'Knowledge, Understanding and Reality: Some Questions Concerning the Philosophy of Bernard Lonergan', *Looking at Lonergan's Method*, ed P Corcoran, Dublin 1974, pp 27-41; 'Reason and Authority', *The Furrow*, Vol 20 1969, pp 454-65; 'The Catholic Church and Divorce' under the title 'Marriage Annulments' in *The Maynooth Review*, Vol 1 1975, pp 45-51; 'The Concept of Infallibility', *Concilium*, Vol 3 1973, pp 65-76; 'The Ontological Argument for God's Existence' under the title 'The Refutation of the Ontological Argument', *The Philosophical Quarterly*, Vol 40 1990, pp 195-212. Section 11 of chapter 9 is due to appear in *The Irish Theological Quarterly* under the title 'John Stuart Mill and the Concept of a Miracle'. A small number of stylistic changes have been made in some of these papers; otherwise they are unchanged.

# 1 Faith and Reason

I

The relationship between faith and reason has been picturesquely described as follows: 'Faith and reason are two sisters who live together in the same house. Faith dwells on high, reason a little lower. But faith will never kill her sister; she will not betray the hospitality accorded to her to dwell alone.'[1]

I need hardly tell you that these are not the words of a contemporary writer. Who would take the trouble nowadays to assure reason that it is safe from attack? Today it is faith that feels threatened. But what the quotation effectively brings out is the character of the relationship between faith and reason as it was traditionally understood. There is the insistence, first of all, that there is no opposition between them. Faith and reason live peacefully together in the same house. It is true that on occasion they may appear to conflict, but this is always due to a misunderstanding concerning either the findings of reason or the content of faith.

Secondly, since faith lives on high, it needs the support of reason. There are certain things which are presupposed by faith — and which must be true therefore for the content of the faith to be true — but are not part of the faith and cannot be known by faith. What we believe by faith, we believe on the authority of God. But this presupposes that there is a God, who

---

1  Monsabre: quoted in *The Teaching of the Catholic Church*, ed GD Smith, London 1948, 12.

has spoken to man and whose word is to be trusted. So faith depends on reason to establish the existence of God, the fact of revelation and the reliability of God's word. These constitute the preamble of faith — the ladder which reason supplies to enable us to reach faith.

The third point is that while we need this ladder to ascend to the level of faith, we do not need it in order to remain there. We rely on reason to establish that there is a God who has spoken to man, but we then believe on the authority of God, not the authority of reason. The believer throws away the ladder, so to speak, once he has climbed it. The certainty of faith is not measured, therefore, by the certainty of the rational arguments which support it.

This, more or less, is how we were taught to understand the relationship between faith and reason when we were students studying theology. I cannot say that we accepted what we were taught unquestioningly. We raised problems about it and, no doubt, we were often dissatisfied with the answers given to them. But, looking back, I feel now that the questions we asked were the wrong ones. What concerned us was the ability of reason to do what faith required of it. We wondered if it were possible to prove God's existence. We knew that all sorts of difficulties could be urged against the traditional arguments and we were uneasily aware that modern philosophers were reluctant to believe that reason could tell us anything about God. We wondered, too, if the fact of revelation could be satisfactorily established. Had Hume's arguments against miracles ever been answered? The problems that concerned us were, in other words, philosophical ones — important problems and ones that should be raised by any student of theology. But in our concern with them we never got round to asking the essential theological question, the one which, if asked, would have enabled us to see the other problems in a very different light: was this the correct account of the relationship between faith and reason? Was faith as dependent on philosophical argument as we had been taught?

I call this the essential question because I believe that the answer to it is 'No'. The traditional account of the relationship between faith and reason is seriously defective. As a consequence our understanding of faith was distorted and needless difficulties were created for the believer. But before enlarging on the defects of the traditional approach it is only fair to add that there is also something to be said for it. It is clear for one thing. You may not agree with it, but unlike some modern treatments of the subject, you are never at a loss to know what you are disagreeing with. A more important virtue is its insistence that faith is reasonable. It almost certainly goes too far in this respect, for it makes faith too dependent on rational argument. But one must admire the insistence that faith is not an irrational leap and that one does not have to abandon reason in order to believe. Finally, I think it is correct in holding that there is a preamble of faith not in the sense of preliminaries to faith, as the word 'preamble' suggests, but in the sense of things presupposed by faith and which must be true, therefore, for the content of the faith to be true, but are yet outside the scope of faith. But this is not to say that the content of the preamble is as the traditional theory understood it to be.

What is wrong then with the traditional theory if there is so much to be said in its favour? It seems to me that there is a whole series of objections to be urged against it, but I will confine myself to what I regard as its most serious defects. The first objection may not seem very theological in character, but I believe it to be the most important of all. It is that the traditional account seems a long way removed from the faith of the ordinary believer. The majority of Christians know nothing about the preamble of faith. One might argue, of course, that the traditional theory takes account of this fact, for it does not say that the believer must be able to demonstrate the different elements of the preamble of faith for his faith to be reasonable, but only that human reason must have the capacity to do this. But this doesn't seem to make the case for the traditional theory any better. A belief is not reasonable merely because reasons exist for thinking it to be true. If I had believed before the Derby that Nijinsky was certain to win on the grounds that I had picked him out with a pin, my belief would have been wholly irrational even though very good reasons existed at the time for the belief that this horse would indeed win. The reasonableness of a belief clearly requires that the believer be aware of some good reason in its favour. Hence the faith of the average Christian cannot be made reasonable by arguments or reasons which he knows nothing about.

One might continue to defend the traditional position by saying — 'So much the worse then for the average believer. This only goes to show that his faith is imperfect.' But again this seems to me to be unrealistic. The function of the theologian is to explain the faith as he finds it, not as he would wish it to be. In any event, if we want a model of the Christian faith, we should look not to the theologians, but to the saints. How many of the apostles, for instance, knew anything of the proofs for God's existence or for the divine veracity? No doubt if put to it, they would have been able to formulate an argument to show that Christ was a divine emissary. But what seems certain is that this had little to do with their own belief in Christ as the Son of God. So it seems that the traditional theory explains the reasonableness of faith only at the expense of making the faith of the majority unreasonable. And this is sufficient to condemn it.

A second objection could be stated as follows: the traditional theory insisted that for faith to be reasonable, man must be capable of knowing that God exists by reason alone. This compelled the believer to consider the question of God's existence in isolation from revelation. So when Catholics asked themselves: does God really exist or is he merely a product of man's mind?, they inevitably assumed that the question could be answered only in terms of philosophical argument. This assumption was, I believe, both wrong and dangerous. Wrong, because if God has really spoken to man as we believe, then that is surely the best possible witness to his existence: what better evidence could you have for the existence of God than that he has revealed himself to man? And dangerous, because anyone who confines himself to the philosophical arguments for God's existence is not to be blamed too seriously if he ends up in atheism. If one considers the universe, its existence and the wonderful order which is present everywhere in it, it is easy to believe in a creator. But as soon as one tries to formulate an argument to show that there must be a creator to account for the existence or order of the universe, the whole thing seems to dissolve in doubts and ambiguities. I do not wish to suggest that the arguments for God's existence are devoid of all validity. But anyone who has spent some time studying them, is unlikely to regard them as very useful instruments for producing certainty about the existence of God.

But if you use revelation as a testimony to the existence of God, aren't you in danger of arguing in a circle? How could one know that a revelation had occurred without first knowing that there was a God who was capable of revealing himself? This is obviously a crucial question and I will try to deal with it more fully later on. All I wish to say for the moment is this: every argument for God's existence is based on a real or supposed revelation of God. For if the Christian God exists, the entire universe is a revelation of God to man, though not a revelation in precisely the same sense as the Bible. So in arguing to God, what one is endeavouring to do is to show that the universe or some aspect of it is genuinely revelatory. If it were true, therefore, that one could not identify a revelation as genuine without first knowing that God exists, one could never provide any reason for believing in God, for to try to do so would be to involve oneself in an infinite regress.

A third difficulty with the traditional approach is that the account which it gives of the relationship between reason and faith seems to make no sense. What it says is that the believer needs the help provided by reason to reach the level of faith, but once that level is reached, reason may be dispensed with. The believer then abstracts from the rational arguments that support faith and rests his faith entirely on the authority of God.

One cannot help feeling that the traditional approach is here trying to have it both ways. It is claiming that faith is reasonable and so requires the support of reason, but that any difficulties arising in the rational arguments that support faith do not take from its certainty. But how can faith be both dependent on and independent of reason at the same time? The answer to this difficulty is always given in the form of an image — that of an individual using a ladder to reach a new level and then throwing away the ladder once he has got there. But does this image fit the situation? Can the preamble of faith be dispensed with by the believer, given the role which the traditional theory assigns to it? To answer this question we must ask another: what is the precise character of the relationship between the preamble of faith and the content of faith? There are only two possible answers. The relation can be either logical or psychological. It is psychological if you need the preamble of faith in order to believe, but the truth of the faith is then independent of the truth of the preamble — just as Doubting Thomas needed to see the risen Christ to believe in the resurrection, but the truth of the resurrection is not in any way dependent on Thomas having seen the risen Lord. It is logical if the truth of faith is logically dependent on the truth of the preamble. An example would be the relationship between the truth of the resurrection and the truth of the proposition 'The dead body of Christ is no longer in the tomb.'

Now the relation between the preamble of faith and the content of faith cannot be merely psychological. We don't need a knowledge of the preamble in order to believe since a good many believers know nothing of it. The relation must therefore be logical in character. But this means that the truth of the faith is logically dependent on the truth of the preamble and anything which tends to undermine the validity of the preamble will tend to undermine the faith itself. The believer cannot, in other words, dispense with the preamble as soon as he reaches the level of faith, for if the traditional theory is correct, his faith remains always dependent on reason for support. The image which fits the situation, then, is not that of a climber throwing away the ladder once he has reached a new level, but that of someone sawing off the branch on which he is sitting.

We are now in a position to see the fundamental ambiguity in the traditional theory. When it insists on the necessity of the preamble for faith to be reasonable it is treating the relation between the two as logical. But when it claims that the believer can dispense with the preamble, it is treating it as merely psychological. And there is no way of resolving this inconsistency. If the traditional theory were to plump unreservedly for the logical character of the relationship, it would be destroying faith, or at least seriously distorting it, since the certainty of faith would then derive from reason rather than from God. Whereas if it were to decide that the relationship is not logical after all, it would be destroying itself, since the preamble would not then be necessary for faith in any sense.

## II

One could extend this list of objections, but perhaps it would be more useful if at this stage we adopted a different approach. Let us instead try to get some little way inside the mind of the people who put forward the traditional theory. How did a theory with so many defects exercise such a strong hold on Catholic thought for so long? As students why did it never occur to us to question its validity? The answer, I believe, is simple enough. The traditional account of the relationship between faith and reason was a consequence — I should say almost a necessary consequence — of the traditional understanding of revelation. Faith is man's response to divine revelation. Now revelation was traditionally understood as the communication of propositions and the result of revelation was a body of truth which had been communicated by God to man. Faith was therefore the acceptance of these truths by the individual. But how was the individual believer to know that these propositions were worthy of acceptance? The only possible answer is that he would have to show by rational argument that there is a God who has revealed these things to man. Once you accept the propositional view of revelation you are committed to the traditional theory of the relation between reason and faith. The only alternative is to say that faith is irrational, that it is simply the blind acceptance of certain propositions for which no justification can be provided.

As we all know this propositional view of revelation is now outmoded. The Second Vatican Council has taught us that revelation is God revealing and communicating himself to man, not communicating propositions merely. The primary purpose of revelation is to allow us to enter into a fellowship, a personal communion, with God, rather than to increase our store of information. This restoration by the Vatican Council of the biblical concept of revelation has enormous implications for theology and for the Christian life and it may be some time before we have fully appreciated all of them. But one implication seems obvious enough — it demands a rethinking of the nature of faith and particularly of the relationship between faith and reason. If faith is our response to God's revelation of himself, it makes no sense to say that we need to be able to prove God's existence for our faith to be reasonable. Why should we need to have God as the conclusion of an argument if by faith we are already in contact with him as a person? You don't need to prove the existence of someone you already know.

There is a well-known distinction in philosophy between knowledge by acquaintance and knowledge by description.[2] You have knowledge by acquaintance of someone if you are personally acquainted with him; you have knowledge by description alone if, though not personally acquainted, you are in possession of certain facts about him. Of course, knowledge by acquaintance includes knowledge by description, since one could not be personally acquainted with someone without knowing certain facts about him. The point I wish to make, however, is this: the most that philosophical argument can provide about God is knowledge by description. And this sort of knowledge is insufficient for faith if faith is directed towards the person of God rather than towards a set of propositions. And not merely is it insufficient, it is unnecessary since it is included in the knowledge of God given to us by faith. In other words, if faith really brings us into personal contact with God, we don't need the knowledge of God which is to be gained from rational argument. But if faith does not do this, then rational argument cannot make good that defect.

This distinction between knowledge by acquaintance and knowledge by description goes some distance towards ending the dispute between Catholic theologians and the followers of Karl Barth on our knowledge of God. When Barth says that 'God is always the One who has made himself known to man in his revelation, and not the one man thinks out for himself and describes as God',[3] what he says is perfectly acceptable if we understand him as referring to knowledge of God by acquaintance. And indeed that is what Barth must be referring to since he is concerned with the knowledge that saves, the knowledge

---

2 I am using this distinction not precisely in the sense in which it was used by Bertrand Russell, who introduced it to philosophy, but in the more colloquial sense explained by Jane Austen in chapter 21 of *Sense and Sensibility* where Lucy says 'I have not known you long, to be sure, personally at least, but I have known you and all your family by description a great while; and as soon as I saw you I felt almost as if you were an old acquaintance.'

3 *Dogmatics in Outline*, London 1949, 23.

of God that is essential to faith. When Barth's opponents, on the other hand, assert that there is also a natural knowledge of God apart from revelation, then again what they are asserting is true provided one understands it as referring only to knowledge of God by description. I am not suggesting, of course, that this distinction removes all the differences between Barthian and Catholic theologians on the question of our knowledge of God. But neglect of the distinction by both parties to the dispute has needlessly exaggerated the difference between them.

There is no question then of proving God's existence as a preliminary to faith. A proof is superfluous if faith does what it claims and puts us in personal contact with God, and it is inadequate if faith doesn't do this. Still less is it necessary to prove God's truthfulness. The demand for such a proof is in fact quite incompatible with faith. It is equivalent to saying 'I will not accept the reliability of God's word unless it can be proved to me that what he says is true.' To realise how far removed this is from the attitude of mutual trust that is demanded by faith one has only to visualise a husband or wife saying it about his or her partner. The demand for proof of reliability is an expression not of trust, but of the lack of it. And even if a satisfactory proof is forthcoming, all that has been established is the sort of relationship that exists between a bank and a client who has provided security for a loan — a relationship of trust, if you wish, but based not on personal trust, but on the realities of business. There is no need to emphasise how unlike this is to the response God expects of his people.

This brings us to the third item in the traditional preamble of faith — the fact of revelation. Is it necessary to establish the historical fact of revelation for our faith to be reasonable? This is a difficult and complex question and it would be easy to over-simplify it. A basic preliminary consideration is this: Christianity is a religion that is both historical and trans-historical in character. It is historical because it is centred on Christ, a man who lived at a particular time and place; and it is trans-historical because the Christ we believe in is not simply the man who once lived on earth, but the risen Christ who transcends space and time and who is present here and now in the Church. The historical character of Christianity, which is in many respects a guarantee of the validity of Christian beliefs, has now become a serious obstacle to faith for many people. It isn't merely the problem of establishing the historical facts — though that is problem enough — but that in an era of constant change like the present it is difficult to accept that what happened even fifty years ago has any relevance to the present age, never mind what happened at a distance of two thousand years. The Church has helped to accentuate this difficulty by clinging to the outward forms of the past. Until very recently, when one thought of the Church, the image that came to mind was that of a medieval building in which a man clad in garments from ancient Rome worshipped in a language that has not been used colloquially for nearly two thousand years. We can hardly be surprised if people sometimes treat Christianity as belonging more properly to the museum than to the market place.

There has been a tendency in recent times, particularly in modern Protestant theology, to respond to this problem by minimising the historical character of Christianity by saying 'What happened historically is unimportant, all that matters is our present faith.' But what happened historically clearly cannot be unimportant for Christianity, since the Incarnation is an event which occurred at a particular time and place or it is nothing. The proper response to the difficulty is not to minimise either the historical or the trans-historical character of Christianity, but to give full value to both. Now while at present the tendency may be to minimise the historical character of Christianity, in the past the reverse was the case. The traditional presentation of faith, by overemphasising the historical aspect of Christianity, neglected its trans-historical character. The revelation to which our faith was a response was, according to that presentation, the revelation that took place in biblical times. But if revelation ended two thousand years ago we are back with the propositional view of revelation. What has been revealed to us is not God himself, but certain truths about the revelation of himself to others. For God to reveal himself to us, revelation must be a present reality and it is to this present revelation that our faith is directed.

We don't need to prove the fact of revelation as a preliminary to faith, therefore, since in faith we are confronted with the fact of revelation and our faith is a response to it. For us the fact of revelation is Christ, but not someone seen dimly at a distance of two thousand years, whose life and teachings are laboriously reconstructed by biblical scholars and historians, but the Christ who is present here and now in the Church. Through faith we become contemporaries of Christ. For believers he is a figure from our own time rather than from the past. In Christ are summed up the three elements in the traditional preamble of faith — the existence of God, the truthfulness of God's word and the fact of revelation. Christ is God revealing himself to man — 'To have seen me is to have seen the Father' (*John* 14:9). He is God's Word, and we accept the truthfulness of that Word not by satisfying ourselves of the validity of a philosophical argument but by personal adherence to Christ in faith. And finally, as I have just said, he is the revelation to which our faith is a response. Once we realise that our faith is directed to the person of Christ rather than to a set of propositions, the superfluous character of the traditional preamble of faith becomes immediately apparent. To put it bluntly, it is a mental construction of doubtful validity designed to fulfil a non-existent need.

To say that our faith is a response to a present revelation is not, however, to imply that what happened in history is irrelevant to faith. The truth of Christianity depends on certain historical claims and Christianity would be refuted, therefore, if these claims were shown to be false. As believing Christians we cannot be indifferent to historical research. But this is not to say that our faith is based on the findings of historians. St Paul said to his disciples in Corinth: 'If Christ has not been raised, then our preaching is useless, and your believing it is useless' (1 *Cor.* 15:14). But he himself believed in the resurrection not primarily because he had satisfied himself of its genuine historical character, but because he had met the risen Christ on the road to Damascus. So as Christians we believe in the resurrection because through faith we meet Christ in today's world. We accept the empty tomb because we believe that the risen Christ is present here and now in the Church. This admittedly is not the only reason we accept it. If historical research can undermine the faith, then it follows that it can also corroborate it. And the testimony of history is no doubt an

important corroboration of faith, but it is not the basis of it.
The certainty of faith cannot be derived from the uncertainties
of history.

## III

There is still one important question to be asked about faith
and reason and I will devote the rest of this paper to an attempt
to answer it. The conception of faith that I have outlined leaves
faith self-sufficient so to speak. True, it is still linked to both
reason and history, in that reason or history could show it to be
false, but it does not absolutely require the positive support of
either of them. But how then can we know that our faith has
objective validity? If faith is a response to present revelation,
have we any assurance that revelation is a reality, that it isn't
simply an illusion on our part? How do we recognise this revelation? Is it a special experience which only believers possess?

In an area where there are many uncertainties one thing
can be stated with a fair degree of assurance: faith is not based
on a special experience. This is not to say, of course, that faith
may not involve special experiences, and there can be no doubt
that such experiences do occur in the lives of believers, bringing
home to them the reality of God in a new and more telling way.
But these cannot be the basis of faith. Of their nature they are
exceptional in character and fleeting in nature, whereas faith
must be based on something that is constant and is common to
all believers.

Perhaps the best way to answer our question is by turning
back once more to the apostles. What distinguished them from
the onlookers who refused to believe? Not any special experience.
Some of them did indeed have a special experience on Mount
Tabor, but this was not the basis of their faith. Generally speaking the apostles and disciples had precisely the same experiences
as those who saw Christ and did not believe. What distinguished
them was their way of experiencing, their way of looking at
what they saw. For while unbelievers looked at Jesus and saw
only a man who gave forth human doctrines, his disciples
looked at him and saw the Christ, the Son of the living God,
whose words were the words of eternal life. To have faith,
therefore, is to see things from a special and unique point of
view. St Thomas says somewhere that in faith we see with the

eye of God. To have faith is to see things as God sees them, but in a very imperfect way, of course: 'Now we are seeing a dim reflection in a mirror' (1 *Cor.* 13:12). The believer sees the universe not as unexplainable matter, but as a revelation of God, as a sacrament of God's presence. He sees the Bible not as an interesting historical document, but as the word of God. He sees the liturgy as making Christ present to the community of believers. He sees other people as making demands on him in the name of Christ. And he sees all these things as the revelation of God to man in the person of Jesus.

But having said all that, the same nagging question recurs: has this way of looking at things objective validity or is it merely a delusion? Is it reasonable to look on reality with the eye of faith? Our natural instinct when confronted with this question is to try to provide a justification of faith from outside of faith. This instinct has been reinforced by our theological training, for that is precisely the task which traditional apologetics set itself — to justify faith without presupposing faith. And the traditional preamble of faith was the result of its efforts.

Now I believe this instinct to be false and this effort to be misdirected. In the first place, it doesn't succeed. Of course, it doesn't completely fail either. You *can* make a case for the validity of faith without presupposing faith. But the response of an objective and uncommitted observer to this would be, 'Perhaps', or, 'Not improbable' — not the response that faith requires, which is, 'I believe, Lord, help my unbelief.'

However, the principal objection to traditional apologetics is not that it fails to make good its claim to establish the validity of faith, but that it argues with unbelief on the unbeliever's own terms. What the unbeliever says is that if Christianity is true, then it must be possible to state the case for Christianity in a way that is equally accessible to both the believer and the unbeliever. Traditional apologetics accepted this and the argument is put forward was consequently regarded as *the* case for Christianity. The validity of faith was held to stand or fall by the validity of the case made in apologetics.

This, I think, is quite wrong and in fact is seriously harmful to faith. The certainty of faith derives not from outside faith, but from faith itself. You cannot appreciate the case for the validity of faith unless you are already a believer. In saying this I am not myself presupposing the validity of faith. I am not saying that faith is such that the believer must be mistaken. What I am saying is that faith is such that the unbeliever cannot appreciate fully the case for Christianity. You cannot appreciate the reasons for accepting Christ as the Son of God unless you expose yourself to God's revelation of himself in Christ, and this means accepting the Christian faith.

But doesn't this mean that faith is circular, that you cannot appreciate the truth of the premises of the argument for faith unless you have first accepted the conclusion? The answer, I think, is 'Yes'. There is a circularity involved in faith in that what we regard as evidence for the validity of faith would not appear as evidence at all, or would appear as evidence only in a very dubious sense, unless we were already believers. We agree with the Psalmist that the heavens declare the glory of God and the firmament proclaims his handiwork, but we do so only because we already believe in God; if we didn't believe in God, the heavens would declare nothing but their own glory. Or take Newman's description of the phenomenon of conscience: 'If we feel responsibility, are ashamed, are frightened, it is because there is One to whom we are responsible, before whom we are ashamed, whose claims upon us we fear.'[4] If we didn't already believe in the existence of a God who is guardian of the moral order, we would look upon this interpretation of conscience as a delusion. Or take miracles. What better evidence could you have, one might say, for the validity of faith than the miracles which Christ performed or which have since occurred in the Church? But the trouble is that unless one already accepts faith in at least a minimal sense, these events won't appear as miracles. The unbeliever will either take the view that because of their inherently improbable character, it is highly unlikely that they ever occurred, or else the view that we don't yet know how to explain these events scientifically, but eventually we will be able to do so. We are inclined to say that the unbeliever is being unreasonable, that he is failing to face up to the facts. But he is being unreasonable only on our

---

4 *A Grammar of Assent*, London 1891, 109.

terms, not on his own. A miracle provides evidence for the validity of faith only if you interpret it religiously; and to describe it as a miracle is already to see it from the religious point of view.

Does this circularity mean that faith is irrational? If we are using the normally accepted idea of rationality, then the answer is 'Yes'. Western thought has taken its concept of rationality from Descartes, the father of rationalism, who explained rationality and defined rationalism in one sentence of his work, *A Discourse on Method,* where he laid it down as a rule for himself 'to hold nothing as true that cannot be clearly proved to me'. This innocent-looking rule has taken such a hold on men's minds that nowadays one could say almost that people are born as rationalists; it is part of the air we breathe. What we are inclined to forget is the history of rationalism. We overlook the fact that only a hundred years separate Descartes's *A Discourse on Method* from Hume's *A Treatise of Human Nature.* It took only a hundred years for Descartes's optimism about human reason to be transformed into the melancholy which Hume expresses at the end of Book I of his *Treatise* when he decides that nothing is certain.

During those hundred years men discovered that had Descartes applied his concept of rationality more consistently, then not merely would he have begun his philosophy with a universal doubt, but he would have ended it in the same way. For his idea of rationality is impossibly narrow. It is taken from mathematics and in mathematics it is, of course, true to say that you don't know something unless you can prove it. But mathematics bears little relation to other branches of knowledge. As Hume showed in his *Treatise,* Descartes' concept of rationality produces scepticism not merely about religious faith, but about knowledge in general. The circularity which we have discovered in faith is typical of every aspect of knowledge. Take sense knowledge; philosophers have devoted an enormous amount of energy to endeavouring to prove its objectivity, to showing that there is an external world which possesses the features that our senses reveal to us. And their effort has ended in almost total failure, a failure much more complete than the failure of apologetics to provide an external justification for Christianity. Now there is in fact no difficulty in presenting a case for the validity of sense knowledge. What could be better evidence for its validity than the fact that what our senses have presented us with hitherto has always, or almost always, been really there. But this, of course, presupposes the validity of our senses, for how could we know that what we saw was really there unless we already regarded our senses as reliable? And this circularity is only to be expected, since the certainty of sense perception derives from sense perception itself; it cannot be derived from outside. Or take scientific knowledge: it is now widely accepted that, despite its air of utter rationality, there is no way of providing a rational justification of scientific procedure. In every scientific argument there is an unstated premise on whose truth the validity of the argument depends — that the laws of nature which held good in the past will also hold good in the future. But there is no way of establishing the truth of this premise either within science or outside it. You can only take it on trust. But in another sense there is no difficulty in providing a justification for science. For what could be better evidence for its validity than the tremendous success of science in the past. However, this too involves us in circularity. The past success of science is evidence of its future success only if we assume that the future will be like the past; and this is to assume the validity of the scientific outlook, the very point at issue. Again this circularity is there because the certainty of science derives from science itself, not from outside. Or take ethics: is there any way of justifying ethics, of establishing that moral judgements are objective and not expressions merely of subjective likes and dislikes? The familiar answer is that this can be done only within ethics in the circular fashion I have outlined. If you try to provide an external justification, you inevitably get involved in the fallacy of deriving 'ought' from 'is'. The certainty attaching to moral judgements derives from ethics itself and not from outside.

This circularity which we find in every branch of human knowledge is not just an unexpected fact; it is something that couldn't be otherwise. To prove something is always to leave something else unproven, and our arguments, no matter how far back we push them, always presuppose something that we accept without argument, something whose certainty derives from itself and not from outside. Furthermore, if sense perception or science or ethics are unique and irreducible ways of looking at reality, it is only to be expected that they cannot be justified from outside; such a justification would imply that they were not unique after all, but were reducible to some more fundamental way of seeing reality. It is not surprising then if we find the same circularity in faith, since the eye of faith is certainly unique and irreducible to any other form of knowledge. This circularity is a token of its rationality rather than the reverse.

Well, is faith reasonable then? It is reasonable in the sense of not offending against the negative criteria of rationality, provided we take these criteria from human knowledge as it actually exists and not from some *a priori* model as Descartes did. But there is another more positive sense of rationality in which to say that faith is reasonable is to say that the evidence in its favour warrants the certainty that the believer feels about its validity. Is faith reasonable in that sense? This question I cannot answer for you, since it is a question each person has to answer for himself. Your answer to that question is what constitutes your faith or lack of it, and the decision to believe, like all the great decisions of life, is one that the individual, in the last analysis, must make alone.

# 2 Believing in God

It is a commonplace nowadays that Christians have become confused about their beliefs. This is nowhere more evident than on the question of our knowledge of God. Until recently the Catholic position on this matter was quite clear: belief in God was based on arguments which had withstood the test of time, notably the Five Ways of St Thomas. But the Five Ways have become the victims of what is now called a 'credibility gap'. There is widespread doubt among Catholics whether they provide any good reason for believing in God. If anyone remains unconvinced that such a change has taken place during the last twenty years, he should contrast the consternation which greeted Fernand Van Steenberghen's very mild criticisms of the Five Ways at the Third International Thomist Congress in Rome in 1950 (described in chapter eight of his book *Hidden God*) with the placid reception given to Anthony Kenny's much more devastating critique in his book *The Five Ways* when it appeared in 1969.

But if there is widespread agreement on the unacceptability of the Five Ways, there is little agreement on what should be put in their place. Do we need arguments for God's existence for our belief in God to be intellectually respectable? If we do, are there any good ones? Alternatively, if we don't, how is belief in God to be explained? Is it simply a blind leap as Kierkegaard maintained? These questions confront every believer today and it is difficult to feel certain as to the answers to be given to them.

It would be easy to deplore this situation and say that we have exchanged a position of certainty and clarity for one of uncertainty and confusion. This is indeed true, but it is only half the story. What is also true is that we need to rethink the question of belief in God — and without the stimulus of the present situation I doubt if we would ever get around to doing so. We need, first of all, to rethink the arguments. Nothing discredits a belief so much as putting forward bad arguments in its support and many of the traditional arguments for God's existence have little to be said for them. Secondly, and more importantly, we need to rethink the *relevance* of argument to belief in God. Most of us were brought up to believe that argument is all-important, that without a valid argument for God's existence belief in God would be little better than superstition. The oath against modernism implies that we are required by faith to believe that the existence of God is demonstrable.[1] Whatever about the importance of argument for belief in God, it seems to me that the extreme position of the anti-modernist oath is quite untenable. The insistence on proving God's existence is a feature not of Christianity as such, but of post-medieval Latin Christianity. As Pascal has pointed out, you can search the entire Bible without finding an argument for God's existence.[2] This would be extraordinary if argument was as necessary as the anti-modernist oath takes it to be. It is true that Christian tradition differs somewhat from the Bible in this matter, since you find arguments for God in Christian writers from quite early on, Augustine being the most notable example. But writers such as Augustine and Anselm did not think that belief in God is based upon or depends on the arguments they put forward. Their attitude to these arguments was somewhat similar to that of Francis Bacon who said that the 'purpose of natural theology is to confute atheism but not to inform religion'.[3] Augustine and Anselm formulated argu-

---

1  It is noteworthy that the Vatican I definition on which this part of the anti-modernist oath formula is based speaks only of human reason's natural capacity to *know* that God exists.

2  *Pensées* (Brunschvigg edition) 14, 243. 'C'est une chose admirable que jamais auteur cononique ne s'est servi de la nature pour prouver Dieu'.

3  Quoted in JH Newman, *The Idea of a University*, London 1884, 225. Newman himself adds that he 'has ever viewed natural theology with the greatest suspicion, for it was a most jejune study, considered as a science'.

ments to show the fool who says in his heart that there is no God that he is a fool.

The change came with the introduction of Aristotle's philosophy to the Western universities in the twelfth and thirteenth centuries. One of the principal features of Aristotle's philosophy is his empiricism. He believed that all our knowledge comes to us through the senses, that we have no other source of knowledge. The acceptance of empiricism in the Western universities caused the problem of God to be seen in a very different light. For God is not an object of sense experience. We do not see God as we see tables and chairs. So if all our knowledge comes through the senses, we could know that God exists only by deducing his existence from the data presented to us by the senses. God's existence ceased to be something which one proved merely to confound the atheist and became something which had to be proved for belief in God to be intellectually respectable.

To see the difference Aristotle made you need only contrast what St Thomas said about our knowledge of God with the views of his predecessors and of his contemporaries who were not Aristotelians. Here is St Bonaventure on our knowledge of God: 'God is mostly truly present to the very soul of man and by that very fact he is already knowable'.[4] St Thomas on the contrary says that 'the intellect depends on the senses for its knowledge; and so those things that do not fall under the senses cannot be grasped by the human intellect except in so far as knowledge of them is derived from sensible things ... So beginning with sensible things, our intellect arrives at a knowledge of God, namely that he exists and that certain characteristics are to be attributed to him'.[5] Again St Anselm says: 'I do not seek to understand in order to believe, but I believe so that I may understand'.[6] But St Thomas's position is that 'if we do not demonstrate that God exists, all consideration of divine things is necessarily suppressed'.[7]

The struggle between Aristotelianism and Augustinianism was not decided in St Thomas's lifetime. It lasted several cen-

---

4  *Quaestiones Disputatae de Mysterio Trinitatis* IX, I.
5  *Summa Contra Gentiles* 1, 3, 3.
6  *Proslogion* 1.
7  *Summa Contra Gentiles* 1, 9.

turies, but in the end the Augustinian approach to our knowledge of God was almost completely supplanted by the empiricism of Aristotle and survived in the Catholic tradition only in the work of isolated individuals such as Pascal and Newman. Looking back from our vantage point we are inclined to deplore this and to feel that the loss of the Augustinian tradition was a real impoverishment. At the same time we must be fair to Aquinas and the Aristotelians. They adopted the demonstrative approach to God not because they believed that it was more in accordance with the Christian faith, but because they believed that it was the only possible approach once you accepted the basic truth that all our knowledge comes to us through the senses. So if one is tempted to adopt the Augustinian approach, one must remember that it is a question not merely of different approaches to God, but of different theories of knowledge. What one would not be entitled to do, I think, would be to change one's theory of knowledge merely to leave room for a non-demonstrative knowledge of God. This sort of move would be permissible if we were dealing with a non-controversial aspect of human knowledge such as mathematics. But to adapt one's theory of knowledge so that it leaves room for a belief which many regard as without foundation, is like changing the rules in the middle of a game so as to avoid defeat. Hence if you abandon empiricism, you must provide a justification for your move in general philosophical terms, something which Augustine did but which would be difficult to do nowadays. It is not that empiricism is entirely satisfactory as a theory of knowledge, but that any alternative theory seems highly implausible.

## II

At any rate I have no intention of suggesting that empiricism be abandoned. Instead I wish to raise the question: Does acceptance of empiricism also involve the acceptance of Aquinas's view that God's existence must be demonstrable for belief in God to be reasonable? It is easy to see the logic of St Thomas's position. Once you grant that our knowledge is entirely derived from the senses, it seems to follow of necessity that every item of human knowledge falls into one or other of two categories: (a) facts revealed by the senses, and (b) facts derived by some form of reasoning from the facts revealed by the senses. The existence of God does not come into the first category, so it must come into the second.

St Thomas's model of human knowledge is based not on an examination of what we actually know, but on an idea of what must be the case if empiricism is correct. Here we are reminded of Wittgenstein's advice in the *Philosophical Investigations*: 'Don't say that something must be the case, but look and see if it is so in fact'.[8] Now if we look at human knowledge, we will see, I think, that there must be something wrong with St Thomas's model. If it were correct, we would be forced to conclude that we know almost nothing. The most basic human beliefs, those on which nearly all our other beliefs depend, do not fall into either of the categories I have mentioned. For example, the belief that our senses provide us with reliable information about the external world. There seems to be no way of establishing this despite the best efforts of philosophers and yet it is a belief on the truth of which a great many other beliefs depend. A second example is the belief that other people have minds just as we ourselves have. The only argument in favour of this belief involves an enormous generalisation which by all the laws of logic ought to be illicit. A third example is the belief that the physical laws of nature which have held good in the past will also hold good in the future. The validity of the physical sciences depends on the truth of this belief and yet any argument which has hitherto been put forward in its favour seems to beg the question. A fourth example is the belief that moral judgements are, in some sense of the word, objective. Not merely has this belief not been satisfactorily established, but so far as I can judge, it is in principle incapable of being established; and yet it is a belief on which the character of all our moral judgments depends. Without extending this list any further one can see that if we remove those beliefs which neither express facts revealed by the senses nor are derivable from facts revealed by the senses, the entire edifice of human knowledge would collapse.

What is wrong then with the empirical model of human knowledge? The answer, I believe, is that it is based on a myth

---

8 Cf *Philosophical Investigations*, trans. GEM Anscombe, Oxford 1953, paragraph 66.

— the myth of empirical facts. There are no facts which are immediately given to us by the senses, no facts which are conclusively verified by reference to sense-experience. Every assertion we make, however elementary, goes beyond what is given to us by the senses. Every description of experience transcends experience. The reason is that every assertion or description must include at least one universal term. Even if our description goes no further than to say that this is white, the term 'white' refers not to a quality which is given in experience (if it did, there would be no distinction between something seeming white and being white) but to a disposition to reflect white light so to look white in normal conditions of illumination. In calling something 'white', therefore, we are saying that the term exhibits a certain law-like behaviour characterised by the word 'white'; we are, in other words, implying a theory about the thing. What appears to be a bare fact which is immediately apparent in sense-experience turns out to be an interpretation of experience in the light of a theory. The same holds good of any description however basic or elementary. There is no such thing as a theory-neutral description, such as Husserl sought, since every description implies a theory. As Whewall, the nineteenth century philosopher of science put it, 'there is a mask of theory over the whole face of nature'.[9] The word 'mask' in Whewall's statement could, however, be misleading, since it seems to suggest that theory comes between us and nature and that if we could strip away the theory, we would see nature as it is in itself. This would be true of a false theory or of a false interpretation, but not every theory is false and not every interpretation a misinterpretation. When we theorise, we are not necessarily imposing something on reality; rather we are trying to understand reality. To strip away the theory, therefore, would not be to leave us face to face with reality, but to deprive us of all understanding.

The theories we use in understanding reality are not, of course, taken on trust. Every fact is understood in the light of a theory, but the truth of this theory can be assessed with reference to other facts. However, this process cannot go on indefinitely. The facts with reference to which you assess your

9   *The Philosophy of the Inductive Sciences*, London 1847, Book II, Chapter 2, paragraph 9.

original theory are themselves understood in the light of other theories which must themselves be assessed. But you must eventually arrive at a theory or theories whose truth cannot be established with reference to other facts, just as when you define a term and then define the terms of the definition, you eventually arrive at terms which are indefinable. It might seem that while you must eventually come to a stop in both processes, where you stop is a matter of choice rather than of necessity — while you must leave some terms undefined and some theories unproven, that does not mean that these terms are indefinable and these theories unprovable. But this, I think, is incorrect. For if you define a term, and then define the terms of the definition, and then the terms of the second-order definitions, you eventually come to terms which cannot be defined, which appear too basic to admit of definition. And the same is true at the level of theory. If you attempt to establish a fact and the theory it implies with reference to other facts and other theories, you eventually come to theories which cannot be established, which are too fundamental to admit of being confirmed by reference to further facts. I have already given some examples of these — the theory that our senses are reliable sources of information, that other people have minds, that the future will be like the past, that human actions are objectively right or wrong. These theories function as conceptual frameworks within which less general theories can be confirmed or falsified, but they are not themselves open to confirmation. To put this in terms of experience rather than of theory, these are fundamental modes of human experience, fundamental ways of seeing reality. This is perhaps a better way of putting it, since apart from philosophical reflection, we never advert to these beliefs; normally we are not even conscious of possessing them. To accept the reliability of the senses is to see sensible reality as objective; to accept the existence of other minds is to see other people as centres of consciousness and not merely as automata; to accept that the future will be like the past is to see the physical universe as a system governed by unvarying natural laws; to accept the objectivity of morals is to see others as persons with rights which demand our respect.

One might be tempted to reply to this by saying that even fundamental beliefs or modes of experience must have reasons in their favour since otherwise acceptance of them would be irrational. In fact, however, it is the demand for a further reason that is irrational. You cannot justify a belief or mode of experience in a vacuum, so to speak; you can justify it only by means of a conceptual framework which itself involves some more fundamental belief or mode of experience. To justify anything, therefore, means leaving something else unjustified. This is simply a matter of logic. To find it unsatisfactory is no more rational than to say that the principal of non-contradiction places an intolerable restriction on which can be expressed in words.

What is perhaps controversial in what I have been saying is the suggestion that there is a multiplicity of fundamental modes of experience or ways of seeing reality, and that these are irreducible; that they cannot all be derived, in other words, from one absolutely basic mode of experience. Now this is quite contrary to the usual empiricist outlook which looks on observation as the basic source of knowledge and demands that all our other beliefs be derivable by reasoning from the data presented by the senses. You find the clearest expression of this in Hume, but Hume's views on this question were not at all peculiar to himself; they would have been shared by almost all the classical empiricist philosophers, including St Thomas Aquinas. Hume's remarks are as follows: 'If I ask you why you believe any particular matter of fact, which you relate, you must tell me some reason; and this reason will be some other fact connected with it. But you cannot proceed after this manner, *in infinitum*; you must last terminate in some fact, which is present to your memory or sense; or must allow that your belief is entirely without foundation'.[10]

Apart from the empiricist belief in the primacy of sense knowledge, there are, it seems to me, two other factors involved in producing this sort of outlook. The first is respect for intellectual tidiness, the attitude that the simplest or tidiest explanation is to be preferred; and it is, of course, tidier to believe in one absolutely fundamental way of looking at reality than in many. The second factor is the belief that what is immediately given to us in sense-experience is absolutely

---

10 *An Enquiry Concerning Human Understanding* Section 5, Part I (Selby-Bigge's edition, p 46).

certain and that observation therefore provides us with a copper-bottom foundation for human knowledge in general. Neither of these factors is capable of standing up to examination. In the first place, tidiness as a virtue has its limitations. There is little point in your explanation being tidy if it is also inadequate. That the classical empiricist theory of human knowledge is inadequate is clear from the history of philosophy. Those who consistently try to put it into practice invariably end up as sceptics, like Hume, and conclude that the greater part of human knowledge is without foundation, or as reductionists, like Russell and Ayer, and treat every meaningful assertion as a statement about sense-data or mental states. As theories of knowledge scepticism and reductionism are both entirely inadequate — scepticism because it cannot account for human knowledge, reductionism because it systematically distorts it. As to the certainty of what is immediately given in sense experience — a fact of observation is not necessarily more certain than any other since, as we have seen already, it involves an interpretation of reality in terms of a theory which must itself be established with reference to other facts and other theories. We may conclude then that we have every reason for treating these fundamental modes of experience as irreducible and no reason at all for trying to reduce them all to one.

What I have been saying up to now could be summarised as follows: There are a number of different modes of experience or different ways of seeing reality. These are fundamental and irreducible in the sense that while they provide the basis for all our beliefs, they are not themselves derivable from other beliefs, nor can they be reduced to one absolutely basic mode of experience. It follows from this that they are also unjustifiable — not in the sense that they cannot be criticised; one can consider objections to them and if these turn out to be well-founded, one can reject the mode of experience in question — but in the sense that one cannot provide a positive justification for them. This is only another way of saying that they are fundamental and irreducible. Finally, and this is something I haven't mentioned already, these modes of experience are natural in the sense that we have a strong natural instinct to see reality in these different ways. No matter how strong a set of reasons we have for thinking that a particular way of seeing reality is invalid, this instinct is nearly always too strong for us. There have been many who have been idealists or behaviourists in the abstract, but in practice it is nearly impossible to be other than a realist and a believer in minds.

### III

What I now wish to suggest is that the religious outlook is just such a fundamental way of seeing reality and that it possesses the characteristics I have attributed to every fundamental mode of human experience, namely that it is fundamental and irreducible, that it is unjustifiable and finally that it is natural. To be religious or to accept a religion is to see the world from a unique viewpoint, to interpret one's experience in a unique way. One of the problems here is the difficulty of giving an account of just what the religious viewpoint is. There has never been a satisfactory definition of religion and apparently there never will be because there is no element common to all religions. No matter how you frame your definition, no matter how you describe the religious outlook, some religions will be left out in the cold. But this is really a problem about our understanding of universal terms rather than a problem about religion. For the objects to which a universal term is applicable do not normally possess a common characteristic or set of characteristics; rather they are linked by what Wittgenstein called family resemblances. In other words, the term is understood by reference to a set of characteristics none of which is possessed by all the members of the class of things to which the term is applicable, but every member of the class possesses at least one of them. And this is how the religious outlook is to be understood. One can characterise it by reference to a set of beliefs about God, man and the universe which are shared by nearly all the great religions — that there is a Supreme Being, that the universe was created by him and that everything which exists is therefore to be treated with respect, that the human person is sacred and inviolable, that man survives death, that his status in the afterlife depends on how he has comported himself in this world, that one can address God in prayer and in acts of worship — but there is always the proviso that none of these is absolutely essential and that the absence of some or perhaps even all of them would not imply that an outlook was non-religious.

Now if the religious outlook is in fact a fundamental mode of experience, then the demand for a justification of that outlook from outside of religion is misplaced. Those who make that demand and say that without such justification religion must be rejected are being selective. If they were to make the same demand of every fundamental mode of experience, they would end in complete scepticism. To say this is not, of course, to say that the religious outlook is valid, but it is to say that absence of an external justification for the religious outlook is not a reason for regarding it as invalid.

But surely, you may say, there is a great deal of evidence for the validity of the religious outlook. Cannot one point to the existence and character of the universe, to revelation and miracles, to religious experience and the phenomena of conscience? Doesn't this constitute a solid body of evidence which it is impossible to overlook? This is true in a sense, but the point I am making is that a great deal of what we regard as evidence for the validity of the religious outlook would not appear as evidence at all unless we already accepted that outlook. We agree with the psalmist that the heavens declare the glory of God and the firmament proclaims his handiwork, but we do so only because we already believe in God; if we didn't believe in God, the heavens would declare nothing but their own glory. Or take Newman's description of the phenomena of conscience: 'If we feel responsibility, are ashamed, are frightened, it is because there is One to whom we are responsible, before whom we are ashamed, whose claims upon us we fear'.[11] If we didn't already believe in the existence of a God who is the guardian of the moral order, we would look upon this interpretation of conscience as a delusion. Or take miracles. What better evidence could you have, one might say, for the validity of the religious outlook than the occurrence of miracles? But the trouble is that unless one already accepts the religious outlook, unless one already has faith in at least a minimal sense, these events won't appear as miracles. The person without faith will either

---

11 *A Grammar of Assent*, London 1891, 109.

take the view that because of their inherently improbable
character, it is highly unlikely that they ever occurred or else
the view that we don't yet know how to explain these events
scientifically, but eventually we will be able to do so. A miracle
provides evidence for the religious outlook only if you interpret
it religiously; and to describe it as a miracle is already to see it
from a religious point of view.

Now there is nothing odd about all this nor does it tell
against the validity of the religious outlook. The other
fundamental modes of experience are confronted with precisely
the same problem. There is no shortage of evidence for their
validity, but this counts as evidence only if one already accepts
them as valid. What could be better evidence for the validity of
the scientific outlook, for example, than the tremendous success
of science? But to say that science has been successful is to say
simply that the scientific method has worked well hitherto,
and this is evidence for the future success of science only if we
assume that the future will be like the past, which is to assume
the validity of the scientific outlook — the very point at issue.
Or what could be better evidence for the validity of sense
knowledge than the fact that what our senses have presented
us with hitherto has always, or almost always, been really
there? But this, of course, presupposes the validity of sense
knowledge, for how could we know that what we say was really
there unless we already regarded our senses as reliable. Or
again what could be better evidence for the existence of other
minds than the fact that people talk and smile and display
emotion? But here too you have the same difficulty, for this is
evidence for the existence of other minds only if one assumes
that certain physical occurrences are signs of mental
occurrences, which is, of course, the point at issue. You have
the same difficulty which I mentioned earlier in connection
with miracles — that the evidence you are putting forward will
count as evidence only if the theory for which it is supposed to
be evidence is written into your description of it. Thus when
you describe someone as talking or smiling or showing anger,
your belief that he has a mind is written into your description
of his behaviour. If you were to leave that element out of your
description and describe a smile, say, in a purely impersonal
way as a movement of the lips revealing the teeth, then it is no

longer evidence for anything but itself. So your argument either never gets off the ground or it becomes circular.

And this is typical of any attempt to justify a fundamental mode of experience. Philosophers have often tried to break through the circle. Descartes, for example, tried to prove the validity of sense-experience by arguing from the divine veracity. John Stuart Mill tried to prove the existence of other minds by arguing from analogy. There have been many attempts in recent times to solve the problem of induction — to provide a justification, in other words, for the scientific outlook; and, as we all know, there have been many attempts to justify the religious outlook by arguing to the existence of God. Nearly all these attempts are commonly regarded as failures, and one might go beyond this and say that not merely did they fail in fact, but they couldn't have succeeded because the project in each case was misconceived. It was misconceived for two reasons. Firstly, since the fundamental modes of experience are irreducible, they cannot be derived from other modes of experience and therefore they cannot be justified with reference to other modes of experience. Secondly, the justification would in any case be pointless, since it would be based on some other mode of experience which is itself unjustifiable. Clearly there is little point in justifying a mode of experience by reference to another mode which is as much in need of justification as the first.

I would agree with this for the most part, but I think it is necessary to add a few qualifications. The first is that it would be pointless to justify a mode of experience by reference to another if these modes were on a level; and it is not clear that they are. If what I have been saying is true, then they are on the same level logically and epistemologically, but they are not on the same psychological level. Hardly anyone doubts the reliability of his senses or the existence of other minds, but nearly everyone has had doubts about the validity of the religious outlook at some time or another. Some would argue that this psychological difference indicates that there is also an epistemological difference, that the religious outlook is not merely easier to doubt, but is also, objectively speaking, more doubtful. It seems to me, however, that this psychological difference is due more to practical than to epistemological considerations. One cannot sustain a doubt about the validity of the senses or the existence of other minds for any length of time because the demands of practical life force one to put aside such doubts. But the theoretical difficulties which confront a believer in the external world or in other minds are hardly less numerous or less serious than those which confront a believer in God. Whatever about this, the psychological difference alone would warrant the attempt to justify the religious outlook from outside.

The second qualification is that while it is impossible adequately to justify a fundamental mode of experience, this would not rule out the possibility of providing a partial justification by reference to some other mode of experience. That science has worked in the past, for example, probably provides a partial, though inadequate, justification for the scientific outlook; the argument from analogy provides a partial justification for belief in other minds. So there is still room, I believe, for arguments to God's existence. But these should be construed not as providing a complete justification for the religious outlook — not as proving the God of Abraham and Isaac – but rather as providing some evidence for its validity, as showing that there must be something more to existence than the material world.

# 3 Antony Flew and the Presumption of Atheism

## I

In his book, *God and Philosophy*[1] Professor Antony Flew uses as one of his main weapons against arguments for God's existence a principle which he calls the Stratonician Presumption. This principle, he explains, was first formulated by Strato, second successor to Aristotle as head of the Lyceum. Flew's own formulation is as follows:

> The presumption, defeasible of course by adverse argument, must be that all qualities observed in things are qualities belonging by natural right to these things themselves; and hence that whatever characteristics we think ourselves able to discern in the universe as a whole are the underivative characteristics of the universe itself (3.20).

The presumption then concerns 'all qualities observed in things' and from it we can infer a further presumption about the universe as a whole. Is this a valid procedure? Are we entitled to infer something, whether fact or presumption, about the universe as a whole on the grounds that it is true of all the things which go to make up the universe? It depends obviously on what is being attributed to the universe and to the things which constitute it. If all the bricks in a wall are red, it follows that the wall itself is red, but if the bricks are all three inches

---

1  London: Hutchinson, 1966.

45

long, it doesn't follow that the wall is merely three inches in length. Similarly, if everything in the universe is material, it follows as a consequence that the universe is itself material, but if everything in the universe is finite in extent, it doesn't necessarily follow that the universe is finite. The validity of Flew's reasoning depends, therefore, on the attribute which the Stratonician presumption assigns to things in general. The odd thing, however, is that in the sentence quoted above this attribute is described in two quite different ways. The qualities observed in things in general are presumed to belong to them 'by natural right', but the characteristics we discover in the universe as a whole are presumed to be 'underivative'. Are we to take it that if something belongs by natural right, it follows that it is underived? This is not how we normally use these expressions. We are commonly said to have a natural right to life even though our life has been derived from our parents and a natural right to liberty even though a person rescued from slavery or imprisonment has had his liberty bestowed on him by another. Flew may possibly have been misled into thinking that what is possessed by natural right is necessarily underived, by the fact that a natural right is, in the usual sense of the term, a *right* which is underived. But what we are concerned with here are the qualities possessed by natural right and not the rights themselves.

At any rate, however we may account for his misuse of language, Flew must have been under the impression when formulating the presumption that part at least of what we mean when we say that something belongs by natural right is that it is underived. His position then is that since the qualities belonging to things in general are presumed to be underived, the qualities of the universe as a whole must be presumed to be underived. This *looks* like a valid inference but we need not enter here into the question of its validity, since there is a more fundamental question to be answered first: since we are concerned with the qualities observed in things in general, why must we be content with a mere presumption? Can we not decide whether the qualities observed in things are in fact derived or not? One cannot however attempt to transform the presumption into an established fact without realising immediately that the thing cannot be done — not because there is insufficient evidence to show that the presumption is true, but because there is an abundance of evidence to show that it is false. This point hardly needs elaboration. One has only to consider for a moment the qualities found in (a) human artefacts, (b) living beings and (c) inanimate objects to realise that Flew's presumption is almost entirely false of class (a), largely false of class (b) and partly false of class (c). So obvious is all this that it suggests that we have misinterpreted Flew. But if the presumption doesn't mean what it says, what are we to suppose it to mean? I can offer one suggestion. What Flew intended to say is that the qualities we observe in things must be presumed not to be derived from outside of nature, that is, are not conferred on them by a supra-mundane agent; and hence that the qualities possessed by the universe as a whole are not derived from the activity of a supernatural being. Admittedly if this is what Flew intended to say he chose an extraordinary means of expressing it, but as interpretation it possesses the following virtues: It transforms the presumption into something which is not obviously false. Secondly, it transforms it into a genuine presumption and not something whose truth or falsity could fairly easily be determined. Lastly, it provides a further explanation, though hardly a justification, of why Flew chose to use the expression 'belonging by natural right' as a partial synonym for 'underivative'.

But though this interpretation makes sense of Flew's position, it does not free him from difficulty. What we now understand him to be saying is that since the qualities we observe in things in general are presumed to have a natural origin, the same is to be presumed of the qualities possessed by the universe as a whole. But this sort of reasoning will not stand up to careful scrutiny. If all the parts of a complex whole are understood to have a common origin, whatever that origin may be, one cannot presume something about the origin of its parts without thereby presuming something about the origin of the whole. Hence one is not *entitled* to presume something about the origin of the parts unless one is already entitled to make a similar presumption about the origin of the whole. There can be no question therefore of deriving the presumption concerning the whole from the presumption concerning the parts, since the second presumption is not justified unless the first is; and hence the first cannot derive its justification from the second. To state this in concrete terms: One cannot presume that the universe as a whole (or its qualities) do not owe their existence to a creator on the grounds that the parts of the universe with which we are best acquainted (or their qualities) are presumed to be uncreated, since one is justified in accepting the presumption concerning the parts only if one is already justified in accepting the presumption concerning the whole; hence the presumption concerning the entire universe is justified independently of the presumption concerning its parts or it is not justified at all.

One can, of course, reply to this objection by saying that one does not have to accept that the entire universe had a common origin: one can always envisage the possibility that part of the universe owes its existence to a creator while the rest exists independently. It follows that in presuming something concerning the origin of part of the universe one is not thereby presuming something concerning the origin of the whole, so that one may be entitled to make the first presumption without necessarily being entitled to make the second. This indeed is correct but it provides no comfort for Professor Flew, for Flew's own argument requires the supposition that the entire universe had a common origin. If we take the contrary proposition seriously, then the presumption concerning the part of the universe with which we are best acquainted — an infinitesimal part of the whole — provides no justification for a similar presumption concerning the entire universe. So the upshot is that since Flew cannot have it both ways, he cannot have it either way. If he accepts the commonly accepted and, I suppose, reasonable supposition that the universe was either created or designed in its entirety or not at all, then his argument begs the question: if he rejects this supposition then his argument is so weak as to be of no account.

In saying this we are not, of course, ruling out the possibility of arguing to some truth or presumption about the universe as a whole on the basis of what is true or presumed of the things which go to make up the universe. What we are saying merely is that one cannot presume something concerning the universe as a whole on the basis of a presumption concerning the things which go to make it up, if the second presumption presupposes the first. But there are many things which can be asserted or presumed of part of the universe without thereby presuming them of the universe as a whole.

Flew's argument fails, therefore, but this does not rule out the possibility that his presumption about the universe may be justified without it. Are we in fact entitled to presume that the characteristics possessed by the universe as a whole have all a natural origin? The answer to this must be 'No'. What we are considering may well be true, but we are not entitled to presume it without argument. To presume it is to presume that the God of theism does not exist; and the presumption that he does not exist is surely as unwarranted as the presumption that he does. The presumption moreover implies that all arguments from the world to God are unsuccessful. Flew would no doubt point out that the presumption does not prejudge the issue, since if an argument for God's existence should turn out to be free from defect, the presumption would have been overthrown. But this does not remove the air of irrationality which surrounds his position. For if the presumption is to be used to defeat these arguments, then all arguments from the world to God are rendered impossible by definition; the arguments have been refuted by the presumption that their conclusion is false, and there is, of course, no argument which is not open to this sort of 'refutation'. But if the presumption is not so used, then what is the point of formulating it in the first place?

## II

As we might anticipate, however, Flew's practice in this matter is somewhat better than his theory. He does not sweep aside the arguments for theism by simply presuming the falsity of their conclusion. Instead he brings forward three further justifications for the Stratonician presumption in an attempt to show that the argument from order is based on a premise which cannot be known to be true and must be presumed to be false. The version of the argument which he examines is that put forward by Aquinas in the *Summa Contra Gentiles*.[2] There

---

2 The quotation which Flew examines is taken from the section where Aquinas is attempting to prove, not the existence of God (he has already done this), but his uniqueness. Flew does not mention this nor does he indicate that at two points in the quotation a sentence has been omitted.

Aquinas asserts of the elements which make up the universe that 'of themselves they are diverse and exhibit no tendency to form a pattern'. But, Flew counters, how could Aquinas possibly know this:

> To know what tendencies they possessed 'in themselves', as opposed to knowing what they do and will under various universal conditions, you would presumably have to study them: either separated from the universe, which is manifestly senseless: and/or without any Divine control, which is a notion which the theist himself would want to rule out (3.25).

The point Flew seems to be making here in a rather roundabout way is that one of the premises of the argument from order cannot be known to be true if the conclusion is true; for if the universe is in fact subject to divine control, we have no means of knowing what it would be like if left to its own devices. Flew describes this objection as one of those with which Hume 'devastated' the argument from order in Section XI of his *Enquiry Concerning Human Understanding*. A more detached disciple of the master might perhaps have recognised that far from devastating the argument, this criticism does not even get to grips with it. The proponent of the argument bases his case, not on what the universe would be like if divorced from divine control, but on what it is like here and now. And he is enabled to this by the fact, unnoticed by Flew, that order admits of degrees. The universe is indeed naturally ordered, but this does not mean that it is ordered to the maximum extent or that the amount of order it contains is incapable of being increased. This planet, as we all know, contains a great deal of order which cannot be explained by the operation of the laws of nature alone. And it is this that provides the basis for the conclusion which the theist reaches concerning the origin of the natural order of the universe.

To see the precise import of Flew's objection let us imagine for a moment a universe in which everything is naturally red — not merely on the surface, but through and through so that there is no other colour to be seen. And let us suppose further that an inhabitant of this universe argues to God's existence on the grounds that the stuff of the universe of itself has no tendency to redness and hence that its colour can be explained only by postulating the existence of a creator. Now *this* argument would be open to Flew's objection. Since every element of the universe is red by nature, the proponent of the argument for the existence of a creator can provide no evidence for his contention that the presence of red in anything can be explained only by positing a supra-mundane agent as its cause. Indeed in asserting this he is presupposing the point at issue, since his premise would not be true unless his conclusion were true. But the proponent of the argument from order is in a quite different position. He can argue that whenever we discover order in the world which is not due solely to the operation of natural laws, we invariably find that it has been brought about by the activity of an intelligent being; one may conclude, therefore, that the natural order of the universe is also due to a being endowed with intelligence. There are no doubt serious difficulties in this argument, though whether these can be successfully overcome is a question which need not detain us here. What we may legitimately conclude is that Flew's criticism goes no distance towards showing the argument to be ineffective.

### III

Flew's next effort to justify the Stratonician presumption is based on a very similar form of reasoning. He is again arguing from the uniqueness of the universe, but his claim this time is that its uniqueness rules out the possibility of knowing not only what it is like 'in itself', but also what is probable or improbable concerning it.

> It is put that it must be immeasurably improbable that there could be so much order without Design.... But we, alerted to the context by that capital, ask: 'How does he know what is probable or improbable about universes?' For his question, like the earlier overweening assertion about the tendencies which things possess or lack 'of themselves', presupposes that he knows something which not merely does he not know, but which neither he nor anyone else conceivably could know. No one could acquire an experience of universes to give him the necessary basis for this sort of judgment of probability or improbability; for the decisive reason that there could not be universes to have experience of (3.29).

This argument has several odd features. In the first place it seems quite incompatible with the argument put forward by Flew in his initial formulation of the Stratonician presumption. There he inferred a presumption concerning the entire universe on the basis of what could be presumed of the things which make it up. But if this is permissible, why cannot one argue from what is probable of the things which make up the universe to what is probable of the universe in its entirety? The fact that we are speaking in one case of a presumption and in the other of a probability will not affect the validity of the reasoning.

A second peculiarity about this argument is that it runs counter to the well known fact that scientists are constantly making assertions about what is probable or improbable of the universe. It is probable that the universe as we know it began with the explosion of the primeval atom, that the same physical laws apply throughout the universe, etc. Flew can scarcely believe that these statements cannot conceivably be known to be true; but if not, how does he propose to reconcile them with his argument?

This last point suggests that something has gone wrong with the argument, so let us take a closer look at it to see if we can spot the defect. Its central contention seems to be that to know what is probable of a class of objects we need to be acquainted with several members of the class, since if we are acquainted with only one, then we have no means of knowing which of its characteristics are peculiar to itself and which typical of the class to which it belongs. The reasoning here seems plausible; the only difficulty is that it has nothing to do with the argument from order. For what that argument concludes to is not something which is probable of universes in general, but the probable explanation of a feature of this particular universe. And a knowledge of several universes is not only not required to reach this conclusion, it would not be even mildly helpful. For suppose we did have a knowledge of other universes. How would this help us to settle the point at issue? If these other universes also exhibited order, the argument for a designer would not be any the stronger, since the crux of the argument is not the amount of order in the universe but whether natural order is ever sufficient to prove a designer. And if the other universes did not exhibit order, this would not make it any less likely that our own ordered universe had been designed.

Flew may have been misled into thinking that the argument from order requires a knowledge of other universes by the fact that it seems to imply something about all possible universes — namely, that if they are ordered, then it follows that they have been designed. But this implication refers only incidentally to universes; it is really a statement about things in general. What it says is that if anything displays order, then it is likely to have been designed; universes come into it only because they are capable of being ordered.

And this point should also make it clear how we are enabled to arrive at judgments of probability about the universe even though it is unique. For while the universe is unique as a universe, it is not unique in many other respects. It is the only member of the class of universes, but not the only member of the class of things which are subject to change, or which are extended, or which exhibit order in their make-up. So there is nothing to prevent us arriving at a judgment of probability about, say, things which change and then applying this to the universe as a whole. This application *may be* improper since the universe is unique in certain respects and therefore might possess some characteristic which other changing realities lack or lack something which they possess. But this risk is present in every application of a general principle to an individual case, since there is no member of a class which is not unique in some respect. There is therefore no warrant for saying that the uniqueness of the universe rules out from the very beginning the possibility of applying a general principle to it.

## IV

Flew makes one more effort to justify the Stratonician presumption. The argument from order, he claims, illustrates a fallacious form of reasoning to which he gives the picturesque title 'My-best-friend-is-a-Jew-but Gambit'. This type of reasoning bases its conclusion 'on evidence the best of which, if anything, points in the opposite direction' (3.27). This is a surprising accusation to level against the argument from order. The evidence which that argument principally appeals to is the order in the world which is not due simply to the operation of natural laws. And one can hardly say that this evidence points in a direction opposed to the conclusion of the argument. The evidence which Flew is thinking of is, of course, the natural order of the universe. But this provides evidence only for the uncontroversial premise of the argument, which Flew himself does not challenge, namely that the universe is ordered. The controversial premise, the one on which the argument stands or falls, is 'Order implies a designer'. And one cannot regard the natural order of the universe as evidence for or against this premise without begging the point at issue. For if one claims that the natural order of the universe shows that order does not always imply a designer, one is refuting the argument by presuming its conclusion to be false. And if one asserts that natural order confirms the claim that order implies a designer, one is employing the conclusion of the argument to prove one of the premises. In either case one is guilty of a *petitio principii*.

Flew still insists, however, that the evidence available indicates that order does not demand a designer.

> All our knowledge of things, of their natures and tendencies, has to be founded upon and checked against the way those things in fact behave, under whatever conditions they can be available for our study. Yet, if that is so, is it not topsy-turvy to insist that those things cannot naturally do what is, in our experience, precisely what they do do (3.25)

It is difficult to resist the suspicion that Flew is here employing sleight of hand with different meanings of the word 'natural', so as to create the impression that the argument from order asserts something which outrages common sense and is contrary to ordinary experience. For if we give the term 'naturally' its ordinary signification, the proponent of the argument from order does not assert that things cannot naturally behave in an orderly fashion. He would claim that the order of the universe is due to the operation of certain laws which are in fact the laws of nature. The possibility that the presence of these laws in nature is due to the activity of a designer does not take from the fact that they are natural laws: to claim otherwise would be no more sensible than to claim that nature is non-existent if the universe has been created. If, on the other hand, by 'naturally' we mean 'without the assistance of an intelligent designer', then the proponent of the argument does claim that things cannot naturally behave in an orderly manner, except perhaps in certain exceptional cases which can be accounted for by chance. But to assert this is not to assert anything contrary to common sense or ordinary experience. And to dismiss it 'topsy-turvy' without further argument is to succumb to the temptation to which the Stratonician presumption exposed Flew from the beginning — of refuting the argument from order by simply presuming its conclusion to be false.

V

Flew does not appeal explicitly to the Stratonician presumption when criticising the other arguments for God's existence, but it does appear to underlie what he says about the nature of explanation in his treatment of the cosmological argument. For Flew explanation always takes the form of showing that what is to be explained follows from a wider regularity or set of regularities. Every explanation, therefore, however far we bring it, ends in something which is not itself explained — a brute fact, in other words. Two consequences follow from this: the first is that the widely accepted idea, shared even by some naturalists, that theism is more intellectually respectable than any system of naturalism must be ruled out. For while the naturalist must admit the ultimate facts about the universe to be inexplicable, the theist must make the same admission concerning the ultimate facts about God. The second consequence is that the 'Principle of Sufficient reason, the principle that there must be a sufficient reason to explain everything that happens, is not merely false but demonstrably false' (419).

Three comments seem to be called for here. (a) Flew's concept of explanation seems to rule out theism by definition, for it suggests that we cannot, in any line of explanation, get beyond the laws of nature in their most generalised form. In fact, however, his concept of explanation is far too narrow since it takes no account of explanation in terms of free choice. (b) Flew is wrong in thinking that his concept of explanation shows the Principle of Sufficient Reason to be false. If we accept Flew's formulation of the principle as affirming a sufficient reason for everything that *happens*, then the fact that every explanation must end in something unexplained does not imply that what is unexplained must be a happening or event; it could also be a law or a singular fact which does not involve an event or occurrence. If on the other hand, one understands the principle as asserting that there is a sufficient reason for every *fact*, one must take account of the theist position according to which every line of explanation ends ultimately in God who is the sufficient reason for his own existence. Whether this theory is coherent is, of course, debatable, but one is not entitled to dismiss it without argument. (c) Flew's claim that naturalism and theism have the same status as explanations of the universe, since both must end by appealing to facts which cannot be explained, is misleading. It overlooks the fact that what is wrong with naturalism from the theistic point of view is not that it ends by appealing to unexplained facts, but that the facts which it leaves unexplained are ones which demand an explanation. The theist contention is that in our ordinary experience if something displays order which cannot be accounted for by the operation of natural laws or something comes into existence, an explanation is always called for. *A fortiori* we require an explanation for the fact (if it is a genuine fact) that the universe came into existence or displays order at every level. No doubt naturalism may find a means of successfully countering these arguments. But it is not likely to do so if, following Flew's example, it treats these difficulties to its own position as if they were non-existent.

In his preface to *God and Philosophy* Flew expresses the hope that someone will defend theism against his attack by 'developing a systematic and progressive apologetic, genuinely beginning from the beginning'. If this means answering all Flew's arguments, it may well be regarded as an unreasonable request, particularly in view of the fact, so clearly illustrated by this essay, that an argument which takes only a paragraph to express may take several pages to answer. Perhaps Flew will forgive us then if we apply an amended version of the Stratonician presumption to his own book and presume that the qualities we have discovered in the section with which we are best acquainted are present throughout the entire work.

# 4  Knowledge, Understanding and Reality — Some Questions Concerning the Philosophy of Bernard Lonergan

## I

B ernard Lonergan's project in *Insight* is expressed in the famous slogan which, in his own words, 'sums up the positive content of the work'.[1]

Thoroughly understand what it is to understand and not only will you understand the broad lines of all there is to be understood, but you will have a fixed base, an invariant pattern, opening upon all further developments of understanding.[1]

Two things strike one immediately on reading this — the magnitude of the claim that is being expressed and the vagueness of the language that is used to express it. It is a claim concerning all of human knowledge, concerning not merely everything that is already known, but everything that ever will or could be known. If it is true, then it could scarcely avoid being extraordinarily important. But what precisely is being claimed? The terminology used is extremely vague and Lonergan, despite the importance which he attaches to this slogan, offers no further elucidation of it. What does 'the broad lines of all there is to be understood' mean, for instance? We would normally

1  B Lonergan, *Insight*, London 1957, XXVIII.

57

take it as referring to the essential points or basic elements of all there is to be understood, but it hardly makes sense to say that an understanding of understanding will give you an understanding of the essential points of, say, the Theory of Relativity, even if you have no previous knowledge of physics. And it makes even less sense to say that every item of human knowledge has the same set of essential points as every other — which is what Lonergan's principle would seem to imply.

  In the second part of the slogan the metaphors appear to have got mixed. It is not so easy to see how an understanding of understanding could provide you with either a fixed base or an invariant pattern, but when the base or pattern is supposed to function like a door or window and *open upon* something, then the problem of interpretation becomes difficult indeed. Why, in any event, should Lonergan have thought it necessary to introduce these two new metaphors? He could have expressed his basic principle simply as: 'Thoroughly understand what it is to understand and you will understand the broad lines of all there is to be understood and of all future developments of understanding'. If this formulation does not differ in meaning from the formulation that was actually adopted by Lonergan, he would hardly have rejected it in favour of the latter. But if the two formulations are not equivalent in meaning, then it appears that an understanding of understanding will not, in Lonergan's view, provide you with the broad lines of all further developments of understanding, but with something weaker — 'a fixed base, an invariant pattern'. This position hardly makes sense, however, since Lonergan clearly looks on the structure of the act of understanding as something constant. And if this is so, then the relationship between understanding and what has already been understood will be no different from the relationship between understanding and what has not yet been, but will eventually be, understood. Thus if an understanding of understanding will now provide you with an understanding of the broad lines of the structure of deoxyribonucleic acid, something discovered only in 1953, then an understanding of understanding would have provided you with the same insight or information in 1950, since the character of understanding has not changed in the meantime.

How then are we to explain Lonergan's formulation of his

basic principle? He may have felt that it would be implausible to assert that an understanding of understanding would provide you with an understanding of all further developments of understanding and so he watered down the claim by speaking instead of 'a fixed base, an invariant pattern, opening upon all further developments'. This would account for the change in terminology, but it hardly inspires confidence in the validity of the principle. However, there does not appear to be any alternative explanation.

The air of absurdity which surrounds the principle when it is applied to concrete instances of understanding may suggest that it should be interpreted as referring not to the *content* of what is understood, but to its *form*. Thus it could be argued that every item of human knowledge has the same general form as every other and that one can, therefore, know in advance the general form of every new development of human knowledge. But it is difficult to be sure that this is Lonergan's position and even more difficult, if this is his position, to see how it makes sense. Lonergan's fundamental point is that an understanding of understanding will provide you with the basis for an understanding of reality as whole or, as he himself puts it, that 'metaphysics is derived from the known structure of one's knowing'.[2] But if the known structure of one's knowing concerns merely the form of human knowledge — the aspect of knowledge that is derived from the mind as opposed to the aspect that is derived from reality — what reason is there for thinking that this tells you anything about reality? One could of course adopt the Kantian distinction between reality as it is in itself and reality as it appears to us and argue that reality as it appears to us must necessarily conform to the structure of one's knowing. But Lonergan appears explicitly to reject this distinction in its Kantian sense.[3]

## II

Perhaps it would be a help to interpretation if at this stage we were to enquire what sort of principle Lonergan's basic principle is intended to be. Is it an inductive principle? Or if not, is it analytic? Or if neither of these, is it synthetic *a priori*? Oddly

---

2 *Ibid*, XXIX.
3 Cf *Ibid*, 339-42.

enough Lonergan doesn't deal with this question, but we may, I believe, go some distance towards answering it for ourselves. It seems clear, first of all, that the principle is not intended to be analytic. An analytic proposition is one whose denial involves a contradiction, and there seems to be no contradiction involved in the denial of Lonergan's basic principle and Lonergan makes no attempt to show that there is — something that would be incomprehensible if he believed it to be analytic. The same sort of reasoning would appear to exclude the idea that the principle is to be regarded as synthetic *a priori*. A statement expresses a true synthetic *a priori* proposition only if its denial, though not self-contradictory, is somehow inconceivable. And whatever about the truth of Lonergan's principle, its falsity does not appear inconceivable, nor does he ever suggest that it is.

Is it an inductive principle, then? This is a more plausible suggestion than the others, for we can easily visualise the principle being argued for in an inductive fashion. This could be done by comparing the structure of the act of understanding with a number of items of human knowing, thereby showing, or at least endeavouring to show, that the broad lines of these different items are reflected in the structure of the act. But Lonergan himself does not adduce any such evidence and if he regarded the principle as an inductive one, he could hardly have failed to do so.

Well if the principle is neither inductive, nor analytic, nor synthetic *a priori*, what is it? The answer, I believe, is that it is the expression of a philosophical theory concerning the relationship between knowledge and reality. It must be admitted that, aside from the fact that this seems to be the only remaining possibility, there is little evidence one can offer in favour of this view, for philosophical theories need to be supported by arguments and Lonergan leaves his basic principle, at least at the point where he formally enunciates it, devoid of argumentative support. However, at a later stage in *Insight* an argument appears which, though not specifically put forward in support of the basic principle, appears to exhibit the reasoning that underlines it. This is so brief that one can scarcely credit that an essential point would be argued for in such a casual way. But at any rate it is the nearest thing to an argument in support of the principle to be found in the pages of *Insight*. It runs as follows:

Knowing and the known, if they are not an identity, at least stand in some correspondence and, as the known is reached only through knowing, structural features of the one are bound to be reflected in the other.[4]

This argument is not itself sufficient to establish the truth of Lonergan's principle, for even if there is an isomorphism between knowing and the known, it may be too slight to warrant the claim that a knowledge of the structure of knowing or understanding will provide you with a knowledge of the broad lines of all there is to be known or understood. However, if the argument is sound, it would go some distance towards showing that Lonergan's basic principle is correct.

But is the argument sound? What it says is that since the known is reached only through knowing, structural features of the one are bound to be reflected in the other. But why should the fact that A is reached only through B mean that A and B must have structural features in common? When stated thus in general terms, the reasoning does not seem at all plausible. But perhaps this is to distort the argument, for Lonergan may be using the term 'reach' in a special sense. If he is, however, he hasn't told us so. 'Reach' is one of those elusive metaphorical terms which Lonergan is fond of employing, but not of elucidating. Nevertheless he may be using it here to refer exclusively to the special way in which, through knowledge, one 'reaches' that which is known. But if so, then the statement 'The known is reached only through knowing' is equivalent to 'The known is reached in the manner exclusive to knowing only through knowing'; and this is a vacuous statement, a tautology which could not form the basis for any significant conclusion. If, on the other hand, 'reach' is being used in the ordinary sense of 'to make contact with', then the statement is equivalent to 'We make contact with the known only through knowing'. And this is to render the statement false, for we make contact with reality in all sorts of ways other than by knowing it.

Could the term 'only' not be omitted from the argument and this difficulty thereby avoided? Perhaps the best way to answer this question is by raising another: Why was 'only' inserted in the argument in the first place? Lonergan's point is surely that

4 *Ibid*, 115.

as the known is reached through knowing, there must be an isomorphism between the two. If there are other ways of reaching the known apart from knowing, this would not detract from the necessity for an isomorphism between knowing and the known. But why then was the word 'only' ever inserted in the premise? The answer, in my opinion, is that if it were omitted, then the conclusion would be that there is an isomorphism not merely between knowing and the known, but between the known and any human activity that puts us in contact with it. And this, to say the least, sounds implausible — or it could be made plausible only by rendering the isomorphism so weak as to be of no account. To avoid this awkward consequence the word 'only' has to be inserted. But the premise is thereby rendered either tautologous or false.

### III

Clearly Lonergan's argument as it stands has little or nothing to be said for it. But it may be premature to dismiss it immediately as worthless, for the argument can, I believe, be reformulated in such a way as to avoid the difficulties which I have urged against it. The reformulated version runs as follows: unless there is an isomorphism between knowing and the known, reality would be unknowable. But it is not unknowable. Therefore, this isomorphism must exist.

What are we to make of this? The crucial point is obviously the truth of the first premise. Why should the lack of an isomorphism between knowing and reality render reality unknowable? One reason why someone might be inclined to think this is that since human knowledge must, in some sense, mirror reality, there must be a structure common to the two. But to say that there must be an isomorphism between knowledge and reality is not at all the same thing as to say that there must be an isomorphism between knowing or understanding and reality — just as to say that there must be an isomorphism between a photograph and its object is not to say that there must be an isomorphism between the object photographed and the operation of the photographic mechanism. Knowledge is one thing, knowing is something else.

Why should it be thought then that there must be an isomorphism between knowing and the known for reality to be knowable? Perhaps the most plausible reason is this. The human cognitive faculties are not passive agencies which simply mirror reality; rather they actively organise the data presented to them. Thus what is seen is organised in a way characteristic of the sense of vision; what is heard is organised in a way characteristic of the sense of hearing and so on. This is equally true of knowing or understanding. Our knowledge is organised in a way that is characteristic of human intelligence and in that sense there is an isomorphism between the known and our manner of knowing it. However, this is not something inherent in the known; rather it is imposed on it by the cognitive faculty. What is inherent in the known is merely the capacity to be organised in this way. In that very qualified sense then there is an isomorphism between knowing and the known, but it would appear to be much too weak a sense for Lonergan's purpose. For to say that reality is knowable only if the data it supplies to the mind is capable of being organised in the manner characteristic of human knowing is to say very little, perhaps nothing at all. What would it mean to say that the data supplied by reality are incapable of being thus organised — that, say, reality is incapable of being described by means of universal terms. If such a supposition is meaningless — and I suspect that it is, seeing that one cannot even express it without applying certain universal terms to reality — then it would appear that to say that the data supplied by reality have the capacity to be organised in the manner characteristic of human knowing is to say nothing at all. Even if this is not so, it would seem to be much too slender a basis for the claim that if we understand what it is to understand, we will understand the broad lines of all there is to be understood.

## IV

So far I have been concerned with the meaning of Lonergan's basic principle and the reasons for believing it to be true. I now wish to examine its significance for Lonergan's philosophy as expounded in *Insight*. The principle, as we have seen, is concerned with understanding. This concept is central to the entire work. Two other related concepts seem equally central and important. These are the concepts of knowing and insight. Now at this stage we come across a strange lacuna in *Insight*

— that even though we are told that the main purpose of the book is to enable us to know what it is to know, to understand what it is to understand, to gain an insight into insight, there is no attempt made to analyse these terms or to examine their meaning or to work out their relationship to each other or to cognate terms. Lonergan has failed, in other words, to engage in even the most elementary conceptual analysis for the central concepts of his philosophy.

There is, however, a fairly obvious answer to this charge. What could be more familiar to us, it might be asked, than knowing or understanding or having an insight? As Thomas Reid said in reply to Hume: 'To a man that understand English, there are surely no words that require explanation less.'[5] We all know perfectly well what they mean, so why waste time with a tedious explanation or examination of them? But as an answer to the charge this is unsatisfactory. It is one thing to know what a term means; it is quite a different matter to give a correct account of its meaning. Or to put this in a slightly different way — it is one thing to be able to use a concept correctly in making judgments; it is quite another to be able to give a correct account of its use. We all know what the word 'true' or the word 'good' means, for example, but we would be in immediate difficulties if someone were to ask us for an account of their meaning. Nor is this surprising, seeing that philosophers have been in disagreement about these concepts of centuries. But the important point is that while in the ordinary course of events we don't need to be able to give a correct account of these concepts to be able to use them to make true judgments — it is sufficient to know what they mean simply — this is not true at the philosophical level. Philosophy is a second order activity in the sense that the philosopher is concerned not – or at least not solely — to make true judgments by means of philosophical concepts, but rather to make true judgments about them; hence it is necessary for him not merely to know how to use such concepts, but also to be clear about their content and character. Otherwise confusion is likely to occur.

It appears to me that through failing to engage in the sort of

---

5 *Esssays on the Active Powers of Man*, Edinburgh 1788, V, VII. Reid was here discussing the meaning of 'ought' and 'ought not'.

linguistic or conceptual analysis I have mentioned, Lonergan has misunderstood the character of the basic concepts of his philosophy. To illustrate this point I shall quote two short passages — the first from *Insight*, the second from *Method in Theology*.

> The present work falls into two parts.... The first deals with the question, What is happening when we are knowing? The second deals with the question, What is known when that is happening? (p XXII).

> Transcendental method ... brings to light our conscious and intentional operations and thereby leads to answers to three basic questions. What am I doing when I am knowing? Why is doing that knowing? What do I know when I do it. (p 25).

I do not believe that anyone who had examined the concept of knowing could have written either of these passages. They appear to me to constitute a typical example of what Wittgenstein had in mind in writing, 'when we do philosophy we are like savages, primitive people, who hear the expressions of civilized men, put a false interpretation on them, and then draw the queerest conclusions from it.'[6] Presumably what Wittgenstein means is not that this always happens when we do philosophy, but that it is always liable to happen. For when we do philosophy, language, as he puts it, goes on holiday, that is to say, words and expressions are taken from the context in which they are normally used and placed in a highly artificial philosophical context where they may easily be misinterpreted. Now in the two passages which I have just quoted from Lonergan, the word 'known' has clearly lost its way while on holiday, for we never use it as Lonergan uses it here. Take the question 'What is happening when we are knowing?' Do we ever speak in this way? Would we ever say, for example, 'When I was knowing Pythagoras's theorem, the telephone rang'? The answer, clearly, is that we would not. And this is not just a matter of linguistic convention. We do not speak in this way because, if we did, our remarks would be devoid of sense. If someone were to say 'When I was knowing Pythagoras's theorem, the telephone rang', we would immediately conclude

6 *Philosophical Investigations*, trans GEM Anscombe, Oxford 1953, paragraph 194.

that either he had inadvertently used the word 'knowing' for a word such as 'studying' or 'learning' or that he was a foreigner whose knowledge of English was defective. Or take the first line of the poem *The Lake Isle of Innisfree* — 'I will arise and go now'. Yeats couldn't have written 'I will arise and know now', for if he had he would have been uttering nonsense. But if knowing is doing something, as Lonergan asserts, there would be no reason why one shouldn't arise and do it.

This sort of misunderstanding of the character of the concepts of 'knowing', 'understanding' and 'insight' occurs frequently in Lonergan's work. For example he speaks of insight as an activity (*Insight*, p X) and elsewhere as an event (p XXII). And he also speaks of 'conveying an insight' (p IX) and of 'having an insight' (p 3). But while you can observe an event, you cannot have it; and while you can perform an activity, you cannot convey it. Here again there has been a misinterpretation of the character of a concept. In other places Lonergan appears to identify knowing and understanding. Again, this sort of error could scarcely survive an examination of the use of these terms. To say that you know someone is not to say that you understand him; and to say that you understand a proposition is not to claim that you know it to be true. Knowing and understanding are closely related, but not identical.

V

How important is all this? I would not wish to claim that all the points I have made are of great importance for an evaluation of Lonergan's philosophy. Some of them are perhaps of no great significance in themselves. But they are symptoms of something that is significant — namely that Lonergan appears to have misunderstood the character of the concepts which are central to his philosophy. And this must raise doubts about the validity of the entire enterprise.

The purpose of the enterprise is to provide us with an understanding of understanding, an account of the dynamic structure of the act of understanding. This involves two presuppositions about understanding — and indeed about knowing and insight as well, but in the interests of simplicity I shall concentrate on understanding. Both these presuppositions are apparently accepted by Lonergan without examination or argument. The first is that understanding is a uniform activity, that it is something like walking or typing or climbing, except of course that it occurs in the mind. Whenever you engage in walking or typing or climbing, you always do more or less the same sort of thing. So it would, I suppose, make sense to refer to the 'dynamic structure' of the act of walking or typing or climbing, though it is difficult to see what is the point of the word 'dynamic' here, since the structure of an act is presumably dynamic by definition.

There are, however, other human activities such as working, housekeeping and gardening, to which this sort of terminology does not apply. We do not speak of an act of working or an act of housekeeping or an act of gardening, for what each of these terms refers to is not a specific activity, but a whole range of diverse activities. There would be no sense, therefore, in enquiring into the dynamic structure of the act of housekeeping, for there is no such thing, though one could perhaps enquire into the different dynamic structures of the various acts which come under the generic title of housekeeping, such as cooking, cleaning, dusting and washing-up. Now understanding would seem to be far more akin to working or gardening or housekeeping than it is to walking or typing or climbing. The mental activities associated with understanding would appear to be as many and as diverse as the different types of problem and different sorts of subject matter to which the human mind applies itself. Think of the difference between understanding a word and understanding a sentence — a sentence can usually be understood the first time you encounter it whereas a new word has to be explained — between understanding a language and understanding a work of art — acquiring an understanding of a language is largely a matter of memory, but memory plays only a minor role in understanding a work of art — between understanding a subject like philosophy and understanding a person. I do not see how anyone who contrasts these different instances of understanding could seriously take the view that there is a uniform mental activity associated with understanding which has a specific dynamic structure.

Lonergan's second presupposition about understanding is that it is an act. He constantly refers to it as such. The expression 'an act of understanding' occurs twenty-four times in the first hundred pages of *Insight*. (He also refers, though not so frequently, to acts of knowing and acts of insight.) This second presupposition is, I believe, as unwarranted as the first. There are no such things as acts of understanding. In saying this I am not, however, making a statement of empirical fact. It isn't as if I had ransacked my mind and discovered no traces there of acts of understanding; it is a question rather of the impossibility of assigning any coherent meaning to the expression 'an act of understanding'. Modern linguistic philosophy has familiarised us with the idea that in discussing philosophical problems we may utter remarks which, while impeccable from the point of view of grammar or syntax, turn out on closer examination to be devoid of sense. Various, though not necessarily conflicting, explanations have been offered as to how this occurs. Bertrand Russell believes that there are different levels of language and that to use a second order concept as if it were a first order one or vice versa is to produce absurdity. Gilbert Ryle attributes the meaninglessness of some philosophical expressions to a confusion between different logical categories, while Wittgenstein in his later writings thinks that it is brought about by failure to advert to the differences between different language games. What all these explanations have in common is the idea that philosophers sometimes lapse into incoherence by using words or expressions in a way that is quite alien to the way they are used in the ordinary non-philosophical contexts which are their original home.

This error seems to me to vitiate Lonergan's treatment of the concepts which are central to his whole enterprise. In non-philosophical contexts we never speak of understanding or knowing or having an insight as acts. This point can be brought out in a number of ways. (Again I shall concentrate on understanding, but the same arguments apply to the other two concepts.)

1. If understanding were an act, it should cease when the mind temporarily ceases to function or when it is concerned with some other topic. But this is not so. A mathematician does not cease to understand differential calculus when he is asleep, nor does a polyglot cease to understand other languages when he is speaking English.

2. Actions occur at a certain point in time and they endure for a certain period of time. We say 'I was reading or typing or daydreaming when the telephone rang' or 'I spent half an hour reading or typing or daydreaming this morning', but it makes no sense to say 'I was understanding Pythagoras's theorem when the telephone rang' or 'I spent half an hour understanding Pythagoras's theorem this morning'.

3. If understanding were an act, then it should make sense to speak of deciding to do it. But this is not the case. We may indeed speak of deciding to study some topic or deciding to try to understand it, but if someone were to say 'I have decided to understand the causes of the English Civil War', we would convict him of a misuse of words.

But if understanding is not an act, then what is it? This is not necessarily a question to which there is a proper answer, for in asking it, what one is seeking is a category, such as 'act' or 'process', which was originally used for describing the physical world and then applied in a somewhat extended sense to the world of minds; and it may well be that there is no such category available which would be suitable for explaining the nature of understanding. Like God, understanding may be such that it is possible to say what it is not, but not what it is. However, I do not think that the situation is quite so desperate as that. If we are asked 'What is understanding?', the correct answer, I believe, is that it is a state of mind. This answer is, however, open to a number of misinterpretations. If we treat understanding as a state of mind, we may be tempted to assimilate it to a certain type of mental state such as a feeling of fear or a sensation of pain. This would be a mistake for two reasons. A feeling or sensation is a conscious state of mind — one cannot have a feeling of fear or a sensation of pain without being aware of it. But not all states of mind are conscious states. One can be habitually afraid of something, eg, travelling by air, without being always conscious of it and to say that one is in love with someone does not imply that one is always conscious of one's love. Now understanding, as is clear from our discussion of the expression 'an act of understanding', is an habitual state of mind rather than a state that is present only so long as one is conscious of it. So to say that one understands something is to assert the existence of a state of mind, but it is not necessarily to say anything about what is passing through one's mind at this moment.

Secondly, a feeling or sensation is wholly internal to the mind of the individual who is the subject of it, but understanding is not. This may appear surprising, since we are inclined to take it for granted that a state is wholly internal to the thing of which it is a state, but in fact not all states are of this kind. The state of being married, for instance, is not wholly internal to the married person, since it depends on another person to whom he or she is married. And in mental states too you find some that are wholly internal to the mind and others that are not. Belief, for example, is a wholly internal mental state whereas knowledge is not. This arises from the fact that the question of what you believe is entirely a matter of your internal state of mind, whereas the question of what you know cannot be answered by reference to your mind alone, but depends also on the way things are. It makes no sense to speak of knowing what is false; hence to say that one knows that it is raining implies something about one's internal state of mind and something about the state of the weather. Now understanding is more like knowing than believing in the sense that it too is not wholly internal to the mind of the person who understands. 'Understanding', as it is normally used, is an 'achievement word' in that it implies success. You do not understand something unless you have *correctly* grasped the nature of the thing that is understood. Thus it would make no sense to speak of someone understanding my motives if he had a completely wrong idea of what my motives are. The question of whether you understand cannot be resolved, therefore, by reference to your mind alone; one must also take account of the character of what is understood.

But in *Insight* Lonergan, under the influence of the idea that understanding is an act, assumes throughout that one acquires an understanding of understanding through introspection.

The dynamic, cognitional structure to be reached is not the transcendental *ego* of Fichtean speculation, nor the abstract pattern of relations verifiable in Tom and Dick and Harry, but the personally appropriated structure of one's own experiencing, one's own intelligent inquiry and insights, one's own critical reflection and judging and deciding. The crucial issue is an experimental issue, and the experiment will be performed not publicly but privately. It will consist in one's own rational self-consciousness clearly and distinctly taking possession of itself as rational self-consciousness. Up to that decisive achievement, all leads. From it, all follows.[7]

But if understanding is a mental state of the type we have described, then there would appear to be insuperable difficulties in the view that its nature can be grasped by introspection. The first difficulty is that since understanding is not wholly internal to the mind, it cannot be fully grasped by mental introspection; indeed introspection can give no guarantee that what is being examined is a genuine instance of understanding, since this depends as much on the character of what is understood as on the internal state of mind of the person who understands. Secondly, since understanding is not a conscious state of mind, it does not appear susceptible to examination by introspective methods. It may seem odd to speak of understanding as a non-conscious state of mind, but while one may be conscious *that* one understands, one cannot be conscious *of* one's understanding in the same way as one can be conscious of thinking or of day-dreaming. This point may be substantiated in a number of ways. Firstly, if understanding were a conscious state, it should cease when one ceases to be conscious or even when one ceases to be conscious of the object of understanding; and this is obviously untrue. Secondly, if understanding were a state of mind that is susceptible to introspective examination, we could never really be in doubt as to whether one understands something or not — just as one cannot be in doubt as to whether one is thinking of something or not – but this is a point about which we are not merely frequently in doubt, but often in error. Lastly, consider what it means to examine a particular instance of understanding — one's understanding of, say, the French Revolution or the twentieth century novel. To examine your understanding of the French Revolution is to do nothing more than to consider the French Revolution. It is to ask yourself such questions as 'Is this what really happened?', 'Is

7 *Insight*, XVIII.

this the correct explanation for the events in question?' Clearly these could not be answered by recourse to introspection.

There are of course certain mental acts associated with understanding, such as thinking, reasoning and calculating, which are to some extent open to introspective examination. But to examine these introspectively is not to examine understanding for the reason that one may do all these things and not understand or, alternatively, one may understand without having done any of them, as in the case of infused understanding. (Whether infused understanding is a reality is irrelevant here; all that matters is that there appears to be no reason for thinking it to be logically impossible.) Introspection may tell you something about the workings of the human mind, therefore, but that is rather different from claiming that it gives you an insight into the invariant structure of understanding.

Finally, I would like to raise a comprehensive difficulty concerning Lonergan's appeal to introspection. The use of introspection as a means of acquiring an insight into the invariant structure of understanding depends for its validity on understanding being the same for everyone; otherwise introspection will reveal nothing more than details of purely autobiographical interest. But how could Lonergan *know* that understanding has an invariant structure which is the same for all if we are dependent on introspection for our knowledge of understanding? In other words, Lonergan's method makes no sense unless he already knows a great deal about how others understand. And this knowledge could not have been gained from introspection.

# 5  Reason and Authority

## I

The controversy surrounding *Humanae Vitae* may now seem to have reached a dead-end. The two parties to the dispute are just as far apart as when the encyclical first appeared, and since there can hardly be anything important left unsaid on either side, it must seem pointless to continue the argument. There is, I think, a good deal of truth in this. To continue the debate along the old lines by arguing the case for or against the papal declaration would at this stage be entirely futile; it could do nothing but exacerbate the feelings of those who hold the opposite point of view. Nevertheless this does not, I believe, justify a policy of silence. The disagreement on the morality of contraception is a continuing source of disquiet to Catholics. There is no likelihood that it will disappear or grow any less acute if we stop talking about it. To ask for silence would be to adopt a passive attitude towards the present division in the Church which would be almost as regrettable as the division itself. What is needed in this situation is not an end to the discussion but a reconsideration of the way in which the discussion has hitherto been conducted. Is there perhaps something wrong with the terms which have governed this debate and if these were altered, would there then be a renewed possibility of agreement?

If we ask what went wrong with the debate, why it tended to produce heat rather than light, an answer is readily forthcoming. The debate never developed into a genuine discussion because the protagonists were talking about different things. Those who supported the Pope conducted the debate at the

level of authority, those who opposed him at the level of reason.
Hence no matter how successful either party was in arguing
its point of view, it had gone no distance towards persuading
the other party that its position was untenable.

This answer is admittedly somewhat oversimplified, but the
qualifications it requires are not sufficient to invalidate it. Not
all the supporters of the encyclical confined themselves to the
argument from authority. But it was noticeable how few of
them attempted to argue the case from reason, and those who
did invariably gave the impression that they were attempting
an explanation rather than a justification of the papal decision.
It seems reasonable to conclude that in general the supporters
of the encyclical did not believe that the authority of the papal
ruling depended in any way on the validity of the arguments
which could be brought forward in its support. Their attitude
was summed up by Archbishop Murphy when he said that 'in
these matters of interpreting the natural law all honesty, all
compassion, all theological acumen is of little account ... We
need the Holy Ghost.'

Equally it would not be true to say that the opponents of the
encyclical ignored the argument from authority. They recognised that *Humanae Vitae* constituted a solemn declaration by
one with authority to teach on moral matters, but they rejected
its central teaching on the grounds that it was based on a 'fallacious understanding' or 'an inadequate concept' of natural
law. This seems to imply that an authoritative judgment on
moral matters need not be obeyed if the reasons accompanying
it are unsatisfactory, or in other words that the rational basis
of the judgment is in the last analysis the decisive factor. This
position appears to me to be just as one-sided and unacceptable
as the previous one. The Christian conscience must give full
weight both to authority and to reason on moral issues. A
moral theology which emphasises either of these at the expense
of the other is no longer a genuine moral theology; if it exaggerates the role of authority, it is transformed into a species of
canon law; if it exaggerates the role of reason, it becomes
indistinguishable from ethics. Moreover, unless we arrive at a
clear view of the relationship between authority and reason in
moral matters, there can be little hope that the debate on the
morality of birth-control will ever reach a successful conclusion.

To obtain a balanced view of the matter we must first see what is wrong with the two extreme views that have been mentioned. The first emphasises authority to the detriment of reason. It holds that once authority has spoken on a moral issue, the obligatory character of its judgment is not in any way dependent on the reasons underlying it. An authoritative moral judgment is binding because it is authoritative, not because it is supported by reason. This view seems to underlie nearly all the statements emanating from supporters of *Humanae Vitae*, though perhaps not all of them would accept it were it put to them explicitly. But the curious thing is that it is not at all necessary to adopt this view in order to defend the encyclical. In fact by doing so the defenders of the encyclical weakened their case considerably. Why then did they adopt it? To find the answer we must go back to the discussion on the morality of birth-control which preceded the publication of the encyclical. One point emerged from that debate with almost universal acceptance — that the arguments in favour of the traditional position were far from satisfactory. This was confirmed by the reports of the papal commission which revealed that the conservative minority had made only a perfunctory effort to defend the traditional position on rational grounds. Consequently when the encyclical appeared its defenders assumed that since the reasons underlying its teaching were less than compelling, the papal ruling could not be satisfactorily defended except on the grounds of authority alone. In doing so they were implicitly assuming that to attach any importance to reason on this issue would be to negative the role of authority, that in other words the only alternative to the extreme view that authority is decisive independent of reason is the opposite extreme that reason alone is decisive.

The defenders of the encyclical ensured against defeat by refusing to join battle on any other issue but the authority of the papal ruling, but this sort of victory is not one that can be taken very seriously. For the view that authority can be decisive on a moral issue independently of reason is one which is incompatible with any understanding of the character of moral judgment or of the nature of the Church's magisterium. It could appear plausible only if one had failed to take account of the difference between a moral judgment and a judgment on a non-moral issue. A non-moral judgment can be true even if there are no reasons to support it. It might be true, for example, that Napoleon sneezed three times on the morning of Waterloo or that there are planets in other parts of the universe inhabited by intelligent beings even though there is no evidence in support of either statement. The absence of evidence would make it impossible for us to know that these statements are true, but it would not make it impossible for them to be true. Now it is easy to assume that the same holds good of moral questions, but this is not so in fact. One of the special characteristics of moral judgments is that the absence of reasons in their favour makes it impossible not merely for us to know that these statements are true, but for them to be true. If an action is wrong because it involves the killing of an innocent person, for instance, this reason not merely enables us to know that the action is wrong, but actually constitutes its wrongness. Without this reason the action would not be wrong. So unlike a non-moral judgment where the absence of supporting reasons implies merely that we are not entitled to regard it as true, the absence of supporting reasons for a moral judgment implies that it is false.

Moral philosophers explain this by drawing a distinction between independent attributes and consequential ones. An independent attribute is one whose presence in a thing is independent of the presence of other attributes. To decide whether an attribute is independent or not we must ask the question: Is it possible for two things to be alike in every respect except that one possesses this attribute while the other lacks it? If the answer is, Yes, then the attribute is independent. But if the answer is, No, then the attribute in question is consequential, that is, its presence in something is dependent on or a consequence of the presence of other attributes. Now moral terms and indeed all value terms denote consequential attributes in this sense of the term. It would make no sense to say that two paintings or two pieces of music were exactly alike in every respect except that one was good and the other bad. Equally it would make no sense to say that two actions were alike in every respect except that one was right and the other wrong. Actions could not differ in their moral character without differing in other respects as well. To put this in another way, an action could not be morally good or bad unless there were certain features in the action which render it morally good or bad. The truth of a moral judgment, therefore, is logically dependent on the reasons which support it. It is inconceivable that a moral judgment be true without there being reasons for regarding it as true. Conversely, if there are no reasons for regarding it as true, it follows that the judgment is false.

Now this entails that the binding force of an authoritative statement on matters cannot be independent of the reasons underlying it. For if the judgment is devoid of rational support, if there are no valid reasons underlying it, it follows from what we have just been saying that it is false. And, of course, a false moral judgment obliges no one.

There is, however, one possible line of defence against this argument. The fact that one is not aware of supporting reasons for a moral judgment does not entail that there are none. Hence an authoritative moral declaration could be true, and therefore obligatory, even though we are not conscious of any reason for thinking it to be so. This answer assumes that a moral judgment can be supported by reasons of whose existence nobody is aware. And this is indeed possible of moral judgments on individual actions, since an action can have a hidden effect which if it were known, would alter our judgment of its moral status. But is the same thing true of general moral principles? This is the crucial question since authoritative declarations on moral issues are invariably general. Is it possible that a moral principle, which had hitherto been regarded as true, should turn out to be false through the discovery of some fact about it which was previously unknown?

At first glance it may seem that it is. Some years ago it was discovered that smoking can be a cause of lung cancer. Suppose instead that it had been discovered that smoking invariably causes lung cancer. Wouldn't this mean that the principle that smoking is a morally justifiable practice, which had hitherto been accepted, would have turned out to be false? People sometimes use this sort of possibility as the basis of an argument against contraception. They point out that the contraceptive pill has already been shown to have undesirable side-effects. Isn't it perhaps possible that it has far more serious ill-effects which have not yet been discovered, that its use may in the second or third generation produce malformed babies or something of that sort? They take it that if this did happen, the papal condemnation of contraception would have been vindicated. But this is a misunderstanding. Such a discovery would have no bearing on the morality of contraception. This is clear from the fact that if this were the sole reason for regarding contraception as immoral, then a contraceptive technique which did not produce this ill-effect would be morally unobjectionable. The discovery would not have falsified a moral principle, but would have shown that a certain practice, which had hitherto been regarded as coming under one moral principle merely, also came under another one.

And once we consider it, it is clear that the same is true of any such discovery. It would serve not to verify or to falsify moral principles, but to clarify their area of application. For suppose that there is a universally accepted moral principle that all actions which are x are morally lawful and that it is discovered that such actions have an undesirable effect which renders them immoral. Could this ever mean that the original principle had turned out to be false? The answer, I believe, must be, No. For if the undesirable effect is a physical one such as the production of lung cancer or of malformed babies, the connection between practice and effect will be contingent, something which is the case but need not be so. Hence it will not be true to say as a strict statement of moral principle that actions which are x are immoral, since this implies that they are immoral because they are x, when in fact their character of being x has nothing to do with their moral status. If, on the other hand, the undesirable effect is moral rather than physical, that is, if the practice of actions which are x corrupts the person who performs them, then the connection between practice and effect would indeed be necessary — an immoral action of necessity corrupts a person who practises it. But this effect could not be the reason why such actions are immoral since its occurrence presupposes their immorality. An action cannot corrupt unless it is immoral, so the fact that it corrupts cannot be the reason for its immorality. It is clear, therefore, that there can be no such thing as hidden reasons for accepting or rejecting moral principles. Problems of moral principle, like philosophical problems generally, are solved 'not by giving new information, but by arranging what we have always known'.

But even if you overlook this point and refuse to disallow the possibility of a moral principle being supported by a reason of whose existence no one is aware, you would still not be in a position to argue that authority can be decisive on a moral issue independently of reason. For the further question arises as to how those in authority could know that the principle in question is true. If there are no known reasons for thinking it to be so, there can be only one answer to that question — those in authority must have a source of information on moral issues which is denied to everyone else. This involves looking on the Church's magisterium as a sort of oracle. But one has only to consider for a moment how the magisterium actually operates to realise that this view of it cannot possibly be correct. For if the function of the magisterium is to transmit the information it receives from the Holy Spirit, what is the point of conciliar debates or of papal consultations? Or what is the purpose of theology, seeing that theological problems could be solved immediately by an authoritative statement? Or why do we distinguish between infallible pronouncements of the magisterium and non-infallible ones? It is clear, therefore, that the authority of the magisterium is due not to its having access to a special source of information, but to the fact that it receives supernatural guidance in making judgments on certain issues. Here as elsewhere grace perfects nature rather than supplants it. Hence those who exercise the magisterium must arrive at authoritative moral judgments in the natural way, that is, by basing their judgments on reasons. It follows that authoritative statements on moral issues require the support of reason not merely because without it they could not be true, but also because without it they could not be known to be true by those who enunciate them.

But how much rational support is required? According to the other view that has been mentioned reason must be capable of establishing the truth of the principle independently of authority; there must, in other words, be a conclusive reason or set of reasons in favour of the principle. But this view, like the one we have just been considering, is confronted by two insuperable obstacles, one ethical, the other theological. In the first place it is not at all clear that the truth of any moral principle can be conclusively established by reason. If you assume the truth of a general theory of ethics such as utilitarianism or the natural law theory, then no doubt satisfactory arguments can be provided for certain moral principles. But these arguments are not probative unless the truth of the general theory is also established; and if there is anything certain in ethics, it is that there is no such thing as an ethical theory that is supported by arguments which come anywhere near being conclusive. To demand that authoritative declarations on moral issues be supported by conclusive reasons is to lay down a condition which strictly speaking cannot be fulfilled; and this seems sufficient to invalidate it.

In any event this view seems to be ruled out by the fact that it would render authority superfluous. For if an authoritative moral declaration is not binding unless there are compelling reasons to support it, we do not need authority to tell us what is right or wrong; reason alone is sufficient. One might argue that not everyone would be capable of seeing these reasons for himself and hence authority is required to bring home the truth of certain moral principles to those who might otherwise be in error. But this reduces the role of authority to that of passing on the findings of moralists and obviously this is something which could be carried on without any help from the Holy Spirit. Besides the primary purpose of the moral teaching of the magisterium is not to give us guidance on those questions which reason alone would be capable of solving, but on those concerning which, despite the best efforts of reason, some doubt still remains. And this implies that the support from reason which declarations require can be something less than conclusive.

Would any degree of rational support then be sufficient? Would an authoritative moral declaration be binding if there is any genuine moral reason in its favour? This view is attractive at first glance, but seems to be ruled out by the fact that there can be a genuine moral reason in support of a principle which is obviously false. It is not difficult to think of moral reasons in support of the view that euthanasia or suicide or even killing of the innocent can be morally permissible. The fact that a moral judgment is false does not imply that there are no genuine reasons in its favour, but only that such reasons are seriously outweighed by reasons to the contrary. An authoritative moral statement clearly requires some *positive* support from reason; the reasons in its favour must not be completely negatived by reasons pointing in the opposite direction.

As an answer to the problem we have set ourselves then I would suggest the following: an authoritative moral statement requires that there be a reason or reasons in its favour which are not outweighed by reasons to the contrary. We are dealing here with inconclusive reasons or arguments — ones which suggest the truth of something or, more precisely, render its truth more probable without actually establishing it. And what we are saying is that the minimum support from reason which authority requires for its moral declarations to be obligatory is that there be at least one inconclusive reason in its favour which is not outweighed by a reason or reasons which tend to show that it is false. Admittedly this is rather vague and leaves several questions unanswered. Would any sort of positive reason be sufficient in the absence of reasons to the contrary? When could it be said that reasons for are outweighed by reasons against? I do not propose to deal with these questions here, nor do I know if they can be satisfactorily answered. What does seem certain is that there are no clear-cut answers to them. To expect such is to demand a clarity which the subject does not really possess.

## II

In dealing with the relationship between authority and reason on moral issues we have, for purposes of simplicity, confined ourselves to those issues which are not dealt with in revelation and which have not been the subject of an infallible declaration by the Church. No doubt what we have said would also have implications for these other types of moral issues, but we will not consider them here. What I now wish to do is to apply our findings to the birth-control debate. There are, it seems to me, two very obvious conclusions to be drawn concerning it. The first is that to defend the traditional position it is not sufficient to point to the authoritative character of the papal ruling. Authority here, as we have just seen, is not decisive without the support of reason. If one fails to argue the case from reason, like so many of those who came out in support of *Humanae Vitae*, then one has failed to make a real case for the traditional point of view. The second conclusion is that if one wishes to make a case against the traditional position, it will not do to confine oneself to showing, as so many have done, that the arguments in its favour are unsatisfactory. This still leaves it an open question whether the papal ruling receives sufficient support from reason to render it obligatory. The kernel of the dispute then is the relative strength of the reasons for and against the traditional view. There are two questions to be raised; Firstly, are there genuine reasons in its favour? Secondly, if there are, are these reasons outweighed by reasons to the contrary?

If a defender of the traditional position were asked for reasons to support his view, he would point to the customary arguments, adding in all probability that while these arguments may not be demonstrative, they do at least provide inconclusive reasons for thinking that birth-control is always immoral. There is, however, a danger of confusion here. It is easy to fall into the trap of thinking that if an argument is not demonstrative, it does at least provide an inconclusive reason for thinking its conclusion to be true. This *may* be the case, but it is not necessarily so. The ontological argument of St Anselm, for example, either demonstrates the existence of God or provides no valid reason for thinking that he exists. It either succeeds absolutely or fails completely, and the same can be true of an ethical argument. What we must ask ourselves, therefore, is whether the usual arguments are capable of providing inconclusive reasons in favour of the traditional view. We are not concerned, strictly speaking, with the validity of these arguments, but with the question whether, on the assumption that they are not demonstrative, they do provide some reason for thinking their conclusion to be correct.

There are three arguments which merit consideration. The first is the traditional one which holds that contraception is immoral because it frustrates the natural purpose of the sexual faculty and is therefore contrary to nature. (There are different ways of formulating this argument, but this has no bearing on its validity.) This is usually held to be undemonstrative on the grounds that the mere fact that it frustrates nature does not show that contraception is immoral, since man is constantly frustrating nature in other areas without incurring moral blame. But couldn't one argue that the fact that contraception

frustrates the natural purpose of a faculty is at least an indication that it is contrary to the will of the creator and hence
that it is immoral? This is a difficult question to answer. This
version of the faculty argument would still be faced with serious
difficulties, but it may be that these would not undermine it
completely. However, even if it is true to say that the faculty
argument provides a genuine, though inconclusive reason for
regarding contraception as immoral, this is not the same thing
as saying that it provides a reason for thinking that it is
intrinsically immoral, which is the point at issue. The fact that
a reason is inconclusive means that in some circumstances it
could be outweighed by reasons to the contrary; hence there
would still be a real possibility that contraception might
sometimes be morally justified. But this question obviously
needs to be clarified by further discussion before one could
arrive at a definite opinion about it.

The second argument is based on the undesirable consequences of contraception. It is doubtful if anyone looks on
this as a demonstrative argument, but many seem to regard
it as providing some support for the traditional view. This, I
believe, is a mistake. For the undesirable consequences on
which the argument is based are the consequences of an *indis-
criminate* use of contraception, whereas the question at issue
is the morality of contraception in certain clearly defined
circumstances within marriage. There is no evidence that this
restricted use of contraception would have any such undesirable
results. The consequences argument seems, therefore, to
provide no genuine reason for thinking that contraception is
always immoral and so may be disregarded.

The third argument is of fairly recent vintage. It is based on
the claim that if contraception is judged to be sometimes morally
permissible, there will then be no reason for looking on more
obvious forms of sexual immorality as immoral. But even if
this claim is well founded, and it is not at all clear that it is, it
still would not constitute a genuine reason for looking on
contraception as intrinsically evil. For the argument is based
on the assumption that to accept the traditional view is
somehow to confer validity on the reasons which are used to
substantiate it. But this is obviously without foundation — the
reasons underlying the traditional view do not derive their

validity from the fact that this view continues to be accepted. One might accept this and continue to argue that to reject the traditional view is to reject the reasons underlying it and this leaves one with no reasons for rejecting more obvious forms of sexual immorality. But the point is that if these reasons are in fact invalid, they will still be invalid whether or not one continues to regard contraception as immoral; acceptance of the traditional view will not make up for the shortcomings of the reasons underlying it. The third argument then seems to have no more probative value than the second.

This leaves us with one possible reason for accepting the traditional view. What of the reasons to the contrary? These have been debated so fully during the discussion before and after the encyclical that they hardly merit more than a mention here. The first is based on the principle that personal values take precedence over impersonal ones. But to regard contraception as always immoral is to ensure that in certain circumstances personal values will be sacrificed to purely biological considerations. Supporters of the traditional view reply to this by arguing that contraception always involves a suppression of personal values since it prevents intercourse from being a proper expression of married love. But it is difficult to avoid the suspicion that no one would be tempted to accept this view if he were not trying to argue a case. The experience of married couples suggests the opposite, that it is the fear of an unwanted pregnancy which prevents the marriage act from being an expression of love; and a question of this kind should normally be decided by experience rather than by *a priori* considerations.

The second contrary reason points to the fact that man is universally regarded as having a right to adapt nature for his own ends. Why should the marriage act be an exception to this? The usual reply is that it is the inviolability of human life which makes the marriage act an exception to the general rule. But it is not easy to see how the inviolability of human life could be extended in this way, since it is derived from the inviolable right to life possessed by the individual person, whereas before conception occurs there is no person present to possess such a right.

The third contrary reason is concerned with an apparent inconsistency in the traditional view, which regards the use of the contraceptive pill as sometimes permissible (for therapeutic purposes) and a contraceptive intention as sometimes permissible (with exclusive use of the safe period), but looks on the use of the contraceptive pill with contraceptive intent as always immoral. It is difficult to see how the intrinsically evil character of the act is to be accounted for if it does not reside either in the means or in the end. I do not know of any serious attempt to answer this argument.

This survey of the rational arguments has been far too sketchy to permit a decisive verdict. But it is, I think, sufficient to illustrate the serious difficulties which face anyone who tries to show that the reasons opposing the traditional view are outweighed by the reasons which support it. It seems impossible to avoid the conclusion that until these difficulties are overcome — if that is possible — the issue is still in doubt despite the papal intervention. It has often been claimed, of course, that the papal declaration put an end to whatever doubt may have existed before it was made. But this is to assume that authority can be decisive on a moral issue independently of reason. A doubt whether the conditions are fulfilled for previous authoritative declarations to be obligatory cannot be resolved by a further authoritative declaration, since this last declaration would be just as subject to doubt as the previous ones. To suggest otherwise would be like saying that a doubt whether the bridegroom was already married could be resolved by having the couple go through the marriage ceremony a second time. The doubt about the morality of contraception concerned the rational support for the authoritative declarations and it could be resolved, therefore, only at the rational level.

Some will find this conclusion unpalatable on the grounds that authority is undermined if its moral declarations are not binding unless a certain condition is fulfilled. But this seems no more plausible than to say that civil authority is undermined if its laws must be in accordance with reason before they can bind the individual citizen. In both cases there is a presumption that these conditions are fulfilled and one must act in accordance with this unless there are serious reasons to the contrary. But such reasons do seem to be present in the question of birth-control. One may disagree with this view, of course, but what seems certain is that one cannot refute it by simply appealing to authority.

# 6 The Concept of Infallibility

## I

There have been two notable attempts to show that the concept of infallibility, as traditionally understood, is not susceptible of rational employment in theology. In his book, *Infallible? An Enquiry*, Hans Küng has argued on the basis of an examination of language that the traditional concept is incoherent. Language, he claims, is of its very nature an inadequate expression of reality. Every propositional utterance is 'subject to ambiguity, distortion, misunderstanding and error'.[1] To speak of a proposition as infallible is like speaking of a square that is circular, for 'every proposition can be both true and false, depending on its aim, circumstances, meaning'.[2] But if there can be no infallible propositions, then there can be no authority which is infallible in the traditional sense, for the only way in which such an authority could exercise its infallibility would be by uttering propositions which are infallible.

What Küng's argument amounts to, therefore, is that the traditional doctrine of infallibility must be rejected *a priori*; it is false not just as a matter of fact but as a matter of principle, for the concept of infallibility which it employs makes no sense. This argument is in my opinion unsound. It contains two defects, either of which is sufficient to invalidate it. Nonetheless it raises several important points about the concept of infallibility and an examination of it should shed some light on the topic

---

1 Hans Küng, *Infallible? An Enquiry*, London 1971, p 139.
2 *Ibid*, p 141.

under discussion.

The first thing wrong with the argument is that it fails to distinguish between a propositional formula and a proposition. The concept of a proposition is not an easy one to define and philosophers are in some disagreement about it, but one thing seems undeniable — that a proposition is not to be identified with the propositional formula or set of symbols which is used to express it. This is clear from the fact that different propositional formulae can express the same proposition — eg, 'Two plus two equals four' and '2 + 2 = 4' — while the same propositional formula can express two or more different expressions — eg, the oracle's advice to Pyrrhus: 'Aio te, Aeacida, Romanos vincere posse'.

Now the crucial part of Küng's critique of language — the part on which the validity of his argument depends — makes sense only if it is understood to refer not to propositions, but to propositional formulae. Thus when he writes that 'every proposition can be both true or false, depending on its aim, circumstances, meaning', this is not merely true but platitudinous when understood of propositional formulae, but it is false if understood of propositions themselves. For example, the statement 'The sun is shining' expresses a false proposition as I write, but it expressed a true proposition yesterday. But this does not mean that a true proposition has become false, for it will always remain true that the sun was shining on the day in question. What has happened is that a propositional formula which yesterday expressed a true proposition now expresses a different proposition which is in fact false. The proposition which it expressed yesterday is still true, but one now requires a different propositional formula to express it. Equally when Küng writes, 'A previous study of mine on the problem of Church definitions went beyond the statement made above the propositions can be true or false and concluded that they can be true and false',[3] what he is saying is true of propositional formulae, but false of propositions. Thus the expression 'Queen Elizabeth never married' is true when understood of Elizabeth I, but false when understood of Elizabeth II. But this means not that the same proposition is true and false, but that the

---

3 *Ibid*, p 140.

same propositional formula expresses two different propositions, one of which is true, the other false.

Küng is, of course, correct in thinking that every proposition which is genuinely informative and not a mere tautology is capable of being either true or false. But this in no way implies that the traditional concept of infallibility is incoherent. For the possibility of a proposition being false remains only so long as its truth has not been established. What the Vatican I definition claims is that a proposition, when asserted in certain circumstances by the Pope, is thereby guaranteed to be true so that its being false is no longer a real possibility. Küng's account of the limitations of language makes clear how easily such propositions may be misunderstood, but it does nothing to show that the Vatican I claim concerning them must be rejected as a matter of principle.

The second defect in Küng's argument is doctrinal rather than linguistic, and may be illustrated by the following quotation from his book: 'Both supporters and opponents (of the Vatican I definition), the majority and the minority, assumed that the promises given to the Church were related to infallible propositions ... they all without exception assumed that the promises given to the Church depended on infallible propositions.'[4]

Here again Küng has overlooked a crucial distinction. It is one thing to assume that the infallibility of the Church can only be exercised in the assertion of propositions; it is quite a different thing to assume that such propositions are infallible. The Fathers at Vatican I made the first assumption, but not the second. The Vatican I definition says nothing about infallible statements or propositions. It ascribes infallibility to the Pope and Church alone. Of the solemn definitions of the Pope and the Church it says, not that they are infallible, but that they are irreformable, that the Church cannot subsequently revoke them. Infallibility and irreformability are clearly different characteristics. Infallibility is necessarily connected with truth and falsity, irreformability is not. A law could be irreformable (the divine law presumably is) but it would make no sense to speak of a law as infallible. Hence in stating that the Pope and

---

4 *Ibid*, pp 124-5.

Church can speak infallibly in certain circumstances, the Vatican Council was not maintaining that what they said on those occasions consisted of infallible propositions.

But could one not argue that this follows as a matter of course from the Vatican definition, since Pope or Church could not be said to speak infallibly if the propositions they assert were not infallible? This position seems plausible at first glance, but I believe that we have only to consider it briefly to realise that it is untenable. Modern linguistic philosophy has familiarised us with the idea that in discussing highly abstract problems such as those of philosophy and theology, we may utter remarks which, while impeccable from the point of view of grammar and syntax, turn out on examination to be devoid of sense. One way in which this may happen is when we commit what Gilbert Ryle calls a 'category mistake', that is when we allocate a concept to a logical category to which it does not belong. If we were to describe a sound by means of a colour concept – 'a yellow scream' — and intend our remark to be taken literally, then we would be guilty of a mistake of this kind. A rather more endearing example is contained in the story about the African colony where, shortly before independence was granted, people came to the local missionary and inquired anxiously whether independence would be delivered to them by a government official or whether they would be able to collect it at the bank. More sophisticated examples may be found in the writings of philosophers and theologians. Thus Bernard Lonergan in his book *Insight* frequently mentions 'acts of knowing' and 'acts of understanding'. The logical impropriety of these modes of expression becomes clear when we consider the remarks, 'I was understanding when you came into the room' or 'I was knowing when the bell rang'. If knowing and understanding belonged to the category of actions, these would be perfectly intelligible utterances, whereas in fact it is impossible to attach any sense to them.

Now to speak of infallible propositions is to commit, it seems to me, that sort of category mistake. Infallible propositions are impossible not in the way in which it is impossible for water to freeze at $10°$ or to boil at $90°$, but in the way in which it is impossible for screams to be yellow or for independence to be obtained over the counter. The impossibility is logical rather than factual. Only a person can err in the sense of accepting a proposition as true when in fact it is false. And therefore only a person or a community of persons such as the Church can enjoy immunity from error of this kind. We say that a proposition is erroneous or incorrect or false, but we never say that it errs, for to err is to do something that only a person or something akin to a person can do.

But what if a proposition were free from the possibility, not of erring, but of being erroneous? Would this not enable one to ascribe infallibility to it? The answer is no, because there would then be no intrinsic difference between an infallible proposition and a merely true one. A proposition which is true cannot possibly be false any more than an even number cannot possibly be uneven; in each case you are dealing with mutually exclusive characteristics. Hence if an infallible proposition is one which cannot be false, 'infallible' is merely a misleading synonym for 'true'; and this cannot be what is meant by those who claim that the power of enunciating such propositions is a supernatural gift which was bestowed on the Church by Christ. The ability to assert true propositions may not be the most obvious of human characteristics, but not even in the case of higher ecclesiastics would one be tempted to regard it as a supernatural gift.

A persistent opponent may still argue, however, that the difference between an infallible proposition and a true one is that the impossibility of being false is only conditional for a true proposition, but it is absolute for an infallible one. A proposition that one believes to be true may always turn out to be false, for the belief that it is true may be incorrect. and this means that the impossibility of the proposition being false is never absolute but always dependent on its being genuinely true and not merely believed to be such. An infallible proposition, on the other hand, simply cannot be false; the infallible judgment of the Pope or Church is sufficient to ensure this.

This, I am afraid, is an attempt to create a distinction where none exists. For the impossibility of an infallible proposition being false is itself dependent on the authority which declares it being genuinely infallible and not merely thought to be such. And the belief that this authority is infallible cannot itself be justified by reference to the declaration of an infallible authority without involving oneself in a vicious circle or an infinite regress. The truth of an 'infallible proposition' is therefore dependent on the truth of another proposition which is not itself 'infallible'. Hence the impossibility of being false is no more absolute for an 'infallible proposition' than for a proposition which is true but not 'infallible'.

Before ending this section it might be added that while the phrase an 'infallible proposition', if interpreted strictly, involves a category mistake, it is often used as a convenient shorthand for 'a proposition which has been infallibly declared to be true by the Pope or the Church'; and of course it then involves no logical impropriety. But the point is that if we use the term 'infallible proposition' in our explanation of the doctrine of infallibility, we are in danger of thinking that infallible propositions constitute a class of super-propositions which differ intrinsically from non-infallible ones; and hence that a separate question arises about their possibility. But this, as we have seen, is a false problem. If the concept of infallibility is incoherent, it is not because propositions cannot be infallible.

## II

The second attempt to show the impossibility of any rational use of the concept of infallibility in theology was made by the Church of Ireland divine, George Salmon, in his book *The Infallibility of the Church*. Despite its age and faded scholarship this is still the most acute critique of the Vatican I teaching on infallibility, though this is perhaps less a commendation of Salmon than a reflection on his rivals. Salmon's aim is less radical than Küng's. What he seeks to show is not that the concept of infallibility is incoherent, but that one cannot have an adequate reason for believing any doctrine which employs it. His argument may be summarised as follows: Catholics accept the infallibility of the Church because they believe that without an infallible teacher there can be no certainty on matters of revealed religion. Now infallibility will provide certainty only if the doctrine of infallibility is itself certain. But its certainty cannot be based on the infallibility of the Church without involving oneself in a vicious circle and it cannot be based on something else without admitting that certainty can, after all, be reached on matters of revealed religion without recourse to infallibility. Hence a Catholic can never have an inadequate reason for believing the doctrine of infallibility to be true.

A man may say 'I am absolutely certain that I am right in my religious opinions, because I believe what the Pope believes, and he is absolutely certain not to believe wrong'. But then comes the question, 'How come you to be absolutely certain that the Pope is absolutely certain not to believe wrong?' It is not possible to answer this question without being guilty of the logical fallacy of arguing in a circle.[5]

This argument, like Küng's, will not stand up to serious examination. All that Salmon has succeeded in showing is that a Catholic who believes that without infallibility there can be no certainty cannot provide a reason for believing in the Church's infallibility without being guilty of either inconsistency or of the fallacy of arguing in a circle. He has given us no reason for thinking that belief in infallibility of necessity involves the belief that without infallibility there can be no certainty concerning revelation. If these two beliefs are logically independent of each other — and there seems to be no good reason for thinking that they are not – then arguments for infallibility cannot be ruled out a *priori* as logically invalid.

What *is* true, however, is that Catholics have often argued that without recourse to infallibility there can be no certainty in matters of religion. Thus Bishop BC Butler has recently tried to establish the reality of the Church's infallibility by claiming that 'if the Church's power to define infallibly is denied, then the Church is *unable* to proceed from understanding to unhesitating judgment, and revelation is not effectively transmitted'.[6] This type of argument leaves one completely open to Salmon's attack. And what is equally true is that defenders of infallibility have a compelling motive for wanting to argue in this way. For if certainty is attainable without infallibility, then the Church does not absolutely need infallibility for carrying out of its mission — it may still be a useful aid, but it can no longer be regarded as an essential requirement. And this means that the case for infallibility is enormously

---

5 George Salmon, *The Infallibility of the Church*, London 1888, revised edition 1952, p 21.
6 BC Butler, 'The Limits of Infallibility', *The Tablet*, vol 225, p 399.

weakened. If the Church could not function properly without infallibility, then, granted its divine origin, it must have been endowed with it. But if infallibility is not an essential requirement, then the case for the Church's infallibility rests entirely on the far from unambiguous testimony of Scripture and tradition.

That defenders of infallibility have a compelling motive for arguing that infallibility is required for certainty is, however, a different thing from claiming that the doctrine of infalli-bility logically implies this; and unless the latter claim is true, Salmon's argument is unsound. In fact Salmon gives the game away himself when he considers Bishop Clifford's contention that the doctrine of infallibility is based, not on the infallible teaching of the Church, but on the testimony of Scripture. Having considered the weaknesses in Clifford's attempt to derive infallibility from Scripture, Salmon concludes, quite rightly, that infallibility cannot provide certainty if it is itself based on arguments whose validity is doubtful. But the point is that Clifford's argument has merely turned out on examin-ation to be less than probative, whereas Salmon's original claim was that any such argument must of its very nature involve a logical fallacy. The fact that Salmon has to examine Clifford's argument to show that it is inadequate is enough to indicate that his original claim was unwarranted.

### III

Despite this Salmon's argument is of considerable significance and should not be dismissed by saying simply that it establishes nothing more than that defenders of infallibility are sometimes inconsistent. It draws attention to two significant facts about infallibility. The first is that infallibility is of no value for the attainment of certainty unless it is itself certain. The second is that defenders of infallibility tend to put forward circular arguments in its support. A further examination of these points must, I fear, raise serious doubts about the usefulness of the concept of infallibility in explaining the nature of the Church's teaching authority.

An appeal to the infallible teaching of the Church will provide certainty on matters of doctrine only if one is already certain that the Church is infallible. And this latter certainty, as Salmon has pointed out, cannot itself be based on infallibility without involving oneself in a vicious circle; it must therefore be based on other grounds. Now the certainty on which infallibility depends goes well beyond infallibility itself. To be certain that the Church is infallible one must be certain that Christ was a divine emissary, that he founded a Church, that he set up a teaching authority within it, that he had the power to endow this authority with the gift of infallibility and that he did in fact do so. Since the Church could not be infallible unless all these things were true, it follows that certainty concerning their truth cannot be based on the infallibility of the Church.

This places a considerable restriction on the scope of infallibility; it means that it has no power to provide certainty in a whole area of doctrine which includes some of the most important and basic elements of Christian belief. Furthermore, even within the area of doctrine where it can function, the exercise of infallibility does not produce certainty, but rather presupposes it. For the defining authority must first be certain that the doctrine has been genuinely revealed before it can define it. To suppose otherwise is to conjure up the extraordinary hypothesis of a Pope or Council defining a doctrine and imposing it on the faithful without themselves being certain beforehand that it had been revealed. It follows that a claim, such as Bishop Butler's, that without infallibility certainty is impossible is not merely not true of Christian doctrine in general; it isn't even true of any particular aspect of it. Certainty about doctrine is a presupposition of the exercise of infallibility rather than a consequence of it.

Nevertheless, infallibility could still carry out the more modest role of providing believers with an assurance that much of what the Church solemnly proclaims is true. It can do this, however, only if the evidence for infallibility itself warrants certainty, since an assertion of infallibility which is itself uncertain obviously cannot provide certainty on other matters of doctrine. It does not fall within the scope of this article to evaluate the evidence for the infallibility of the Church, but one thing seems evident — if Christ did endow the Church with infallibility, he would surely have made it abundantly clear that he had done so. The whole point of infallibility is to provide a secure means of ending doubt on matters of doctrine.

And this it cannot do if the presence of infallibility is itself doubtful. For Christ to grant infallibility to the Church in a merely implicit way — and arguments for infallibility often suggest this — would be equivalent to giving something with one hand while taking it back with the other. It would be to endow the Church with the means to put an end to doubt on matters of doctrine, but in such a way that the means can never function effectively. The question to be asked about the doctrine of infallibility, therefore, is not simply whether there is evidence to support it, but whether the evidence is anywhere near as clear-cut as the character of the doctrine itself demands. In this instance inadequate evidence is hardly better than no evidence at all. And one cannot help asking: If the evidence is so convincing, why has the doctrine been so controversial?

The second significant point which emerged from Salmon's critique of infallibility was the danger of putting forward circular arguments in its support. Salmon believed that any argument in favour of infallibility must inevitably be circular in character. This claim, as we have seen, cannot be sustained, but it is not entirely unwarranted. For a defender of infallibility will almost inevitably fall back on the authority of the Church to bolster up his argument if he finds that on its own it is incapable of providing certainty. However, this inevitability is not logical, for there is no *a priori* reason why arguments for infallibility must be inadequate. If they are so in fact, then this is a contingent matter, which could have been otherwise.

A much greater danger of circularity occurs when one considers the conditions which must govern the exercise of infallibility. Here there is the same need for certainty as there is concerning the presence of infallibility in the Church. Infallibility will provide certainty only if one is already certain, not merely that the Church is infallible, but also as to where one finds the infallible voice of the Church. To say that the Church is infallible is to say very little until one has answered the questions: Who in the Church is infallible? In what circumstances? Concerning what subject-matter? Each of these questions can be answered only by answering a series of sub-questions which generate their own difficulties. Take the first, for instance. It is commonly held that a General Council is one of the infallible voices of the Church. But who has the power to convoke a

General Council? Who decides its membership and on what principles? Must it be genuinely representative of the Church as a whole and could it be such if the laity, not to mention ordinary clergy, are excluded from any active role in it? Even if it is representative of the Church of its time, how far, if at all, can a Council held at one period be held to represent the Church of another period? How are decisions on doctrinal matters to be arrived at — by simple majority, moral unanimity or something in between? (A very real question in view of the eccentric way in which membership of General Councils was proportioned between different areas in the Church; at Vatican I, for instance, almost thirty per cent of the bishops present were from Italy.) Most important of all, who is to answer these questions and how can we tell if the answers are correct? Unless they can be answered with certainty, no exercise of infallibility by a General Council will provide certainty on a matter of doctrine.

One might say in reply that the answers come from the non-infallible teaching of the Church; the fact that the teaching is fallible does not mean that it is uncertain, while at the same time it rules out the danger of circularity in argument. But even if we overlook the other difficulties here — and this is to overlook a great deal — does this not deprive infallibility of any real meaning? What assurance can a claim to infallibility give if the validity of the claim is dependent on a whole series of propositions whose truth is not vouched for by infallibility? The conclusion of an argument cannot be more certain than the premises on which it depends. So what is to be gained by calling a doctrine infallible if its infallibility is so dependent on the non-infallible teaching of the Church? In any event if the non-infallible teaching of the Church can provide certainty on so many difficult matters, then what use is infallibility? It seems to provide no compensation for the many difficulties it creates.

The recent history of the Church would appear to confirm these considerations. Infallibility was not exercised by either the Second Vatican Council or by Pope Paul in his attempt to give a definitive answer to the problem of birth-control. Yet would anyone claim that the authority of the Council's teaching was thereby lessened or that the birth-control controversy would have ended if *Humanae Vitae* had been infallibly proclaimed? Or does anyone seriously think that the difficulties which beset the believer today on matters of faith could be removed by a series of papal or conciliar definitions? Fallible man cannot be provided with an absolute assurance against error. The pilgrim Church has indeed been assured that it will reach its goal; but this does not mean that any particular step is in the right direction.

# 7   The Catholic Church and Divorce

D r Maurice Dooley, in his informative article on marriage annulments in *The Furrow*, is severely critical of efforts by theologians and canonists to modify the Catholic Church's present marriage discipline.[1] Unfortunately, he makes little effort to examine the numerous complex issues involved and offers no arguments against these new approaches beyond saying that they have been condemned by the Congregation of the Doctrine of the Faith. This type of reasoning will scarcely appear conclusive to anyone who takes cognisance of the fact that many of the important changes which have recently occurred in the Church's teaching and practice were originally opposed by the Vatican.

What makes this lacuna in Dr Dooley's article the more regrettable is that there *is* a serious case to be made against this new thinking. Much of it is characterised by a notable degree of woolly-mindedness. This appears to derive not so much from the difficulty of the subject matter, nor from any lack of intellectual acumen on the part of those who discuss it, but from the convention — still accorded deference by Catholic theologians — that the Church cannot admit to having been wrong on an important question of doctrine or morals. I will not argue the point that this view makes no sense when

---

1 'Marriage Annulments' in *The Furrow*, vol 26, no 4 (April 1975), pp 211-19.

measured against the facts of history; indeed I fail to see how anyone who takes even a moderately impartial view of history could need any persuasion on the matter. Instead I will try to show how this convention has served to distort the recent debate amongst Catholic theologians concerning the character of Christian marriage.

The Catholic Church, as everyone knows, is opposed to divorce. What this means in practice is that a Catholic who is validly and sacramentally married cannot marry again during the lifetime of his spouse unless

a  the Church judges that something which is essential to marriage has always been lacking in this particular union; or

b  the marriage was never consummated and the Pope dissolves it.

The Church will not, in other words, permit a Catholic to marry again because his marriage has irretrievably broken down.

But in practice more and more Catholic marriages have been breaking down and more and more Catholics have been obtaining divorces and remarrying civilly. In the United States, for instance, about 120,000 Catholic marriages end in divorce each year.[2] And since, as Dr Dooley informs us, only a tiny proportion of these obtain ecclesiastical annulments, it is a fair presumption that each year more than 100,000 divorced Catholics remarry outside the Church. Many of these people are estranged from the Church as a result and many more are condemned to the permanent anguish of never participating with their children in the reception of the sacraments.

It is this intolerable pastoral situation which has led Catholic moralists to rethink the Church's position on marriage. But once the principle that the Church cannot have been wrong on an important issue is accepted, the only form such rethinking can take is through a development of the notion of non-consummation or an extension of the number of components which are

---

2  I owe this information to an article entitled 'Divorce: Doctrine et Pratique Catholiques aux Etats-Unis' by CE Curran in *Recherches de Science Religieuse*, tome 61 (1973), n 4, p 592. By a Catholic marriage is meant a marriage which is valid in the eyes of the Church and in which at least one of the spouses is a Catholic.

regarded as essential to marriage. Catholic moralists have thus been endeavouring to get certain aspects of marriage breakdown accepted as grounds for a declaration of nullity or a decree of dissolution by treating them as evidence of the absence of something which is essential to marriage or of the presence of psychological impotence. They have argued, as Dr Dooley tells us, that a broken marriage can be declared never to have been a marriage at all because of the absence of love between the partners or because one of the partners is incapable of behaving lovingly towards the other; or, alternatively, that the marriage can be dissolved because, through some lack of maturity on the part of one of the spouses, it was never psychologically consummated.

This form of reasoning, however laudable the intentions of those who propound it, appears to me to be almost totally devoid of merit. Its most serious defect is that it is lacking in intellectual honesty. To claim that there would be no substantial change in the Church's teaching if the same verbal formula can be used to describe both the old position and the new is to employ the sort of tactic one expects from a certain type of politician, but not from people whose first concern should be honesty and truth. Marriages cannot be declared never to have existed merely because they have turned out badly. Nor does it make any sense to say that the physical consummation of a marriage is so closely linked to something called psychological consummation — a notion which seems to have been invented by theologians for the express purpose of indulging in verbal sleight of hand with theological formulae — that the Church's power to dissolve a marriage because of the absence of the first necessarily includes the power to dissolve a marriage because of the absence of the second. Should the Church decide to change its teaching on marriage, then any attempt to conceal this fact by playing around with words will serve merely to bring theology into disrepute.

A second serious defect in this form of reasoning is that it is designed not so much to meet the needs of couples whose marriages have broken down as to enable the Church to go as far as possible to meet these needs without losing face. But if the Church *can* change her teaching, then the question of loss of face is entirely irrelevant. The Church was instituted for the sake of man, not man for the sake of the Church. If the Church is prepared to place the question of loss of face above the genuine needs of human beings, then it has ceased to serve the purpose for which it was founded. Of course, it could be argued that the only way to persuade the Church to adopt a new position on marriage is to show how this change can be effected without her suffering any loss of face. This may well be so, but it has nothing to do with the proper task of a theologian. His function is to seek the truth on matters of faith and morals. If he should don the mantle of an ecclesiastical politician and concern himself with what is possible rather than with what is true, then he has failed to live up to his calling.

But having said that, it is time to quote Dante's opinion as expressed in *The Divine Comedy*, that the sins of the warm-hearted are weighed in a different scale from those of the cold-hearted. The authors of these new approaches are aware of the human problems which arise from the Church's present marriage discipline. The deficiencies in their thinking are due to an entirely undersandable tension between their sympathy for those who have come into conflict with the Church's marriage laws and their sense of loyalty to the teaching authority of the Church. Unfortunately, the same cannot be said of Dr Dooley, who shows an astonishing lack of awareness of the problems involved in the Church's present discipline on marriage. To read him one would never suspect that this discipline has given rise to the most serious pastoral problems, causing a huge and continuing exodus of people from the Church; that many experienced canon lawyers now believe that the whole system of marriage tribunals is no longer viable, either in principle or in practice, and should be scrapped; and that the most widely-held opinion amongst scripture scholars and theologians is that Catholic marriage discipline is based on a far too rigid interpretation of the moral teaching of the New Testament.[3]

3 For a discussion of the inadequacies of marriage tribunals consult *Divorce and Remarriage for Catholics* by Stephen J Kelleher, Garden City, New York, 1973, and 'Farewell to the Tribunal' by Leo M Groghan, *America*, vol cxxiii (1970), pp 227-29. The teaching of Jesus on divorce is discussed by Wilfrid J Harrington in two articles in *The Irish Theological Quarterly*: 'Jesus' Attitude Towards Divorce', vol. xxxvii (1970), pp 1990-209, and 'The New Testament and Divorce', vol xxxix (1972), pp 178-87. There is a useful survey of recent litera-ture by Séamus Ryan in 'Survey of Periodicals', *The Furrow*, vol 24 (1973), pp 150-56.

I cannot claim to be an expert in either theology, scripture studies or canon law, so I do not propose to develop any of these points here. (Those who wish to study them further should consult the authorities referred to in the footnotes.) Instead I will concentrate attention on an even more serious difficulty in the Church's teaching on marriage, one which has puzzled me for many years, but to which I have yet to find even the beginnings of a solution. The difficulty, to put it briefly, is that the Church's teaching appears to me to be deeply inconsistent. In theory at least this is a greater difficulty than the others, since a doctrine which runs counter to the available evidence may still be true, though that is improbable, but a doctrine which is inconsistent cannot be true, since it is contrary to the laws of logic. Furthermore, the inconsistency is not a minor one. The Church's teaching on the indissolubility of marriage appears to me to suffer from inconsistencies which are so serious as to be quite incapable of being cleared up without recasting the entire doctrine.

The first inconsistency concerns the Church's attitude to civil divorce. She has invariably opposed any attempt by the State in what may be loosely termed the Catholic world to set up divorce machinery on the grounds that marriage is a permanent institution which may be dissolved only by the death of one of the partners. Early last year, for instance, she engaged in a bitter struggle in Italy to have the 1970 divorce law repealed. The Italian hierarchy explained the Church's position in February 1974 by declaring: 'Marriage is by nature indissoluble, not only as a sacrament, but also as a natural institution'[4] But the Church herself is prepared in certain circumstances to dissolve valid marriages or, to put this bluntly, to grant divorces. This fact is not widely appreciated — largely, I suspect, because in expositions of Catholic teaching it is obscured by misleading terminology — but that it is a fact is not open to doubt:[5] The Church claims the power to dissolve a valid marriage:

a  if at least one of the partners to the marriage is unbaptised, a condition which is fulfilled in the majority of marriages which take place throughout the world; or

---

4  Reported in *The Times*, 24 February 1974.
5  There is a good example of this type of obfuscation in a document entitled 'The Church's matrimonial Jurisprudence', which has recently been published

b  if the marriage, though contracted between baptised persons, has not been consummated.

The church thus claims very extensive powers of dissolution while at the same time maintaining that marriage is in the nature of things indissoluble. Furthermore she forbids the State — on the grounds that it cannot be done — to do something which she is prepared to do herself. And finally she claims, in relation to marriages which are not Catholic or even Christian, a legal right which she denies to the State in relation to marriages which are purely civil in character.

No doubt it may be argued that the Church's opposition to civil divorce is justified by the fact that the provision of divorce facilities by the State inevitably weakens the family as an institution and is therefore detrimental to the general welfare of the citizens. This is an extremely important argument, but it is one that is difficult to evaluate since the evidence which is available concerning it is in the nature of things rather limited and is also somewhat ambiguous. But whatever about the merits of the argument, it has nothing to do with the Catholic position on indissolubility as it is based not on the *incapacity* of the State to grant divorces, but on the *inexpediency* of its so doing. Moreover, it cannot be used to justify a blanket prohibition on divorce, since the question whether something is inexpedient is one that may require a different answer in different societies or at different times within the same society. In any event, the argument may be turned against the Church's marriage discipline, for if it is inexpedient to grant civil divorces, it may be inexpedient to grant ecclesiastical divorces as well.

The second serious inconsistency in the Church's teaching on marriage is that it lays down that a Christian sacramental marriage is especially indissoluble in that it cannot be dissolved even by the Church and at the same time concedes that the

by a working party of the Canon Law Society of Great Britain and Ireland. This states that 'the doctrine of the indissolubility of marriage ... professes that by the law of God a marriage, once truly constituted, may not be dissolved by any human authority so that the parties are each free to enter another marriage'. It then adds in a footnote that 'it will be appreciated that no account is here taken of marriages which are dissolved either "in favour of the faith" or because they are not consummated'. This is as if one were to state categorically that all numbers are rational and then add in a footnote that no account is here taken of those numbers which are irrational.

Church has the power to dissolve one form of Christian sacramental marriage, namely marriages which have not been consummated. There is no scriptural or patristic warrant for this practice and theologians have long since ceased to argue that consummation is so central an element that the marriage cannot be said to have been really effected until consummation takes place. Of course, it is easy to see that a non-consummated marriage is in some sense incomplete, but a marriage can be incomplete in other and equally serious ways — if the couple have ceased to love or even to tolerate each other, for example. It seems to make no sort of sense to say that the Church has the power to dissolve one kind of marriage, but not the other. The claim that the Church's power to dissolve marriages which are sacramental in character extends only to non-consummated marriages would, in the circumstances, appear to be entirely arbitrary. To be consistent she should admit either that no form of Christian sacramental marriage can be dissolved or else that her power to dissolve is much more extensive than had hitherto been realised.

The third inconsistency in the Church's teaching on marriage concerns the relationship between it and the teaching of Christ on divorce as related in the New Testament. The Church is accustomed to claim that her position on indissolubility is imposed on her by the very words of Christ himself and that she cannot change it therefore without being untrue to her founder. One problem with this claim is that it is difficult to feel certain concerning the precise import of Christ's words. Did he assert, as the account of his remarks found in *Mark* and *Luke* suggests, that divorce and remarriage is always immoral; or was he saying rather, as *Matthew* seems to imply, that it is immoral except in certain circumstances? Or did he intend, as some modern Catholic scholars believe, that his remarks on indissolubility should be understood as expressing an ideal to which his followers should aspire, but not a command which they are morally obliged to obey? This difficulty is further complicated by the question whether Christ was putting forward an 'interim morality', devised — on the assumption that the end of the world was at hand — for the short period which remains for mankind, or a morality with permanent and unchanging validity.

My opinion on this matter carries little weight and I will not presume to put it forward here. However, I am deeply impressed by the fact that the moral teaching of Jesus is given in nearly every instance in a general or sweeping fashion with no mention of possible exceptions — 'I say to you do not swear at all'; 'If anyone strikes you on the right cheek, turn to him the other also'; 'Let him who has two coats give to him who has none.' But it is clear from the gospels that no one was more aware than Jesus of the necessity for a humane interpretation of moral principles and no one has denounced a legalistic approach to morality more vehemently than he. Does this not suggest that to champion an absolute prohibition on divorce is to display an outlook not far removed from the legalism which he found so reprehensible in the religious leaders of his time.

However one approaches the teaching of Jesus on divorce, there seems to be no way of interpreting it which does not render it incompatible with the Church's teaching on the indissolubility of marriage. One can make a case for the claim that he ruled out divorce completely or, alternatively, for the claim that he did no more than draw the attention of his disciples to the fact that marriage is a permanent commitment. What one cannot reasonably argue is that he declared that every marriage is capable of being dissolved except consummated unions between baptised persons. The Church's position is, in other words, either too weak or too strong. If one interprets Christ's words literally, then she has already departed in a number of important ways from the teaching of her founder; if one interprets his words in a more nuanced fashion, then she has been guilty of legalism.

If there is any substance in the points which I have been making, then the Church has no option but to think again about its position on indissolubility. This reappraisal will need to go much deeper and be much more disturbing than the stop-gap attempts criticised by Dr Dooley. It will be a question not of developing doctrine, but of re-evaluating the moral teaching of the New Testament and re-thinking the Catholic tradition on indissolubility in relation to it. Perhaps this is merely another way of saying that the Church will have to learn to take the parable of the lost sheep seriously.

# 8  The Ontological Argument for God's Existence

## I

The ontological argument for God's existence has probably provoked more discussion than any other argument in the history of philosophy. But we still seem some distance from having a final verdict on it, for while it is widely believed that the argument is unsound, there is little agreement as to what precisely is wrong with it. The standard 'refutations' all seem deficient in one way or another. Yet there is, I believe, a fatal flaw in the argument, a logical blunder so elementary and so central to the reasoning as to extinguish any hope of keeping the argument alive either by restructuring it or by raising doubts about the character of the alleged fallacy. That such a defect could have remained undetected for so long may seem highly implausible, but I hope to establish the point in the course of this article. However, there is no likelihood that my criticism, even if it turns out to be justified, will bring discussion to an end, since it leaves untouched several important philosophical questions thrown up by the argument. What I shall try to show simply is that the type of reasoning which the ontological argument employs is so irredeemably flawed that no version of the argument can provide any good reason for believing its conclusion to be true.

My contention is that the ontological argument begs the question. This claim is not of course original. It was made in a particularly memorable way by Schopenhauer and it has been repeated recently by Michael Roth. But Schopenhauer and Roth disagree as to where the defect occurs in the argument and I believe that both of them are mistaken. Schopenhauer's criticism is contained in the following passage:

> Considered by daylight, however, and without prejudice, this famous Ontological Argument is really a charming joke. On some occasion or other, someone excogitates a conception, composed out of all sorts of predicates, among which however he takes care to include the predicate actuality or existence, either openly stated or wrapped up for decency's sake in some other predicate, such as *perfectio, immensitas*, or something of the kind ... The predicate reality or existence is now extracted from this arbitrary thought conception, and an object corresponding to it is forthwith presumed to have real existence independently of the conception.[1]

The ontological argument would indeed be no more than a joke if Schopenhauer's understanding of it were correct. But the argument does not proceed by taking a conception composed of different predicates and arbitrarily adding to it the notion of existence. Instead it takes the conception of a greatest conceivable being and *argues* that unless it contains the notion of existence, this conception is incoherent. For Schopenhauer the argument simply smuggles the notion of existence into an already existing conception, whereas what the argument actually does is to claim that if you subtract the notion of existence from the conception of a greatest conceivable being, there is no conception left, since it then collapses into incoherency.

Michael Roth's criticism is based on the claim that Anselm's argument begins by offering a definition of God, namely, that God is that than which nothing greater can be conceived. But what, he asks, is the *definiendum* of that definition? Clearly it cannot be the concept of God, since Anselm goes on to argue that the greatest conceivable being cannot exist in the understanding alone, which is equivalent to saying that it cannot be merely a concept. The only remaining possibilities are that the *definiendum* is the bearer of the name 'God' or that it is the

---

1  A Schopenhauer, *The Fourfold Root of the Principle of Sufficient Reason*, trans K Hellebrand (George Bell, London, 1889), pp 11-12.

name itself. But either interpretation, he argues, involves a *petitio principii*. If we take the definiendum to be the bearer of the name 'God', we are presupposing that the name has a bearer, which of course is to presuppose that God exists. But if we take it to be the name 'God', then the only understanding of the definition which is at all consonant with the reasoning employed by the argument is to say that it should be construed extensionally as follows: there exists an entity such that it is the name 'God' and has as its defining characteristic the property of being true of that entity than which nothing greater can be conceived.

> However, given the standard interpretation of the 'is true of' relation, a name X is true of bearer Y only if Y exists. Thus the definition becomes equivalent to the previous definition of the being who is the bearer of the name 'God'. Hence, it begs the question.[2]

This objection is unsuccessful for two reasons. The first is that it mistakenly assumes that the identification of the greatest conceivable being with God is an essential part of the ontological argument. But it is clear that this identification is quite extraneous to the proof that the greatest conceivable being exists and could equally well be made at the end when the existence of the greatest conceivable being has, as it is claimed, been established. The reason why the identification of the greatest conceivable being with God is usually made at the beginning rather than at the end is that this is how the argument is expounded by Anselm, but there is nothing to prevent this move being delayed until after the conclusion has been reached. On the assumption that 'the greatest conceivable being' is a definition of God, one could then treat the *definiendum* either as the bearer of the name 'God' or as the name 'God' with its definition construed extensionally. In neither case is there any danger of begging the question, since — presuming the argument is otherwise sound — the reality of the greatest conceivable being has already been established.

The second reason why the objection is unsuccessful is that the claim 'a name X is true of bearer Y only if Y exists' seems

---

2  Michael Roth, 'A Note on Anselm's Ontological Argument', *Mind*, LXXIX (April 1970), p 271.

highly questionable. There is little difficulty in supplying what look like effective counter-examples to it. Thus the name 'Traveller' is true of Robert A. Lee's horse even though Traveller has ceased to exist and the name Heathcliff is true of a central character in *Wuthering Heights* even though Heathcliff never existed. One could perhaps try to preserve Roth's point by arguing that Traveller exists as an historical figure and that Heathcliff exists in fiction. But does this not leave one free to claim that God exists in much the same fashion as an object of religious belief or as an entity in the universe of discourse? It seems clear that we frequently use names to refer to non-existent entities without in any way presupposing or implying that they exist. Thus, we use 'Apollo' to refer to the Greek Sun-God and we use 'Nessie' to refer to the, presumably non-existent, Loch Ness monster. There seems to be no good reason therefore for thinking that to identify the greatest conceivable being with God before proving that God exists is to be guilty of a *petitio principii*.

## II

Nevertheless, I believe that Schopenhauer and Roth are right in thinking that the argument presupposes what it is trying to prove, even though they do not point out correctly where this defect occurs. To explain just how the argument goes wrong it will be necessary to say something first about the character of the reasoning which it employs. This will be put in very general terms as it is intended to apply, with minor modifications, to all the standard versions of the argument. Perhaps the best way to understand the ontological argument is to treat it as a *reductio ad absurdum*, as an attempt to prove that the greatest conceivable being exists by showing that the hypothesis that the greatest conceivable being does not exist leads to absurdity. However, the absurdity is not that this hypothesis implies two contradictory propositions, $p$ and not-$p$, but that it implies that the existence of the greatest conceivable being is logically impossible and this contradicts something that is assumed to be true, namely, that it is logically possible that the greatest conceivable being exists.

There are two main elements, then, in the argument — the assumption that it is logically possible that the greatest conceivable being exists and the inference from its non-existence to the logical impossibility of its existence. The essential structure of the argument may therefore be set out as follows:

> It is logically possible that the greatest conceivable being exists.
> But if it did not exist, its existence would not be logically possible or, equivalently, if its existence is logically possible, then it actually exists.
> Therefore, it actually exists.

The first premise is the one on which I wish to focus attention, for here, I believe, is where the fatal flaw in the argument is to be found. This premise is usually treated by supporters of the argument as an assumption which it is rational to accept so long as there is no good reason for thinking that the notion of a greatest conceivable being is incoherent. As Leibniz put it, 'We are entitled to assume the possibility of any being, and above all of God, until someone proves the contrary.[3] But Leibniz himself felt that to treat the first premise as an assumption leaves the demonstration of God's existence imperfect and he put forward an argument in its support. CD Broad, on the contrary, thought that the first premise was false and he put forward two arguments – one the mirror-image of Leibniz's — to prove that this was so.[4] However, we need not enter into that controversy here, since what Leibniz and Broad are concerned with is the internal incoherence of the notion of a greatest conceivable being. And this point, though important, is not necessarily decisive. For even if Leibniz is right in thinking that the notion *is* internally coherent, that does not establish the truth of the first premise. This may seem implausible, but it can be shown to be correct if we take the argument and reverse the order of the premises. It then reads as follows:

> If it is logically possible that the greatest conceivable being exists, then it actually exists.
> But it is logically possible that it exists.
> Therefore, it actually exists.

3  GW Leibniz, *New Essays Concerning Human Understanding*, trans and ed Peter Remnant and Jonathan Bennett (Cambridge, 1981), p 438.
4  See CD Broad, *Religion, Philosophy and Psychical Research* (London, 1957), pp 179-80.

Clearly the second premise of this argument cannot be true, granted the truth of the first premise, unless the conclusion is true. It follows that the second premise must be asserting something more than that the notion of a greatest conceivable being is internally coherent. For if this were all that it is asserting, then it could not be rendered false by the non-existence of the greatest conceivable being, since it would make no sense to say that the internal coherence of a notion depends on something external to the notion, namely, on whether or not the notion is exemplified. In asserting that the existence of the greatest conceivable being is logically possible, therefore, the argument is asserting both that the notion of a greatest conceivable being is internally coherent *and* that such a being actually exists. Now this means that one is not entitled to assert the second premise unless one already knows, or has good reason for believing, that there is a greatest conceivable being. The argument goes no distance, therefore, in establishing the existence of such a being, since the evidence for its existence which it provides is not evidence at all unless one already knows, or has good reason for believing, that its conclusion is true. And this is equivalent to saying that it provides no evidence.

We can now see both why the argument proved so difficult to refute and why at the same time it is totally devoid of probative force. Both features derive from the fact that the second premise (in my original formulation) alters the truth-conditions which govern the first premise. The expression 'logically possible', when it first occurs in the argument, appears to be used in the conventional sense as referring to the internal coherence of the notion of the greatest conceivable being. As a consequence, it seems reasonable to regard the first premise as true unless it can be shown that there is some logical incompatibility between the different constitutive elements of this notion. But the second premise then asserts that the first premise is not true unless the greatest conceivable being actually exists. This, if correct, means that we could not know that the existence of the greatest conceivable being is logically possible unless we know that it actually exists, so that in asserting the first premise we are assuming what we are trying to prove.

## III

It would be unrealistic to expect supporters of the argument to accept this as a genuine refutation without a struggle, so let us consider what they might say in reply. There are, it seems to me, two possible lines of defence. The first is to claim that my objection to the argument proves too much, for if it were sound, it would follow that all *modus ponens* arguments, and perhaps all purely deductive reasonings, are guilty of begging the question. The logical structure of the ontological argument, as I have outlined it, is as follows: $p$. But if $p$, then $q$. Therefore $q$. Now if one is not entitled to assert $p$ here unless one first knows, or has good reason for believing, that $q$ is true, then every *modus ponens* argument begs the question. And this conclusion is so implausible as to amount to a *reductio ad absurdum*.

Indeed Peter Geach has claimed that there is no such fallacy as that of begging the question.

> Bad logic books list 'begging the question' as a fallacy. This objection, however, is a mere confusion, and in the court of logic it should be denied a hearing: if the conclusion really is implicit in the premises, then the argument is logically as good as can be — the conclusion really and indefeasibly follows from the premises.[5]

In one sense Geach is right. Begging the question is not strictly a fallacy, since every argument which includes the conclusion in its premises is formally valid. But logicians who speak of the fallacy of begging the question are obviously using the term 'fallacy' in a somewhat wider sense. What they mean is that an argument which begs the question, though not formally invalid, is devoid of probative force. That they are right about this is clear from the fact that no argument of the form '$p$, therefore $p$' provides any good reason for believing its conclusion to be true.

But what is it about '$p$, therefore $p$' that deprives it of probative force? It is often claimed that there are two conditions which need to be satisfied for an argument to prove its conclusion, namely, that its premises must be true and that it must be formally valid. But both these conditions are satisfied by arguments of the form '$p$, therefore $p$' whenever $p$ expresses

---

5   Peter Geach, *Reason and Argument* (Oxford, 1976), p 18.

a true proposition, so clearly something else is required. It might be thought that the third condition is that we must *know* the premises to be true. But this will not do. That I do not know the premises to be true is a defect in me if they are in fact true; it is not a defect in the argument. Thus a non-mathematician will be unable to say whether the premises of a mathematical proof are true or not, but this does not mean that the proof is in any way unsatisfactory. If I do not know the premises to be true, then the argument is ineffective for me in the sense that it does not present me with anything which I can recognise as a good reason for accepting its conclusion. But it is not necessarily ineffective for anyone else. However, if one needs to know the truth of the conclusion in order to know the truth of the premises, the argument will always be ineffective for everyone. The premises in this case cannot provide anything which can be recognised as a good reason for accepting the conclusion, since they cannot be known to be true unless the conclusion has already been accepted. What is required in an argument, therefore, is not that I, or anyone else, would know the premises to be true, but that it must be *possible* to know this without first knowing the conclusion to be true. Arguments of the form '*p*, therefore *p*' fail to satisfy this condition and are consequently useless.

We are now in a position to see why some *modus ponens* arguments beg the question while others do not. When *p* strictly implies *q*, it is impossible for *p* to be true unless *q* is true. But it is not always impossible to know that *p* is true without knowing that *q* is true. Thus the fact that a triangle is equilateral strictly implies that it is equiangular, but one does not need to know that it is equiangular in order to know that it is equilateral. One could therefore legitimately argue that since this triangle is equilateral and a triangle is equilateral only if it is equiangular, it follows that this triangle is also equiangular. On the other hand, on the presumption that one understands the terms involved, one could not know that six is not an odd number without knowing that it is an even number. Hence to try to prove that six is even by arguing that is not odd and a number is not odd, only if it is even, is to beg the question.

Now the ontological argument, as I have outlined it, suffers from the same defect. If it is correct to say that the existence of the greatest conceivable being is logically possible only if it actually exists, then one would need to know that it actually exists in order to know that its existence is logically possible. A supporter of the argument might contest this on the grounds that the logical possibility of the greatest conceivable being is related to its existence in precisely the same way as the equilaterality of a triangle is related to its equiangularity. We can know that a triangle is equilateral without knowing that it is equiangular, so that in inferring its equiangularity from its equilaterality we are not begging the question. Similarly, it might be argued, we can know, or at least have some grounds for believing, that the existence of the greatest being is logically possible without knowing that it actually exists, so we are not open to the charge of *petitio principii* in inferring its existence from its actuality.

However, the two cases are not parallel. To think that they are is to overlook the point, which has previously been made, that the second premise of the argument alters the truth-conditions which govern the first premise. Normally when we say that the existence of the greatest conceivable being is logically possible, what we mean is that the notion of a greatest conceivable being is internally coherent in the sense that the different constitutive elements of that notion are logically compatible with each other. But if the existence of the greatest conceivable being is logically possible only if it actually exists, then two conditions must be fulfilled for its existence to be logically possible. These are (1) that the notion of a greatest conceivable being be internally coherent and (2) that the greatest conceivable being actually exists. If (2) followed from (1), then the logical possibility of the greatest conceivable being would be related to its existence in precisely the same way as the equilaterality of a triangle is related to its equilaterality and the ontological argument would not be open to the charge of question begging. But (2) does not follow from (1) and though most versions of the argument assume that it does, none has argued the point explicitly. What they have argued is that the denial of (2) implies that it is logically impossible that the greatest conceivable being exists or, equivalently, that (2) follows from something that looks very like (1), namely from 'It is logically possible that the greatest conceivable being exists'.

But on examination it turns out that logical possibility is being used in such a way that 'The notion of a greatest conceivable being is internally incoherent' does not imply 'The existence of the greatest conceivable being is logically possible', so that no reason has been adduced for thinking that (2) follows from (1).

This point will be developed more fully when I come to deal individually with each of the standard versions of the argument. For the moment I shall restrict myself to arguing that (2) clearly does not follow from (1) and that therefore no argument that it does could possibly be sound. For to say that (2) follows from (1) is equivalent to saying that the internal coherence of the notion of a greatest conceivable being depends on whether the notion is exemplified or not. But this claim is surely itself incoherent, since it implies that the internal coherence of a notion depends on something external to the notion. Whether a notion is internally coherent depends simply on its content. If we say that it depends on some other factor, then we are talking not about internal coherence, but about something else.

One might try to counter this by arguing that the notion of a greatest conceivable being is unique in that part of the content of the notion is that there is something corresponding to it; hence if this notion is not exemplified, it is incoherent. But this cannot be correct, for the expression 'greatest conceivable being' is part of the content of the proposition 'There is a greatest conceivable being' rather than the other way round. In any event it makes no sense to say that it is part of the content of a notion that something is the case or, equivalently, that it is part of the content of a non-propositional expression that some proposition is true. To say that part of the content of the notion of a greatest conceivable being is that there is something corresponding to it is a muddled way of referring to the notion of a necessarily existing being. But the non-exemplification of this notion would still leave it an open question whether or not it is internally coherent.

The upshot of all this is that while it may be plausible to claim that the existence of the greatest conceivable being is logically possible and also plausible to argue that if the greatest conceivable being does not exist, then its existence is not logically possible, one cannot conclude from this that the

greatest conceivable being exists. For logical possibility is being
used here in two different ways and if we iron out the ambiguity,
the plausibility either of the claim or of the argument disappears. Thus if by the logical possibility of the greatest conceivable being we mean simply that the notion of a greatest
conceivable being is internally incoherent, the argument that
the non-existence of the greatest conceivable being would render
its existence logically impossible collapses. But alternatively if
we mean that the notion of a greatest conceivable being is
internally coherent and that the greatest conceivable being
actually exists, then to claim that the existence of the greatest
conceivable being is logically possible is to assume what one is
trying to prove.

IV

The second way of defending the argument against my criticism
is to claim that nothing more has been shown than that a
potted version of the argument begs the question. But this is
very different from proving that all the standard versions of
the argument, and indeed every possible version of it, suffer
from the same defect.

The only way to deal with this objection is to examine all the
standard versions of the argument to see if they conform to the
model which I have proposed. There are, I suggest, six versions
which are treated as standard in recent discussion. These are
the non-modal arguments of Anselm, Descartes and Leibniz
and the modal arguments of Hartshorne, Malcolm and Plantinga. All but one of these, I shall argue, assert both that the
existence of the greatest conceivable (or absolutely perfect)
being is logically possible and that its existence would not be
logically possible unless it actually exists. The one exception is
Descartes's argument which employs the notion of a true and
immutable nature in place of that of logical possibility. But
this, as we shall see, does not save Descartes from the fallacy
of begging the question.

I shall begin with Anselm and proceed in chronological
fashion. Anselm's argument may appear to escape the charge
of *petitio principii*, since it does not assert that the existence of
the greatest conceivable being is logically possible, but claims
instead that the greatest conceivable being exists at least 'in

the understanding' ('in intellectu'). But this expression is ambiguous. It could be intended in a purely psychological sense, so that to say that the round square exists in my understanding means simply that I understand the words 'the round square'; or it could be intended in a logical sense, so that to say that something exists in the understanding means that this thing is logically conceivable.

In his original formulation of the non-modal argument in the second chapter of the *Proslogion* Anselm seems to employ the expression in the purely psychological sense, for he says of the Fool that 'when he hears of this he understands, and whatever is understood is in the understanding'. But in his *Reply* to Gaunilo he asserts that 'in no understanding is a being than which a greater is conceivable a being than which a greater is inconceivable'.[6] The claim that this is in no understanding must mean that it is logically inconceivable, for we do understand the words of logically incoherent expressions, such as 'a round square' or 'a married bachelor'. Indeed Anselm would be in no position to assert that in no understanding is a being than which a greater is conceivable a being than which a greater is inconceivable unless he understood what these words mean. In any event the logic of his argument rules out the purely psychological interpretation. For what Anselm wants to show is that if the greatest conceivable being exists in the understanding, then it also exists in reality — 'If a being than which a greater cannot be conceived is in any understanding, it does not exist in the understanding alone'[7] or, equivalently, if the greatest conceivable being does not exist in reality, then it does not exist even in the understanding. But it would make no sense to say that the non-existence of the greatest conceivable being makes it impossible to understand the words of the expression 'the greatest conceivable being'. If his argument is not to be deprived of all semblance of plausibility Anselm must be understood, then, as claiming that the non-existence of the greatest conceivable being makes its existence logically inconceivable.

His argument may be set out as follows:

---

6  St Anselm, *Reply to Gaunilo* in A Plantinga (ed), *The Ontological Argument* (London, 1968), p 17.

7  *Ibid*, p 17.

The greatest conceivable being exists at least in the understanding. But if it exists in the understanding, it exists in
reality. Therefore it exists in reality.

Anselm offers the following *reductio ad absurdum* argument
in support of his second premise:

If that, than which nothing greater can be conceived, exists in
the understanding alone, the very being, than which nothing
greater can be conceived, is one, than which a greater can be
conceived. But obviously this is impossible.[8]

Anselm is arguing here that the supposition that the greatest
conceivable being is a logically possible but non-existent entity
leads to a contradiction. I do not think that he is right about
this, since there appears to be no satisfactory way of formulating
this contradiction. It cannot be expressed by the propositions
'There is a greater conceivable being' and 'It is not the case
that there is a greatest conceivable being', since the supposition
that the greatest conceivable being is a logically possible but
non-existent entity clearly does not imply 'There is a greatest
conceivable being'. Nor can it be expressed by 'There is a coherent notion of a greatest conceivable being' and 'It is not the
case that there is a coherent notion of a greatest conceivable
being', for, as we have seen already, it makes no sense to say
that the non-exemplification of a notion implies that the notion
is incoherent.

But Anselm's argument will not work even if we overlook
this difficulty. The conclusion of his *reductio ad absurdum*
argument is that a greatest conceivable being cannot contingently not exist; if its existence is logically possible, then it
actually exists. Now this means that one cannot assume that
its existence is logically possible without assuming that it
exists, so that in asserting that the greatest conceivable being
exists at least in the understanding Anselm is begging the
question.

It might be argued in reply that Anselm is not assuming
that the existence of a greatest conceivable being is logically
possible, but concluding that it is, on the grounds that there is
no good reason for thinking that the notion of a greatest

---

8  St Anselm, *Proslogion* in Plantinga, *op cit*, p 16.

conceivable being is incoherent. But even if we grant this point, it can save Anselm from the charge of begging the question only at the expense of undermining his *reductio ad absurdum* argument, since the contradiction which is supposedly implied by the hypothesis that the greatest conceivable being does not exist cannot be construed as internal to the notion of a greatest conceivable being. In any event, the conclusion of that argument is now evidently false, since it makes no sense to claim that the internal coherence of a notion depends on its being exemplified.

Descartes's ontological argument is often regarded as a poor relation of Anselm's, but there are significant differences between the two. Anselm begins by assuming that God exists at least in the understanding, but Descartes obviously thinks that this is an inadequate foundation on which to build an argument for God's existence and that as a consequence Anselm's argument can only yield the trivial conclusion 'The idea of God is the idea of an existing being'.[9] His own argument is based on the claim that God, or the supremely perfect being, possesses a 'true and immutable nature'. This is a stronger claim than that the existence of God is logically conceivable, since Descartes makes it clear that ideas which are 'put together by the mind', even when logically coherent, do not represent natures which are true and immutable.

Descartes does not seem to have formulated any very satisfactory criterion for distinguishing between ideas which represent true and immutable natures and ideas which do not. But it is easy to see why the distinction between the two is so crucial to his argument. First, it enables him to defend himself against Gaunilo-type objections by arguing that the idea of an existent dragon or of a supremely perfect island do not represent true and immutable natures and cannot therefore be used to prove *a priori* that such beings actually exist. Second, it enables him to argue that whatever can be clearly and distinctly understood to belong to the true and immutable nature of anything can be truly affirmed not simply of the nature, but of the thing itself. This, if correct, would enable him to make the transition

9  See 'Reply to Objections I' in *The Philosophical Works of Descartes*, trans Haldane and Ross (Cambridge, 1976), p 19.

from the idea of God as a supremely perfect being to the conclusion that God exists.

Whether Descartes's true and immutable natures can carry out the role which he assigns to them is, of course, highly debatable. But it is a question which we need not consider, since it can be shown that even if they do, his argument is still unsuccessful. Descartes's most formal statement of the argument is in his *First Replies*, where it is set out as follows:

> That which we clearly and distinctly understand to belong to the true and immutable nature of anything can be truly affirmed of that thing.
> We clearly and distinctly understand that to exist belongs to God's true and immutable nature.
> Therefore, it can be truly affirmed of God that he exists.[10]

The first premise implies that if a certain feature is clearly and distinctly understood to belong to the nature of something, but cannot be truly affirmed of that thing, then its nature is not true and immutable. This in turn means that if existence is clearly and distinctly understood to belong to God's nature, then we could not know that God's nature is true and immutable unless we already know that he exists. Hence Descartes, in asserting in the second premise that God possesses a true and immutable nature, is begging the question.

One might try to rebut this objection by arguing that a satisfactory criterion for picking out ideas which represent true and immutable natures might enable us to know that God possesses a true and immutable nature without first knowing that he exists. But this can be shown to be incorrect by considering the question: would the fact that the idea of God satisfy this criterion imply that God exists? If it did, then we could not know that the idea of God satisfies this criterion unless we already knew that he exists. If it did not, then in the light of Descartes's first premise, this criterion would provide a necessary, but not a sufficient, condition for an idea being such that it represented a true and immutable nature. On either eventuality for Descartes to affirm that the idea of God represents a true and immutable nature would be to beg the question.

---

10  See *ibid*, p 19.

Leibniz's ontological argument is the most straightforward of all the standard versions and also the most straightforwardly fallacious.

> ... it is tacitly assumed that this idea of a wholly great or wholly perfect being is possible and does not imply a contradiction. Even that remark enables us to prove something, namely, that *if God is possible he exists*.[11]

Leibniz goes on to offer a proof that the idea of God as all-perfect being is logically consistent. But this, even if successful, would be insufficient for his purpose, for it would show no more than that the idea of an all-perfect being is internally coherent. And since, as we have seen, there are no grounds for thinking that the non-existence of an all-perfect being implies that the idea of such a being is incoherent, there are equally no grounds for thinking that the coherence of the idea implies that the all-perfect being exists. To provide a justification for the claim that if God is possible, he exists, Leibniz must understand the possibility of God as including both the internal coherence of the idea of an all-perfect being and the further claim that such a being exists. And this, of course, means that to assume that God is possible is to beg the question.

## V

Let us now turn to the modal form of the argument. The Hartshorne version has been formalised by Hartshorne himself and runs as follows: ('$q$' here is to be understood as 'There is a perfect being' or 'Perfection exists', 'N' is the symbol for 'It is necessary (logically true) that' and '$\rightarrow$' stands for strict implication)

(1)  $q \rightarrow Nq$      "Anselm's Principle": perfection could not exist contingently

(2)  $Nq \text{ v} -Nq$      Excluded Middle

(3)  $-Nq \rightarrow N-Nq$      Form of Becker's postulate: modal status is always necessary

(4)  $Nq \text{ v} N-Nq$      Inference from (2), (3)

---

11  G Leibniz, *op cit*, p 438.

| | | |
|---|---|---|
| (5) | $N-Nq \rightarrow N-q$ | Inference from (1): the necessary falsity of the consequent implies that of the antecedent (Modal form of *modus tollens*) |
| (6) | $Nq \vee N-q$ | Inference from (4), (5) |
| (7) | $-N-q$ | Intuitive postulate (or conclusion from other theistic arguments): perfection is not impossible |
| (8) | $Nq$ | Inference from (6), (7) |
| (9) | $Nq \rightarrow q$ | Modal Axiom |
| (10) | $q$ | Inference from (8), (9)[12] |

(7) asserts that the existence of a perfect being is logically possible. If this meant no more than that the notion of a perfect being is internally coherent, then its employment as a premise might well be defensible. However, it can readily be shown that logical possibility has to be understood here in a stronger sense. From (3) and (5) it follows that $-Nq \rightarrow N-q$. But it is an axiom of modal logic that $-p \rightarrow -Np$. (If a proposition is not true, then it is not necessarily true.) Hence $-q \rightarrow -Nq$. But if $-q \rightarrow -Nq$ and $-Nq \rightarrow N-q$, then $-q \rightarrow N-q$ or, in other words, if there is no perfect being, then the existence of a perfect being is logically impossible. Now, as we have seen already, it makes no sense to say that the fact that there is no perfect being implies that the notion of a perfect being is internally incoherent, since by definition the internal coherence of a notion depends on its content alone; it cannot depend on the existence of something exemplifying it. Hence if the logical impossibility of a perfect being has to be understood as meaning that the notion of a perfect being is incoherent, then $-q \rightarrow N-q$ is false and one of the propositions from which it has been deduced has to be rejected. But there is another interpretation available, for $-q \rightarrow N-q$ may be understood as saying that if there is no perfect being, then it is logically impossible for a perfect being to exist in the sense that it is logically impossible for it to come into existence. This seems to preserve the truth of $-q \rightarrow N-q$, since something which came into existence could scarcely be a perfect being. The problem now is that one could not know, or have good reason for believing, that the existence of a perfect being is logically possible in this sense, unless one knew, or

---

12  See Charles Hartshorne, *The Logic of Perfection* (Lasalle, 1962), p 50.

had good reason for believing, that a perfect being actually exists, so that in asserting (7) Hartshorne is begging the question.

Hartshorne is aware that (7) is the vital step in the argument, but thinks that it can be given an external justification.

> The postulate of logical possibility (7) is in my view the hardest to justify. One way of doing this is to employ one or more of the other theistic proofs, some forms of which demonstrate that perfection must be at least conceivable.[13]

But even if Hartshorne were right in thinking that some of the theistic proofs demonstrate that the notion of a perfect being is at least conceivable, this would not resolve the difficulty. For all that would have been established is that the notion of a perfect being is internally coherent, that its constituent elements are logically compatible with each other. However, premise (7) of Hartshorne's argument is not true unless $q$ is true, that is to say, unless the perfect being actually exists.

The Malcolm argument has been schematised by Plantinga as follows:

(1) If God does not exist, His existence is logically impossible.
(2) If God does exist, His existence is logically necessary.
(3) Hence God's existence is logically impossible or it is logically necessary.
(4) If God's existence is logically impossible, the concept of God is contradictory.
(5) The concept of God is not contradictory.
(6) Therefore God's existence is logically necessary.[14]

(4) explains what it means for God's existence to be logically impossible. This explanation unwittingly exposes the confusion inherent in the argument, for it renders (1) untenable and makes Malcolm's argument in support of (1) irrelevant. His argument in support of (1) runs as follows:

> If God, a being greater than which cannot be conceived, does not exist, then he cannot *come* into existence. For if He did, He

---

13  *Ibid*, p 51.
14  See A Plantinga, 'A Valid Ontological Argument' in Plantinga, *op cit*, p 161.

would either have been *caused* to come into or have *happened* to come into existence, and in either case He would be a limited being, which by our conception of Him He is not. Since He cannot come into existence, if He does not exist, His existence is impossible.[15]

This argument has nothing to do with the internal coherence of the concept of a greater conceivable being. What it says rather is that there is a logical incompatibility between our conception of a greatest conceivable being and the hypothesis that such a being comes into existence. But if this is understood to mean that if God does not exist, his existence is logically impossible, then (4) is false and (5) is irrelevant.

Malcolm is clearly employing two different notions of logical impossibility. According to the first, the existence of something is logically impossible if it cannot as a matter of logic exist. According to the second, the existence of something is logically impossible when it does not exist and cannot as a matter of logic come into existence. That these are different notions is clear from the fact that a thing may be logically impossible in the second sense without being logically impossible in the first. This ambiguity in the argument is an irreparable defect. For if logical impossibility is understood throughout in the first sense, (1) is rendered untenable, since it is not true that the non-existence of the greatest conceivable being makes the concept of a greatest conceivable being contradictory. But if it is understood throughout in the second sense, then (4) and (5) must be replaced by 'God's existence is not logically impossible (in the second sense)'. And since God's existence would be logically impossible in this sense if God did not exist, this new premise presupposes that God exists.

The Malcolm and Hartshorne versions, though they differ somewhat in the way in which they develop the argument, are, I believe, essentially the same. They both characterise God/the perfect being as a being whose existence, if he exists, is logically necessary and then proceed to argue that if such a being does not exist, then his existence is logically impossible. But if this is so, as we have seen, one could not know that his existence is logically possible unless one already knows that he actually

---

15  N Malcolm, 'Anselm's Ontological Arguments' in Plantinga, *op cit*, p 146.

exists. This difficulty is in no way lessened if necessary existence is understood in terms of possible worlds. A being which, by definition, exists of necessity is one which exists in every possible world or in none. It follows that if God/the perfect being does not exist, then he does not exist in any possible world, so that one could not know that he exists in some possible world without knowing that he exists in the real world.

Plantinga has offered a rather different version of the modal argument. He believes that the Hartshorne-Malcolm versions prove no more than that there exists of necessity a being which in some possible world is the greatest conceivable being, but is not necessarily the greatest conceivable being in the real world. To get round this difficulty he distinguishes between the greatness of an entity and its excellence. A being's excellence, he stipulates, depends in a given world only on the properties which it has in that world, whereas its greatness in that world depends not only on those properties, but also on the properties which it possesses in other worlds. For a being then to have a maximal degree of greatness in a given world it has to have maximal excellence in every possible world.

Plantinga's modal argument runs as follows:

(1) It is possible that there be a being that has maximal greatness.
(2) So there is a possible being that in some world W has maximal greatness.
(3) A being has maximal greatness in a given world only if it has maximal excellence in every world.
(4) Therefore, there exists a being that has maximal excellence in every world, that is, a maximally great being.[16]

This argument differs from the Hartshorne-Malcolm versions in characterising the perfect being not as a being which exists of necessity, but as a being which necessarily possesses maximal excellence. But while this move may enable Plantinga to escape the difficulty which he detects in the Hartshorne-Malcolm versions, it provides no defence against the charge of committing a *petitio principii*. Implicit in Plantinga's argument is the assumption that if the notion of a maximally great being is

---

16   See A Plantinga, *God, Freedom and Evil* (London, 1976), p 108.

internally coherent, then there is a possible world in which a maximally great being exists. Now it is true that if the notion of a maximally great being is internally incoherent, then there is no possible world in which a maximally great being exists and it is generally true that if the notion of an *x* is internally coherent, then there is some possible world in which an *x* exists. But this is not true when '*x*' denotes something which exists of necessity. For even when the notion of such a being is internally coherent, if it is not exemplified in the real world, then it is not exemplified in any possible world.

It might be argued on Plantinga's behalf that since there is nothing contingent about an absolutely perfect or maximally great being, then if such a being does not exist, it is necessarily non-existent. This is indeed true, but it is necessarily non-existent not because the notion of such a being is internally incoherent, but because it does not actually exist and it is logically impossible for a necessary being which does not actually exist to come into existence. Necessary existence is exemplified in all possible worlds or in none, so that if there are no necessary beings, it is logically impossible for a necessary being to exist. But the logical impossibility in this case derives not from the internal incoherence of the notion of a necessary being, but from the non-existence in the real world of any such being.

Plantinga would be entitled to infer that there is a possible world in which maximal greatness is instantiated from the internal coherence of the notion of a maximally great being only if the non-existence of a maximally great being implied that the notion of such a being is internally incoherent. However, he does not argue that this is so, and, as we have seen, there is good reason for thinking that it is not. But if this inference is not warranted, then his second premise is not deducible from his first unless his first is understood as saying not simply that the notion of a maximally great being is internally coherent, but also that such a being exists in some possible world and therefore actually exists. To avoid a *non sequitur*, then, his first premise must be construed in such a way that it renders the entire argument circular.

This illegitimate move from a weaker to a stronger sense of logical possibility has been found in all but one of the standard versions. It is not present in Descartes's argument where the concept of a true and immutable nature, when applied to God, is equivalent to logical possibility in the stronger sense. But this means no more than that Descartes's argument is a more straightforward instance of a *petitio principii*.

The ontological argument is a hydra-headed monster, so perhaps it will always be premature to write its obituary. Nevertheless, if I have succeeded in showing that all the standard versions exhibit the same error in reasoning, it must be highly unlikely that the arguments can be formulated in such a way as to avoid this difficulty. Certainly the burden of proof rests with those who think otherwise.[17]

17  For a criticism of this paper and my reply see William F Valicella, 'Has the Ontological Argument Been Refuted?', *Religious Studies* 20 (1993), pp 97-110 and PJ McGrath, 'Does the Ontological Argument Beg the Question?' (forthcoming in *Religious Studies*). Further discussion of the ontological argument may be found in McGrath, 'Where Does the Ontological Argument Go Wrong?', *Philosophical Studies*, XXX (1984), pp 144-164, 'The Modal Ontological Argument — A Reply to Kane and Morris', *Mind*, XCV (1986), pp 373-376 and 'The Ontological Argument Revisited', *Philosophy*, 63 (1988), pp 529-533.

# 9  Miracles

I  Miracles as Evidence

Apologists for the great theistic religions, Judaism, Christianity and Islam, have traditionally appealed to miracles in support of their systems of belief. The miracles described in the New Testament, for example, particularly the resurrection of Jesus from the dead, were regarded by Christian apologists as sufficient to establish that Jesus is the Son of God and that Christianity is the true religion. But some contemporary Christian theologians have become wary of this approach. They argue that the New Testament writers do not treat the miracle stories evidentially and that consequently the use of miracles in Christian apologetics is really an abuse. The function of the miracle stories in the New Testament is symbolic rather than evidential. They symbolise in particular the power and the love of God, the importance of Jesus' mission and his victory over death. But to treat them as proofs of basic Christian beliefs is to misuse them.

This account of the New Testament miracle stories is no doubt correct in claiming that to regard them as no more than apologetical aids is seriously to distort them. Many of the miracle stories, particularly those in *John*, contain a symbolism that is clearly theological in character. Nevertheless to treat the stories as if they had no evidential function seems just as great a distortion as to regard them as having a purely apologetical significance. Miracle stories are in fact used evidentially in both the Old and New Testaments. Moses

(*Deuteronomy*, 18:18) vindicates his claim to have been sent from God by predicting a rather gruesome miracle — the destruction of those who had rebelled against him by their being suddenly and inexplicably swallowed up by the earth. 'Hereby you shall know that the Lord has sent me to do all these works, and that it has not been of my own accord.' The prophet Ezechial (*III Kings*, 18) performs a miracle involving spontaneous combustion to prove that 'thou art God in Israel and that I am thy servant, and that I have done all these things at thy word'. Jesus himself on several occasions treats miracles as evidence of his divine mission. When John the Baptist (*Matt*, XI, 4-5) sends him a message, asking 'Are you he who is to come or shall we look for another?', Jesus replies 'Go and tell John what you have heard and seen: the blind see and the lame walk, lepers are cleansed and the deaf hear, and the dead are raised up and the poor have the gospel preached to them'. He vindicates his power to forgive sin (*Luke*, V, 20-25) by miraculously healing the man who was paralysed. When Nicodemus comes to him by night (*John*, III, 2), Jesus does not repudiate his remark: 'Rabbi, we know that you are a teacher come from God; for no one can do these signs that you do unless God is with him'. After the death of Jesus the apostle Peter (*Acts*, II:22) describes him as 'a man attested to you by God with mighty works and wonders and signs'.

But even if miracle stories had not been treated evidentially in the Bible, it would not follow that it is an abuse for later writers to use them as evidence for the authenticity of the Christian message. There is nothing objectionable in finding a significance in an historical episode that was not recognised by the writers who originally described it. Indeed the authors of the four gospels frequently cite events in the Old Testament as prefiguring events in the New even though they would not have been seen in this way by the Old Testament writers themselves. If the New Testament miracle stories do provide good evidence for the claim that Jesus was sent by God, then it would be extraordinarily remiss of a Christian apologist not to cite it. The only serious question that arises concerning the use of miracle stories as evidence therefore is not whether this way of treating them conforms to the way in which they were originally understood, but whether these stories are sufficient to establish that miracles have in fact taken place.

In any event, Christian apologists are in no position to dispense with miracles as evidence for the divine origin of Jesus' mission, for if they do, they have nothing to put in their place. One who claims to be sent from God, must surely substantiate that claim if he or she is to be taken seriously. An unsupported claim to be a divine emissary establishes nothing, since anyone can make it. If the evidential use of miracles is excluded, then there is no means of distinguishing between one who speaks with divine authority and one who merely claims to do so; indeed there is no way of knowing whether anyone has ever been given authority by God to speak on his behalf.

It could be argued however that, even if the miracle stories are excluded from the discussion, there is still evidence in support of the claim that Jesus was sent by God. This evidence consists in the fact that Jesus, as depicted in the Gospels, was a man distinguished by great moral integrity and holiness of life. It is going beyond the bounds of credibility therefore to suggest that his claim to be a divine emissary was insincere or that he lacked substantial reasons for making it.

But this argument seems to me to be too weak to be of any real significance. There are at least two major difficulties confronting it. The first is that if we treat the miracle stories as unreliable and therefore as probably untrue, then it is impossible to see how we can have any real confidence in what the New Testament tells us about the character of Jesus? In all four gospels the miracle stories constitute a substantial and integral part of the text. In the Gospel of St Mark, for instance, they constitute nearly a half of the whole — 202 verses out of 456 — and in all four gospels the delineation of the character of Jesus largely derives from them. His kindness and compassion towards those in need, for example, is shown by his miracles of healing and by his feeding of the multitude in the desert. His tact is displayed by the manner in which he saved the newly married couple at Cana from embarrassment. His capacity for friendship is manifested by the tears which he shed on being told of the death of Lazarus. His mildness and lack of vindictiveness is demonstrated by his healing of the servant of the high priest immediately after his arrest on the Mount of Olives. If all these stories have to be discarded as unreliable, then not merely is the status of the evangelists as historical witnesses seriously compromised, but the picture which they draw of Jesus' moral character becomes a very blurred image indeed.

But even if we accept the evangelists' account of Jesus' character and conduct as reliable, the argument cited above can establish no more than that Jesus was genuinely convinced that he had been sent by God. It provides no good reason for excluding the possibility that he may have been mistaken about this. Moral integrity is essentially a quality of mind or character relating to decision-making; it is the disposition to make morally right decisions and to act in accordance with them. But since we cannot *decide* what to believe, there is no *a priori* reason for thinking that people of great moral integrity are less likely than others to entertain unwarranted beliefs. Nor is there any empirical evidence to suggest that they are. History is full of examples of individuals of the highest moral distinction entertaining the most bizarre and unfounded beliefs. Tolstoy and Gandhi, for instance, both came to believe in their later years that sexual intercourse is always wicked, even when engaged in by a married couple with a view to children. Dr Samuel Johnson believed, rather more mundanely, that swallows do not emigrate, but instead spend the winter under water, asleep on the beds of rivers. Plato thought that in an ideal world children would be brought up not by their parents, but by the state. St Paul believed that women are inferior to men and should be subject to them. St Thomas Aquinas went even further and asserted that a woman is a defective male. He also believed that hail, rain and wind are caused by demons. Jesus himself appears to have believed that the world would shortly come to an end.

The Christian apologist who refuses to use miracles evidentially appears to have no alternative but to resort to the plea that the belief that Jesus was a divine emissary, even though it lacks supporting evidence, is somehow not credulous or irrational. But on the face of it this is an impossible position to defend. Is there any way of understanding it that would make it acceptable? There are two possibilities to be considered. The first is that the belief that Jesus was a divine emissary is a matter of faith rather than of reason. This belief, it might be claimed, though not supported by evidence, is not irrational, for though faith transcends reason, it is not contrary to it. But how is faith being understood here? It cannot be taken in its usual sense as meaning believing something on the authority of God, for Jesus' claim to be a divine emissary was not supported by the authority of God unless he was a divine emissary. To say that one believes that Jesus was a divine emissary on the authority of God is thus equivalent to saying that one believes that Jesus was a divine emissary because he was a divine emissary; and this obviously gets us nowhere.

In Chapter One ('Faith and Reason') I described faith as a response to and acceptance of divine revelation — a response not however to a revelation that occurred solely in the past, but to one occurring here and now in the life of the believer. And I argued that faith in Jesus is supported by evidence that is, to a large extent, available only to the believer, that the case for Christianity can, in other words, be fully appreciated only by one who is already a Christian. I now think that this way of justifying Christian belief is unacceptable. There are two things wrong with it. The first is that the sort of reasoning that it appeals to is circular in character. Admittedly not all circular reasoning, as I argued in chapter one, is necessarily defective. There may well be virtuous circles as well as vicious ones. But only in very exceptional cases should circular reasoning be regarded as acceptable, since anything else would be a recipe for total irrationality. It would appear to me that circular reasoning is warranted only in connection with a belief that underpins an important area of human knowledge and is so basic as not to be susceptible of non-circular justification. To permit it in any other circumstances would be to make it difficult, if not impossible, to treat any form of circular reasoning as fallacious. And this would render all reasoning useless, since any proposition whatever could then be provided with rational justification. Now the belief that Jesus was a divine emissary is not one that underpins an important area of human knowledge, nor is it so basic that any non-circular justification is rendered impossible. It cannot therefore be justified by circular reasoning.

The second thing wrong with this conception of faith is that if one cannot appreciate the case for Christianity without being a Christian, then may not this be true of all forms of religious belief? And if every form of religious belief is such that the evidence in its favour can be fully appreciated only by one who already accepts it, then there is no rational means of distinguishing between religious beliefs that are warranted and religious beliefs that are not. Thus even if it is true to say that only a Christian can fully appreciate the case for Christianity, the problem is that a Christian cannot fully appreciate the case for any other form of religious belief and is in no position therefore to judge whether or not the evidence in favour of some religion that is incompatible with Christianity may not be stronger than the evidence in favour of Christianity itself. One must conclude therefore that faith in this sense of the term is no substitute for evidence that is accessible to both believer and non-believer alike.

The only other way in which it could be argued that the belief that Jesus was a divine emissary is not irrational even though there is no evidence in its favour is by claiming that it is a 'basic belief'. In point of fact I know of no religious thinker who has made this claim explicitly. Nonetheless it is not uncommon nowadays for philosophers of religion to argue that belief in God is a basic belief and if this is acceptable, it seems a short step to go on to claim that belief that Jesus was a divine emissary is also a basic belief and therefore does not require evidential support. Basic beliefs are beliefs that are used to substantiate other beliefs, but are themselves too basic to be substantiated. Since every proof depends on something that is left unproven and it is impossible to go back forever in a chain of reasoning, there must, it is claimed, be beliefs that are accepted as true without proof. Without such basic beliefs it appears impossible to make sense of human knowledge. And if such basic beliefs are admitted, then might not the belief that Jesus was a divine emissary be properly regarded as basic?

However, even if it be granted that there are beliefs that are properly basic, it seems out of the question to regard the belief that Jesus was a divine emissary as one of them. A belief is properly basic if one is justified in holding it even though it lacks supporting evidence. Now consider the belief that Jesus really existed. This is clearly a more basic belief than the belief that Jesus was a divine emissary, for the latter belief presupposes the former in the sense that it could not be true unless the former belief was true whereas the former could be true even though the latter belief was false. But the belief that Jesus really existed could not be a properly basic belief, since it would be absurd to suggest that one could be justified in believing that some individual existed two thousand years ago even though there is no testimony of any kind to support that claim. Suppose, to take a parallel case, that someone were to claim that there had been a famous poet in pre-Christian Ireland called MacDara, but that unfortunately his verse sagas had been forgotten before the Irish had learned the art of writing and as a consequence there was now no historical evidence for MacDara's existence. Clearly it would be preposterous for the believer in MacDara to try to justify his belief by claiming that it was properly basic. But it would be equally absurd to claim that the belief that Jesus really existed is not in need of evidential support. And since that belief is more basic than the belief that Jesus was a divine emissary, the latter must also be non-basic. The belief that Jesus was a divine emissary is, in other words, in need of supporting evidence if it is to be rationally justified.

If miracles are to be used evidentially, how should the term 'miracle' be understood? This is a philosophical rather than a scriptural issue. It is a question not of how the miracles attributed to Jesus were understood by the New Testament writers, but rather of how a miracle is to be understood if it is to be capable of providing evidence in support of some religious doctrine. In ordinary speech the term 'miracle' is used rather loosely to mean an event that is so unusual or unexpected as to arouse wonder or disbelief. We say that people had a miraculous escape when they emerge unscathed from a serious plane crash or that someone, in consequence of a new advance in medicine, miraculously recovered from an apparently fatal illness. But miracles understood in this sense would obviously be of no evidential value in religious contexts. To provide evidence for the reality of the supernatural a miracle would have to be the sort of event that cannot be explained in natural terms. Now any event that comes under natural law can obviously be given a natural or scientific explanation. The only sort of event that cannot be explained naturally or scientifically, it would appear, is one that violates a law of nature — an event in other words that is logically incompatible with, or is a counter-example to, a law of nature. However, most writers on miracles have felt that for an event to constitute a miracle it is not enough for it to contravene a natural law; it must also have some religious significance. This second feature of miracles has been expressed in different ways by different writers, but there would be little point in considering these in detail. Instead I shall give provisional acceptance to the definition of 'miracle' provided by *A Dictionary of Philosophy*, since it seems to me to be a fair statement of how the term has been understood in philosophical discussion. It runs as follows: 'A miracle is an act that manifests divine power through the suspension or alteration of the normal working of the laws of nature'.[1] As we shall see shortly, however, there are reasons for thinking that this type of definition is not wholly satisfactory and that it needs to be modified if miracles are to be used evidentially in religious contexts.

## II Are Miracles Possible?

There are two well known philosophical objections to using miracles, when understood in accordance with this philosophical definition, as evidence for some religious belief. The first is the claim that the concept of a violation of a law of nature is incoherent and that consequently miracles, when understood in this sense, are logically impossible. This objection was first formulated by John Stuart Mill in his book *A System of Logic*:

> We cannot admit a proposition as a law of nature, and yet believe a fact in real contradiction to it. We must disbelieve the alleged fact, or believe that we are mistaken in admitting the supposed law.[2]

Mill's argument is so concise that it is liable to be misunderstood. To expound it fully one must first draw a distinction between a law of nature and a scientific principle. A law of nature is what is expressed by a true scientific principle. It follows that while a scientific principle may be either true or false, it makes no sense to speak of a law of nature as false, for if what appears to

---

1 *A Dictionary of Philosophy*, ed A Flew, London 1979, p 217.
2 JS Mill, *A System of Logic*, Book III, chapter 25, sec 2.

be a law of nature turns out to be false, this is enough to show that it is not a law of nature after all, but is instead an unsatisfactory scientific principle which must be either modified or abandoned. The relationship between a law of nature and a scientific principle is thus rather similar to the relationship between knowing and believing. Truth is a constituent element of the concept of knowing, but not of the concept of believing. If you think you know something, but it turns out that what you think you know is false, then obviously you did not really know it, but merely falsely believed it. Likewise if what is taken to be a law of nature turns out to be incorrect, this is enough to show that it is not a genuine law of nature, for the notion of a false or inaccurate law of nature is unintelligible.

Mill's objection to the possibility of miracles may therefore be stated more comprehensively as follows. Any statement that is logically incompatible with a true statement must itself be false, for if two statements, A and B, are logically incompatible with each other, then it is logically impossible that they both be true. It follows that if A is a statement of a law of nature and B any statement that is logically incompatible with A, then since A must be true, B must be false. But any report of a miraculous event that violated the natural law expressed by A would be logically incompatible with A and must also be false. And since every miracle report is, by definition, a report of an event that constitutes a violation of a law of nature, it follows that every miracle report must be false and that miracles are therefore impossible.

There are two fairly obvious ways in which one might try to rebut Mill's argument. The first is to reject his definition of a miracle as a violation of a law of nature. The second is to reject his conception of a law of nature as something that cannot admit of exceptions. However, the problem with the first approach is that if a miracle is not a violation of a law of nature, then it will be explicable in terms of these laws and as a consequence it will be impossible to use it as evidence for any religious belief. If an event is an instance of the operation of a law of nature, then it is susceptible of a scientific explanation and any attempt to explain it in terms of a supernatural intervention becomes redundant.

The second approach has been adopted by a number of contemporary philosophers of religion, including the American, Robert Hambourger, and the Australian, John Mackie. Hambourger suggests that 'the laws of nature should be understood quite literally as principles that govern the operations of *nature*, not as determining what will happen in cases of supernatural intervention'.[3] Mackie makes a similar proposal in slightly different language.

> We might determine that something *is* a basic law of working of natural objects, and yet also, independently, find that it was occasionally violated. An occasional violation does not itself necessarily overthrow the independently established conclusion that this *is* a law of working.[4]

However, neither of these responses is successful. Consider Hambourger's position first of all. If the laws of nature govern only the operations of nature, then supernatural occurrences do not come within the scope of natural law and cannot therefore constitute violations of these laws. For instance, if the event of Jesus walking on water involved a supernatural intervention in nature, then it could not constitute a violation of the principle 'Bodies displace their weight in water', since this principle does not apply to such events. In any event, Hambourger has provided us with no means of telling whether or not an event such as Jesus walking on water is a supernatural event or is instead merely a highly unusual natural event whose occurrence indicates that a principle which had hitherto been taken to express a law of nature is inaccurate and needs to be reformulated.

Mackie on the other hand does not restrict the scope of natural laws, but he argues that the usual way in which we formulate a natural law expresses a law of working of natural objects and that these laws of working may occasionally be violated. By the expression 'a law of working' he apparently means a description of how certain natural objects normally behave and this does not exclude the possibility that in certain very unusual situations they may behave differently. However, Mackie's position is open to the same sort of objections as

---

3  R Hambourger, 'Need Miracles be Extraordinary?', *Philosophy and Phenomenological Research*, vol XLVII, no 3 (March 1987), p 86.
4  JL Mackie, *The Miracle of Theism*, Oxford 1982, p 21.

Hambourger's. If his laws of working are not overthrown by occasional violations, then these so-called violations are not genuine violations, since their occurrence is not incompatible with the truth of the law. In other words, if Mackie's laws of working are compatible with occasional violations, then what they describe is not the way things happen, but the way things usually or generally happen. Thus if we take the principle 'Bodies displace their weight in water' as an account of the way things usually happen, then the event of Jesus walking on water is not a violation of this principle and cannot therefore be a miracle in the sense presupposed by Mill. Besides Mackie has provided us with no criterion for distinguishing between natural 'violations' of these laws of working and supernatural ones.

The failure of Hambourger and Mackie to refute Mill's argument suggests that it is unanswerable. But this impression may be misleading, for his argument also seems to prove too much and consequently to prove nothing at all. Whatever implies something that is false must itself be false. Now Mill's position appears to imply something that is false, for if it is logically impossible for miracles to occur, then it is logically impossible for an omnipotent God to intervene in nature and produce an event that contravenes one of the laws that govern nature. But there is widespread agreement among philosophers that, in the first place, if God exists and is omnipotent, then the only limits on his power are logical limits, for if his power were subject to limits other than logical ones, he would not be omnipotent; and, secondly, that what is expressed by a law of nature is something that is true not as a matter of logical necessity, but merely as a matter of contingent fact. The laws of nature, in other words, are not logical laws. There is nothing logically incoherent or inconceivable about a universe which is governed by laws that are different from the laws that govern the universe that we inhabit. Now if the power of an omnipotent God is subject only to logical constraints and the laws of nature are not logical laws, then it follows that an omnipotent God could suspend or modify a law of nature; and this in turn implies that miracles are not logically impossible.

But this shows, at best, that there is something unsatisfactory about Mill's argument. It does not tell us what is wrong with it, nor does it indicate how miracles should be understood if Mill's objection is to be overcome. There has however been one other recent attempt to answer Mill which, though not successful as it stands, seems to me to point the way towards a successful resolution of the problem. The English philosopher, Richard Swinburne, has argued that a violation of a law of nature is not just a counter-instance to some well established scientific principle.[5] The occurrence of such an event would prove no more than that the way in which this principle has hitherto been formulated is defective and that consequently the principle needs to be reformulated to take account of this event. But suppose the event cannot be repeated despite the most meticulous reproduction of the causal factors that produced it. In that case any attempt to reformulate the scientific principle is bound to fail, for if the event is unrepeatable, then it is also unpredictable and consequently any reformulation of the principle designed to take account of this event will give rise to false predictions. What the occurrence of a non-repeatable counter-instance to a well established scientific principle would prove therefore is not that the principle needs to be reformulated, but that not everything that happens in nature can be brought under general laws. There are no scientific or philosophical grounds for thinking that such anomalous events cannot happen and therefore no good reason for regarding a violation of a law of nature as an incoherent notion.

But this attempt to answer Mill also fails. This can be readily seen if we consider the question: Would the occurrence of a non-repeatable counter-instance to a well established scientific principle mean that the principle needs to be modified if it is to convey a correct account of the relevant natural law? If Jesus walked on water, does the principle 'Bodies displace their weight in water' need to be modified so as to read 'Bodies nearly always displace their weight in water'? If it does, then the event of Jesus walking on water is not a violation of this principle and therefore not a violation of natural law. But if it does not, then one must conclude that natural laws apply only to events that are repeatable and predictable and the event of Jesus walking on water is still not a violation of natural law.

---

5  See R Swinburne, *The Concept of Miracle*, London 1970, pp 29-32.

Should we conclude from this that Mill's objection is unanswerable and that miracles cannot therefore be employed as evidence for religious beliefs? I do not think so. What we should conclude rather is that 'miracle' should not be defined in terms of a violation of a law of nature, since the latter notion is unintelligible. However, there is nothing to prevent us defining it along the lines proposed by Swinburne, but dropping the notion that a miracle defined in this way would constitute a violation of a law of nature. This can be done by treating scientific principles and laws of nature as governing only law-like or non-anomalous events. An event that does not fall under a particular principle cannot constitute an exception to it. Thus if an event occurs which is a counter-instance to a well established scientific principle, but it turns out to be non-repeatable and therefore strictly anomalous, then it does not fall under that principle and cannot therefore constitute an exception to it or to the corresponding natural law. This enables us not so much to rebut Mill's argument, as to treat it as irrelevant.

Even if someone were to insist that natural laws govern everything that happens in nature and that even strictly anomalous events must be understood to fall within their scope, this would not constitute a difficulty. If anomalous events occur and have to be taken into account in the formulation of the laws of nature, they will not constitute violations of these laws. For example, if it were established that Jesus really walked on water, then the relevant natural law, according to this conception, would be 'Bodies nearly always displace their weight in water'. And the event of Jesus walking on water would not constitute a violation of this law. Moreover, the occurrence of the anomalous event could not be explained by reference to this law, so that there would still be room for a supernatural explanation.

There is still however a serious difficulty about defining 'miracle' in this way. If there are such things as strictly anomalous events, then it may well be that they occur naturally. Indeed in the absence of evidence that it was caused by a supernatural agent, considerations of economy would require us to treat any apparently anomalous event as a natural occurrence. This in turn would mean that an anomalous event could never provide evidence in support of a religious belief, for in the absence of evidence for thinking that it was caused by a supernatural agent, it would have to be treated as a purely natural occurrence; and if there was evidence that it was caused by a supernatural agent, it is this evidence that would be supportive of the religious belief rather than the anomalous nature of the event.

But we can, I believe, find a way round this difficulty by taking account of the essentially unpredictable character of anomalous events. Even a complete knowledge of the laws that govern the physical universe would not enable us to bring a anomalous event about, nor would it be of the slightest help in predicting its occurrence. It follows that human agents, using natural resources only, could have no good grounds for predicting the occurrence of an anomalous event, nor could they intentionally bring one about, since there is no way of knowing which human activity would be likely to cause the event to occur. If therefore a human agent, while claiming to act under divine influence, correctly predicted the occurrence of an anomalous event or to all appearances intentionally brought one about, that is, if he announced his intention to bring it about and the event then occurred as the apparent result of his actions, this would constitute a miracle.

But there are two fairly obvious objections to this line of reasoning. The first is that even if some individual predicts, or announces his intention to bring about, an anomalous event and then the event occurs, there is no guarantee that he had any good grounds for his prediction or that he was actually involved in the bringing about of the event. It may be that he was just lucky. Perhaps the event would have occurred in any case and it was purely by chance that it was preceded by the individual's prediction or statement of intention. However, it seems certain that anomalous events are, at best, very rare occurrences. If they were not, then scientists would need to take them into account in making scientific predictions. But scientists do not do this and there appears to be no grounds for thinking that they are open to criticism on this score, something that would be inexplicable if anomalous events were frequent occurrences. Now if anomalous events occur only rarely, then the odds against someone correctly predicting purely by chance just when, where and how an anomalous event would occur are so enormous that the possibility of this actually happening could in practice be discounted. Moreover if the person claiming to act under divine influence correctly predicted, or to all appearances intentionally brought about, a number of anomalous events, the attempt to explain this as simply a series of lucky predictions would be wholly incredible.

The second objection is that even if anomalous events were to occur, they could not provide evidence in support of any religious belief, since there is no means of distinguishing between events that are strictly anomalous and events that, though susceptible of a scientific explanation, cannot in the present state of human knowledge be explained scientifically. To distinguish between the two classes of events one would first have to know how science would develop in the future, for to claim that this particular event cannot, even in principle, be explained scientifically is to lay down limits to the future progress of science. And this claim could not be warranted, since it is a claim to the possession of knowledge that has not yet been discovered.

Swinburne has however already provided an effective answer to this objection. One does not have to foresee the future development of science to distinguish between events that are strictly anomalous and events that are merely not yet susceptible of a scientific explanation. If an event is unrepeatable, then it is impossible for it to be predicted by a genuine law of nature, since any scientific principle that predicts it will also produce false predictions. Thus if an event were such that it could not be repeated no matter how meticulously the conditions that brought it about in the first instance were reproduced, then there would be adequate grounds for thinking that it could not be predicted by a genuine law of nature and that it was therefore strictly anomalous.

This point can perhaps be best brought out by means of an example. In chapter eleven of the Fourth Gospel Jesus is depicted as bringing Lazarus back to life four days after his death by simply uttering the words 'Lazarus, come forth'. Now it seems as certain as anything can be that this event, assuming that it really happened, is non-repeatable. If a person could be brought back to life merely by the sound of the human voice

or by the uttering of certain words, then the revivification of
Lazarus would be regarded not as a miracle, but as a commonplace event. And if an event cannot be repeated no matter how
carefully the factors that brought it about are reproduced,
then it cannot be predicted or explained by reference to natural
law and is therefore strictly anomalous. It might be argued of
course that the conditions that brought about the raising of
Lazarus from the dead have never been fully reproduced, since
one of these conditions is that the words be uttered by Jesus.
But this would still leave it impossible to explain the event in
terms of natural law, for the factors that caused the event
could not then be stated in general terms.

Admittedly an event that is to all appearances non-repeatable
might eventually turn out to be repeatable. Perhaps the
wonder-worker exercised some natural powers which, though
not uniquely possessed by him, are still extremely rare or
perhaps he brought about the miraculous effect by some
mysterious natural means that has since remained unknown.
But these hypotheses can scarcely be taken seriously when
dealing with an event such as the raising of Lazarus. A great
deal is already known about the laws that govern the
preservation and destruction of brain-cells and none of this is
compatible with the claim that an individual who was dead for
several days and whose body was allowed to corrupt in the
usual way had been restored to normal life. Such an event
would conflict with so many basic scientific beliefs that one
could not treat it as susceptible of a natural explanation without
repudiating a large area of contemporary science. This would
appear to be far too high a price to pay for the privilege of
retaining the principle, itself little more than an article of
faith, that every event that occurs in nature may in principle
be given a scientific explanation.

### III  Are Miracle Reports Credible?

The definition of 'miracle' which I am proposing may be stated
then as follows: 'A miracle is a strictly anomalous event that is
either correctly predicted or intentionally brought about by a
human agent claiming to be acting under divine influence'. I
have argued that one would be justified in treating an event as
strictly anomalous if it constitutes a counter-instance to some

well established scientific principle and any reformulation of the principle that takes account of this event will produce false predictions. I have also argued that in certain circumstances it would be irrational to deny that an anomalous event was intentionally brought about by a human agent claiming to act under divine influence. If all this is correct, then there appears to be no good reason for thinking that miracles could not, as a matter of principle, establish that Jesus was a divine emissary or that his religious teaching was sanctioned by God.

But do miracles establish these things as a matter of fact? To answer this question we must take account of the second important objection to the evidential use of miracles — David Hume's famous argument in his *An Inquiry Concerning Human Understanding* about the rationality of believing that any particular event is miraculous. This was directed against miracles conceived as violations of laws of nature, but there is nothing to prevent it from being directed also against miracles conceived in terms of anomalous events.

The first thing to be noted about Hume's argument is that it is concerned with the rationality of believing in miracles on the basis of testimony. He does not consider the rationality of believing in miracles if one has personally witnessed an event that is to all appearances miraculous. But there are two reasons why this limitation takes little from the value of his argument. The first is that the majority of people who believe in miracles base their belief on testimony; only a small minority would claim that they have actually experienced an event that was strictly miraculous. The second is that Hume's argument, as we shall see shortly, may be readily adapted so that it applies also to the belief of those who think that they have witnessed a miracle.

Even if we make no appeal to philosophy, common sense on its own suggests certain principles relating to the rationality of believing in any event on the testimony of others. The first is that it is irrational to believe that the event occurred if it is more likely than not that the witness or witnesses are telling lies. The second is that it is irrational to believe that the event occurred if it is more likely than not that the witness or witnesses are mistaken in reporting what happened. Thus the common sense approach could be summed up by saying that one should not believe that something happened on the basis of testimony if it is more likely than not that the witnesses were either mendacious or mistaken. But how are we to decide the likelihood of the witnesses being both truthful and accurate? Common sense would here suggest that it is a question of character. If the witnesses are serious minded and habitually truthful, then it is likely that they are telling the truth and if they are intelligent and generally critical in their approach to things, then it is unlikely that they were deceived or that they unwittingly misreported what they experienced.

Now Hume would, I believe, agree with this common sense approach so far as ordinary everyday events are concerned, but he makes it clear that he regards it as inadequate for the evaluation of testimony concerning extraordinary events and *a fortiori* inadequate for dealing with testimony relating to miracles. An extraordinary event is, by definition, antecedently improbable, that is to say, it is improbable relative to what we already know about the way things happen; and since this antecedent improbability must be taken into account when evaluating the likelihood of the witnesses to the event being untruthful or mistaken, it is not sufficient to consider solely the character and attainments of the witnesses. Thus if it were antecedently more improbable that a certain event should occur than that the witnesses who reported its occurrence were either untruthful or mistaken, then it would be irrational to believe that the witnesses were telling the truth. Suppose that there were reports from a large number of witnesses, whose veracity and critical acumen there was no good reason to doubt, that a horse existed which was capable of answering problems in elementary arithmetic that were put to him verbally. Hume's reaction would be that the antecedent improbability of a horse being able to understand such problems, never mind answer them correctly, is so great that it would be irrational not to treat these reports with the greatest scepticism. History has vindicated Hume. At the beginning of the twentieth century there were reports from many witnesses that a German horse called Clever Hans could provide correct solutions to arith-metical problems by tapping out the answer with his hoof. There appeared to be no possibility of deception, since Clever Hans was no less accurate when his trainer was absent than when he was present. However, it later transpired that Clever Hans's arithmetical prowess depended on his audience knowing the answer to the problem that had been put to him. When they did not know the answer, Clever Hans did not know when to stop tapping. Clearly he had not been calculating, but rather observing signs made unwittingly by his audience which indicated when he had given the requisite number of taps.[6]

It is not difficult to see how Hume's reasoning concerning extraordinary events may be applied to miracles. Whether we treat a miracle as a violation of a law of nature, as Hume does, or as a non-repeatable counter-instance to a well established scientific principle, as I do, a miracle is antecedently a highly improbable event. Indeed if a miracle is understood to be a violation of a law of nature, then, it is, as we have seen already, a logically impossible event, so that its antecedent probability is zero. But even if we take a miracle to be a non-repeatable counter-instance to a well established scientific principle, it still has a very low antecedent probability, since a well established scientific principle is a principle for which there is a considerable amount of evidence and no hard evidence to the contrary. It follows that the testimony in favour of a miracle would have to be extremely strong for it to be rational to believe that the miracle had in fact occurred. It is now clear how Hume's argument may also be applied to those who believe that they have witnessed a miracle. Even if I were to witness an event that was to all appearances miraculous, it would not be rational for me to believe that it was a genuine miracle, on Hume's reasoning, unless the antecedent improbability of such an event was outweighed by the improbability of my being subject to some kind of deception or being guilty of misinterpreting the data.

Hume's argument concerning miracles may be stated somewhat more systematically as follows. The first step in his reasoning is the claim that 'a wise man ... proportions his belief to the evidence'.[7] Hume would presumably regard this principle as deriving from the meaning of the word 'rational'

---

6    My information concerning Clever Hans is taken from *The Oxford Companion to the Mind*, ed RL Gregory, Oxford 1989, pp 149-50.

7    D Hume, *An Enquiry Concerning Human Understanding*, ed Selby-Bigge, Oxford 1966, p 110.

and therefore not in need of justification (though it is in need of some qualification if allowance is to be made for beliefs that are properly basic). To be rational on this view is, by definition, to believe neither more nor less than is warranted by the evidence. When there is no conflict of evidence, this proportioning of belief to evidence is a straightforward matter. But when there is evidence both for and against a proposition, then we must consider which evidence is the stronger and proportion our belief accordingly. As Hume puts it 'we must balance the opposite experiments ... and deduct the smaller number from the greater, in order to know the exact force of the superior evidence'.[8]

The next step in Hume's reasoning is the claim that belief in a miracle needs to be supported by two different kinds of evidence. Since a miracle, on Hume's conception, is a violation of a law of nature, there must be (a) evidence that the principle that has been violated is a genuine law of nature an (b) evidence that the event that violated it actually occurred. Let us call (a) the scientific evidence and (b) the historical evidence. When a miracle is understood as a non-repeatable counter-instance to a well established scientific principle, three kinds of evidence are required — (a) evidence that the principle of which the apparently miraculous event is a counter-instance is a well established scientific principle; (b) evidence that the event constituting a counter-instance to it actually occurred and (c) evidence that this event is non-repeatable. However, since (a) and (b) is the same in both cases and (c) is neither relevant to the point Hume is making nor particularly problematic, we can devote all our attention to (a) and (b).

The third and final step in Hume's argument is the crucial one. It is that the scientific evidence and the historical evidence relating to any miracle report are necessarily in conflict. If there is a body of evidence in support of the claim that some scientific principle, P, expresses a genuine law of nature, then this evidence makes it antecedently improbable that any event, E, that is a counter-instance to, or a violation of, P has ever occurred. Now if it is antecedently improbable that an event of a certain type occurs, then it is unreasonable to believe a

8  *Ibid*, p 111.

report that such an event has occurred unless the evidence in favour of its occurrence outweighs the evidence for regarding it as antecedently improbable, that is to say, unless the historical evidence outweighs the scientific evidence. It is thus unreasonable to treat an event as miraculous unless the evidence that supports the occurrence of the apparent miracle outweighs the evidence for thinking that the scientific principle of which it is a counter-instance is a genuine law of nature.

Hume now goes on to point out how difficult it would be for this condition to be fulfilled.

> No testimony is sufficient to establish a miracle, unless the testimony be of such a kind, that its falsehood would be more miraculous, than the fact, which it endeavours to establish; and even in that case there is a mutual destruction of arguments, and the superior only gives us an assurance suitable to that degree of force, which remains after deducting the inferior. When anyone tells me, that he saw a dead man restored to life, I immediately consider with myself, whether it be more probable, that this person should either deceive or be deceived, or that the fact, which he relates, should really have happened. I weigh the one miracle against the other; and according to the superiority, which I discover, I pronounce my decision, and always reject the greater miracle. If the falsehood of his testimony would be more miraculous, than the miraculous event which he relates; then, and not till then, can he pretend to command my belief or opinion.[9]

This passage makes clear that Hume's central argument concerning miracles was not designed to show that belief in miracles is always irrational. On the contrary the argument leaves open the possibility that in certain circumstances it would be irrational, when confronted with the evidence, to believe that a miracle had not in fact taken place. Thus if the historical evidence in favour of some supposed miracle was so overwhelming that its falsehood would be significantly more miraculous than the event itself, rationality would require us to believe that the event is likely to have been a genuine miracle. Suppose, say, that someone claiming to be acting

---

9   *Ibid*, pp 115-6.

under divine inspiration were to predict that on a certain date the earth's revolution on its axis would suddenly cease and that as a result the sun would remain in a fixed position in the sky for a period of twenty four hours. Suppose further that there was an enormous amount of contemporary testimony from different parts of the globe, without any dissenting voice, that things had turned out exactly as predicted. The earth's behaviour in these circumstances could scarcely be regarded as other than a non-repeatable counter-instance to well established scientific principles, yet it would appear more miraculous for the evidence relating to it to be false than for this extraordinary event to have occurred. Thus, on Hume's own terms, it would be unreasonable in these circumstances to reject the claim that a miracle had taken place.

However, in the second part of his essay on miracles Hume takes a more radical line. He asserts that 'no testimony for any kind of miracle has ever amounted to a probability, still less to a proof'[10] and even goes so far as to claim that 'no human testimony can have such force as to prove a miracle, and make it a just foundation for any such system of religion'.[11] But it seems clear that Hume has provided no good reason for accepting these claims. It is true that at the beginning of the second part of the essay he cites some further reasons for treating miracle reports with scepticism. For example, he mentions 'the strong propensity of mankind to the extraordinary and the marvellous' and he claims that miracle reports 'are observed chiefly to abound among ignorant and barbarous nations'.[12] But these reasons serve merely to strengthen his previous argument; they provide no basis for more radical conclusions. Even a commentator as favourably disposed towards Hume as John Mackie concedes that 'they are secondary considerations, additional and subordinate to Hume's main argument'.[13] The more sceptical views expressed in the second part of the essay must therefore be regarded as *non sequiturs*.

What of his more measured conclusion — 'that no evidence is sufficient to establish a miracle, unless the testimony be of

---

10  *Ibid*, p 127.
11  *Ibid*, p 127.
12  *Ibid*, pp 118 and 119.
13  JL Mackie, *op cit*, p. 16.

such a kind, that its falsehood would be more miraculous, than the fact, which it endeavours to establish'? Is this warranted by his central argument? Some philosophers think that it is not. There have in fact been three notable attempts to show that Hume's argument is unsound. The first was made by his lesser known Scottish contemporary, George Campbell. Campbell points out that Hume rejects the New Testament stories of the resurrection of Jesus from the dead on the grounds that it is more probable that these accounts are incorrect than that the well established principle 'People do not come back to life once they are dead' should admit of counter-instances. But how, asks Campbell, does Hume know that this principle is well established?

> Now, what has been observed and what has not been observed, in all ages and countries, pray how can you, sir, or I, or any man, come to the knowledge of? Only I suppose by testimony oral or written.[14]

But the difficulty with this answer from Hume's point of view is that there is a certain amount of testimony to the effect that people have sometimes been raised from the dead. This testimony appears to leave Hume in a dilemma. If he rejects it in advance of his argument, he is guilty of begging the question, since he is assuming that it is irrational to believe that people do not come back from the dead in order to prove this very point. And if he accepts it, he cannot claim that it is very improbable that there are counter-instances to the principle 'People do not come back to life again once they are dead'.

Hume did not reply to this objection, contenting himself with telling Campbell in a private letter that 'I had fixed a resolution, in the beginning of my life, always to leave the public to judge between my adversaries and me, without making any reply'.[15] But there was, I believe, an effective answer available to him. He could have said simply that in applying his argument on miracles to the New Testament reports of the resurrection of Jesus he was neither accepting nor rejecting the various reports of dead people having come back to life again; he was simply treating them as problematic, as reports

14  G Campbell, *Dissertation on Miracles*, Edinburgh 1763, p 69.
15  JYT Greig (ed), *The Letters of David Hume*, Oxford 1932, vol. I, p 361.

that are not *known* to be true or, in other words, as soft evidence.[16] This seems to be the only legitimate stance to adopt towards these reports at this stage of the argument, for to treat them as true or credible would be the equivalent of assuming that Hume's argument is of no account; and this would be as illegitimate as assuming that the reports are false. On the other hand, there are innumerable cases where it is known that someone who has died did not come back to life, so that it could be said that all the hard evidence is in favour of the principle 'People do not come back to life again once they are dead'.

The distinction between hard and soft evidence is not drawn by Hume himself. Indeed he seems implicitly to exclude it when he says that 'a miracle is a violation of the laws of nature; and as a firm and unalterable experience has established these laws, the proof against a miracle, from the very nature of the fact, is as entire as any argument from experience can possibly be imagined'.[17] However, this is the language of a philosopher describing a discipline that he has not practised himself. The idea that there is a firm and unalterable experience in favour of the laws of nature is a myth. There must be few, if any, well established scientific principles that have not been 'disconfirmed' at various times by careless observers or incompetent experimenters in the laboratory.[18] These apparent counter-examples usually arouse little scientific interest, since in almost all cases there would be good reason for thinking that the experiment had been bungled or the observation carelessly carried out. But a scientist who decides in advance that all results that contradict a well established scientific principle must be false is acting unscientifically, since he is treating the relevant principle as true by definition. Science, in other words, requires a distinction between hard and soft evidence. Hard evidence is what one takes into account in formulating scientific principles. Soft evidence is not to be ignored completely, for it is genuine evidence, but it is not worthy of acceptance without further confirmation.

---

16  I owe this point to George Schlesinger, 'Miracles and Probabilities', *Nous* 21 (1987), p 220.

17  D Hume, *op cit*, p 114.

18  I owe this point to EJ Lowe, 'Miracles and Laws of Nature', *Religious Studies* 23 (1987), pp 267-8.

In formulating his argument on miracles Hume may therefore treat miracle reports in the same way as scientists treat an unconfirmed report that a well established scientific principle admits of counter-instances. They are not to be rejected out of hand, but neither are they to be accepted without further examination. The distinction between hard and soft evidence serves to show that not only is Campbell's attack on Hume's argument ineffective, but also that Campbell's own position on miracles is incoherent, for if one rejects the distinction and insists, as Campbell does, that all evidence be given the same status, the result will be that there will be no well established scientific principles. And without such principles it would be impossible for an event to be identified with any degree of certainty as a miracle.

A second notable attempt to answer Hume was made by the eighteenth century Welsh clergyman and philosopher, Richard Price. Price claimed that one can point to situations where it would clearly be rational to believe in the occurrence of a highly improbable event on the testimony of just one witness. This shows that the conclusion of Hume's argument admits of counter-examples and that the argument must therefore be flawed.

> The improbability of drawing a lottery in any particular assigned manner, independently of the evidence of testimony, or of our own sense, acquainting us that it *has* been drawn in that manner is such as exceeds all conception. And yet the testimony of a newspaper, or of any common man, is sufficient to put us out of doubt about it.[19]

To illustrate Price's point let us suppose that there is a lottery with just one prize and with one million participants, each of whom has a single chance of winning. The day after the lottery has taken place we read in a newspaper that Jones was the winner. Newspapers sometimes make mistakes, so there is a small probability that the newspaper erred. But the antecedent probability that Jones was the winner is much smaller still; it is in fact just one in a million. Yet we would unhesitatingly accept the newspaper report. Price took this to show that Hume

---

19   R Price, *Four Dissertations*, London 1767, pp 410-11.

was mistaken in thinking that it is irrational to believe in an antecedently improbable event on the basis of testimony unless the falsity of the testimony is more improbable than the event itself.

This objection shows that Hume's general principle on the rationality of believing in improbable events on the basis of testimony admits of counter-examples and that there must therefore be something wrong with it. But is this error so great that Hume's principle should be simply discarded or is it a question rather of formulating the principle more carefully so as to exclude all counter-examples? Price concludes that it is the former and maintains that 'improbabilities *as such* do not lessen the capacity of testimony to report truth'.[20] But this claim is surely incorrect, for it is much more exposed to counter-examples than Hume's principle. When we hear of calculating horses or of people levitating or bending spoons by an act of will or of creatures from outer space landing in someone's backgarden, we would be irrational if we did not treat these reports with the sort of scepticism enjoined by Hume.

How then is Hume's principle to be reformulated if it is to be rendered free from counter-examples? We can, I believe, arrive at a satisfactory answer to this question by considering the difference between Jones winning the lottery and a miracle such as Jesus turning water into wine at the marriage feast in Cana. Both are improbable events, but the difference is that though it is improbable that Jones should win the lottery, it is not at all improbable that someone should win it, whereas it is improbable not just that Jesus should turn water into wine, but that anyone should do so. The difference, in other words, is that Jones's winning of the lottery is a member of a class of events, each of which is improbable, but one of which is certain to occur, whereas the miracle of turning water into wine is a member of a class of events of which it may be said that it is antecedently improbable that any event of this kind should occur.

This difference is sufficient to explain why there is good reason for being sceptical about miracle reports, but no good reason for being sceptical about reports in a reliable newspaper

---

20 *Ibid*, p 238.

that so-and-so has won the lottery. If Jones did not win the lottery, then someone else did. But since every participant in the lottery has an equal chance of winning, there is no good reason for rejecting the report that Jones has won. To do so is equivalent to saying that though someone, whose chance of winning was no better than that of Jones, must have won, the report that Jones has won is not worthy of credence, since his winning is antecedently very improbable; and this is not a coherent position. However, if a miracle report is false, it does not follow that what took place was some equally improbable event. On the contrary, if the report is false, then in all probability either nothing happened corresponding to the report or else some natural event occurred which was misdescribed or misinterpreted by those reporting the miracle. And since either eventuality is antecedently much more probable than that a miracle occurred, there is good reason for being sceptical about the miracle report.

It should now be clear how Hume's principle on the rationality of believing in improbable events on the basis of testimony needs to be qualified if counter-examples to it are to be excluded. Hume himself treats the principle as if it applied to all improbable events, whereas it should be applied only to events which are such that not only is it improbable that this particular event should occur, but equally improbable that there should occur any event of the same type. When the principle is understood in this way, it is no longer vulnerable to the sort of counter-examples cited by Price. It follows that Price's objection does no more than draw attention to a certain looseness in Hume's statement of his position. It does nothing to weaken his argument on miracles.

The third objection to Hume's argument has been put forward by a number of writers, including William Palely, Cardinal Newman and Richard Swinburne. They point out that Hume's assessment of the credibility of miracle reports is heavily influenced by his lack of religious belief. Hence one who believes in a theistic God would be entitled to make a very different assessment of their credibility. A contemporary American philosopher of religion, William Wainwright, makes the point as follows:

Hume implicitly assumed that theism is false. If traditional theism is true, miracles aren't unlikely. Whether violations of natural law are inconsistent with the texture of reality depends upon its nature ... In short, one's assessment of the inherent probability of miracles should be guided by one's convictions about the nature of reality.[21]

But there are a number of ambiguities here and when these are cleared up, this objection loses almost all its apparent force. Firstly, Hume's lack of belief in theism no doubt made him sceptical of all miracle reports, but it did not enter into his central argument on miracles. This contends that miracles are antecedently very improbable not because theism is false, but because a miracle is, by definition, a violation of a law of nature. What creates the improbability is not anyone's special convictions about the nature of reality, but the evidence which supports the relevant scientific principle.

Secondly, the claim that 'if traditional theism is true, miracles aren't unlikely' is plausible if taken to mean that if theism is true, then it is probable that miracles sometimes happen — though even this is rejected by some theists.[22] But in this sense it has little bearing on the point at issue, for even if it is probable that miracles sometimes happen, this consideration does not make it significantly more probable that any individual miracle report is true. It may tilt the scales very slightly in favour of the truth of the miracle report, but this takes little from Hume's point that the credibility of a miracle report is to be assessed by balancing the historical evidence that the miraculous event occurred against the scientific evidence that such an event is antecedently very improbable. On the other hand, should the claim 'if theism is true, miracles aren't unlikely' be taken to mean that if theism is true, then individual miracle reports are not antecedently improbable, then it is indeed highly relevant to Hume's argument but there is no good reason for believing it to be true. And to assert this claim without providing any evidence in its support is merely to assume that the conclusion of Hume's argument is false, which is of course to beg the question.

21  WJ Wainwright, *Philosophy of Religion*, Belmont, California 1988, p 61.
22  See, for example, Paul Tillich, *Systematic Theology*, London 1953, pp 128-31.

The third objection is correct then in asserting that one's assessment of the antecedent probability of any proposition must be made in terms of what one already knows, but mistaken in asserting that this has a significant bearing on Hume's argument. The antecedent improbability of miracles derives almost entirely from the scientific evidence and this cannot be rejected without abandoning all pretence to rationality.

## IV  New Testament Miracles

Are there any miracle reports that meet the requirements laid down by Hume? In view of the vast number of miracles that have been reported in all ages, this question must be answered selectively. What I propose to do here is to consider three different classes of miracle reports — (a) reports attributing miracles to Jesus in the four canonical gospels; (b) reports in the gospels and the epistles of St Paul that Jesus rose from the dead; and (c) miracle-reports emanating in the twentieth century from the Catholic shrines of Lourdes and Fatima. These seem to me to be by far the most important miracle reports to be found in the Christian tradition. If none of them measure up to the standard of evidence laid down by Hume, then it seems unlikely that any Christian miracle-report is worthy of credence.

Almost all the miracles which are described in detail in the four gospels conform to the definition proposed in the earlier part of this paper. There is no serious question therefore concerning their miraculous character. But is the evidence which supports them sufficient to outweigh their antecedent improbability? At first glance it may appear that it is. There are, after all, four apparently independent witnesses to the occurrence of these events. Two of these, if tradition is to be believed, were St Matthew and St John, who were apostles chosen by Jesus and therefore eyewitnesses. The other two — St Mark and St Luke — were closely associated with eyewitnesses if they were not eyewitnesses themselves. There can moreover be little doubt about the sincerity of these accounts. In the first century there was little to be gained, at least in a worldly sense, from being a Christian. Those who professed belief in Christ may therefore be presumed to be sincere.

But this statement of the evidence in favour of the New Testament miracles requires very significant qualification. In the first place, there are not four witnesses to each miracle. Only two miracles — the resurrection of Jesus and the feeding of the multitude in the wilderness — are reported in all four gospels. One miracle — that of Jesus walking on the Sea of Galilee — is described in *Matthew, Mark*, and *John*, but not in *Luke*. The other miracles reported in *John* include some of the most famous of the miracles attributed to Jesus — the changing of water into wine, for example, and the raising of Lazarus from the dead — but they are not reported elsewhere. If we turn to the three synoptic gospels, we find that almost all the miracles reported in detail in St Mark's gospel are also reported in the gospels of St Matthew and St Luke. However, this does not mean that each of these reports is supported by the evidence of three independent witnesses. There is now an almost universal consensus amongst biblical scholars that St Mark's gospel is the earliest of the four and that St Matthew and St Luke incorporated almost all of it into their own gospels. This in turn implies that Matthew and Luke were not eyewitnesses of the events that they describe, since otherwise their dependence on *Mark* would be inexplicable. Luke himself acknowledges at the beginning of his gospel that he was not an eyewitness of the events that he is about to recount and there is nothing in *Matthew* to suggest that its author was an eyewitness, something that would be very difficult to understand if it was written by one of the apostles. The author of St Matthew's gospel cannot therefore have been Matthew the tax collector who abandoned his occupation and followed Jesus (*Matt*, 9:9). We have in fact little hard information about the identity of the four evangelists. The earliest writers who referred to the gospels failed to mention the names of the authors. The attribution of authorship to particular individuals is a comparatively late development.

Was the author of St Mark's gospel an eyewitness? It appears not. Mark's gospel contains a number of geographical errors which could not have been made by anyone familiar with the topography of Palestine. For example, in *Mark* 7:31 we are told that Jesus 'returned from the region of Tyre, and went through Sidon to the Sea of Galilee'. Not only is Sidon completely off the route, but there was no road from Sidon to the Sea of Galilee in the first century AD. It is, as one Biblical scholar has remarked, as if we were told that someone had travelled from Cornwall to Manchester in order to get to London. In 5:1 *Mark* places the country of the Gerasenes on the shores of the Sea of Galilee, when in fact Gerasa is over thirty miles to the south-east and in 6:30-53 he displays confusion concerning the location of towns that were sited on the north western shore of the Sea of Galilee. In 8:23-26 Bethsaida is twice referred to as a village, even though it was a large and prosperous town.[23]

One cannot avoid the conclusion then that the authors of the three synoptic gospels were not eyewitnesses. Furthermore, these gospels were written long after the events which they purport to describe. The date that is usually assigned to *Mark* is c70 AD — approximately forty years, in other words, after the death of Jesus — and *Matthew* and *Luke* were written even later. This time gap is of particular significance for New Testament miracle reports, since they come from an era in which gossip and rumour formed the staple means of spreading the news. As a consequence it is easy to visualise a charismatic figure from that period, such as Jesus, being the subject of extravagant stories which became even more magnified with the passage of time. It is evident moreover that the authors of the synoptic gospels had an uncritical approach to the miraculous and the supernatural. All three assert that Jesus cast out many demons and describe some of these exorcisms in detail. Even a firm believer in the existence of demons would be compelled to wonder if there could have been so many victims of demonic possession in Palestine during the lifetime of Jesus. They also introduce angels into their narratives. Luke describes angels intervening on four occasions, Matthew also on four and Mark on two. But angels belong to the world of mythology rather than to that of historical fact. Matthew even goes so far as to say that on the death of Jesus 'many bodies of the saints who had fallen asleep were raised and coming out of the tombs after his resurrection they went into the holy city and appeared to many' (*Matt*, 27:52-3). Finally, they were not writing history from an impartial standpoint. Mark describes

---

23  My information concerning topographical errors in *Mark* is taken from Denis Nineham, *The Gospel of St Mark*, London 1979, pp 153, 184, 203, 219.

his gospel in its very first verse as the *euaggelion* of Jesus Christ and it is clear from the frequent occurrences of this term in St Paul's epistles that the early Christians used it to describe oral preaching about Jesus. The gospels should be regarded then as more akin to sermons or propaganda tracts than to biographies in the modern sense. They undoubtedly contain some historical material, but this is entangled with myths and legends and it is not always easy to separate the different categories. The historical evidence in favour of the synoptic miracle reports is thus very slight and is hopelessly outweighed by the scientific evidence which renders the miracles they describe antecedently very improbable. There would be nothing improbable, still less miraculous, about all these reports being false.

But even if the synoptic gospels were not written by eyewitnesses, is it not possible that they contain eyewitness material? Some biblical scholars think that they do. And if some of the miracle reports consist of eyewitness material, would this not increase their evidential value significantly? But this suggestion bristles with difficulties. First, there is no certainty that the synoptic gospels contain eyewitness material. The claim that they do is rejected by some reputable scholars.[24] Secondly, even if it was certain that they did contain such material, there would be a problem about identifying it, since there is no satisfactory criterion for distinguishing it from hearsay. Thirdly, even if we could identify it, we would still have no information about the reliability of the individual or individuals responsible for it. But even if all these difficulties were resolved, the possibility that some miracle reports may consist of eyewitness material would still have little bearing on their credibility. What must be remembered is that according to Hume's criterion a miracle report is credible only if its falsity would be more miraculous than the event which it describes. And since there is no certainty that the synoptic gospels contain eyewitness material, it would clearly not be miraculous, or even unlikely, for the miracle reports which they contain to consist entirely of hearsay. Besides, even if they did contain eyewitness material, there would be nothing

---

24  See, for example, N Perrin and DC Duling, *The New Testament*, New York 1982, p 42.

at all miraculous about it being unreliable.

To appreciate how weak is the historical testimony in favour of the synoptic miracle reports one need only consider the fact that even when the synoptics provide information of a perfectly ordinary character about Jesus, this has to be treated with considerable caution. For example, both Matthew and Luke tell us that Jesus was born in Bethlehem. Modern scholars treat this assertion with scepticism, however, and are inclined to think that the only reason why the birth of Jesus is placed in Bethlehem is that it was the home of King David from whom Jesus was supposedly descended.[25] But if the testimony of the synoptics is not sufficient to establish that Jesus was born in Bethlehem, it can scarcely be trusted in relation to events that are antecedently highly improbable.

What of the miracles that are reported exclusively in the Fourth Gospel? This is the only gospel which claims to have been written by someone who knew Jesus personally — 'the disciple whom Jesus loved' (21:24) — identified in Christian tradition as one of the apostles, John, the son of Zebedee. However, the chapter in which this claim is made is now almost universally regarded by scripture scholars as a later addition.[26] Moreover this gospel is generally held to have been written between 90 and 100 AD and this dating would effectively exclude the idea that it was written by one of the apostles or by an eyewitness. One principal reason for dating it after the synoptics is that it clearly reflects a breach in relations between Christians and Jews and there is evidence that this took place about 85 AD. The author of *Luke* and *The Acts of the Apostles* depicts the followers of Jesus in the years immediately after his death not as a separate sect, but as members of the Jewish community in Jerusalem, though there were clearly tensions between them and the Jewish religious authorities. But in the Fourth Gospel the atmosphere is very different. Its author makes frequent use of the expression 'the Jews' — it occurs seventy times in *John* as opposed to a mere six times in the synoptics – and always in a pejorative sense to designate the

---

25  See, for example, Robin Lane Fox, *The Unauthorized Version*, London 1991, pp 31-3.

26  The point is discussed in WG Kummel, *Introduction to the New Testament*, New York 1966, pp 207-8.

opponents of Jesus, the Jewish religious authorities. Moreover, on three occasions (9:22; 12:42; 16:2) he refers to those who are 'put out of the synagogue'. For instance, in 9:22 he states that 'the Jews had already agreed that if anyone should confess him (Jesus) to be Christ, he was to be put out of the synagogue'. All the evidence indicates that the followers of Jesus continued to worship in the Jewish synagogue until about 85 AD, when the Jewish religious authorities in Palestine decided to treat the Nazarenes (ie the Christians) as heretics, thereby effectively expelling them from the synagogue.[27] Many scholars now think that *John* may have been written as a reaction to this event.

For these and other reasons that relate principally to its highly developed Christology it is now generally acknowledged that the Fourth Gospel was probably written some time between 90 and 100 AD. If this dating is correct, then it cannot seriously be treated as the work of an eyewitness. Of course this gospel, like the other three, may be based in part on documents from an earlier period, some of which may contain eyewitness material. But there is no certainty about this and no satisfactory method of establishing which elements in the gospel constitute eyewitness material and which do not. The greater time gap means that the miracle reports in the Fourth Gospel are supported by even weaker historical evidence than those in the synoptic gospels. Indeed the testimony of the Fourth Gospel is scarcely sufficient to establish with any degree of certainty such everyday facts as that Jesus attended a marriage at Cana or that a man called Lazarus lived at Bethany with his sisters Martha and Mary. How then, in view of the antecedent improbability of such events, could it warrant the belief that at Cana Jesus turned water into wine or that at Bethany he brought Lazarus back to life after he had been in the tomb for four days?

It might however appear that I am devaluing the historical worth of the Fourth Gospel unduly by assuming that it was written some sixty years after the death of Jesus. There is, after all, no absolute proof that this is so. It could have been written much earlier. One scholar, Bishop John Robinson, has argued that it should be dated before the fall of Jerusalem in

---

27  The evidence for this is cited in R Brown, *The Gospel According to John*, vol 1, London 1966, pp LXXIII-LXXV and p LXXV.

70 AD and some of those who accept the later dating argue that it contains material from an earlier period. It could even have been written, or at least inspired, by St John the Apostle. But while this may all be true, it has little bearing on the historical evaluation of the miracle reports contained in the Fourth Gospel. It is indeed possible that this gospel is much earlier than is generally believed or that it contains eyewitness material from an earlier age. It is even possible that it was written, or at least inspired, by St John. But those who base their belief in the truth of these reports on the likelihood of these possibilities being realised are overlooking the central point in Hume's argument, which is that belief in a miracle report is not warranted unless the falsity of the report would be even more miraculous than the event which it describes. Clearly there would be nothing remotely miraculous about the falsity of the claims that the gospel was written much earlier than is generally supposed or that, though written after the synoptics, it contains material from an earlier age or that it was written or inspired by St John. On the contrary, if the opinion of Biblical scholars is to count for anything, then most, if not all, of these claims are very unlikely to be true. And if they are false, then the historical evidence in favour of its miracle reports is negligible.

This leaves us with two miracles which are reported in all four gospels — the feeding of the multitude in the wilderness and the resurrection of Jesus from the dead. It might seem pointless to give separate consideration to these reports, since it is of little consequence, in the light of our previous discussion, whether they are attested to by three evangelists or by four. But though this point is valid *vis-a-vis* the feeding of the multitude in the wilderness, there are two things about the resurrection that mark it off from all the other miracles recorded in the New Testament. The first is that it is reported not only by the four evangelists, but also by St Paul, who was acquainted with the original disciples of Jesus and whose epistles were written considerably earlier than any of the four gospels. The second is that the resurrection is the central miracle of the Christian tradition. Indeed St Paul goes so far as to say that if Jesus was not raised from the dead, then Christianity is false (*I Cor*, 15:14). Our evaluation of the miracles reported in the

Gospels would be incomplete therefore if we did not give the resurrection separate consideration.

## V The Resurrection

One difficulty that arises in examining the credibility of the resurrection is that there is no agreement among biblical scholars and theologians as to how the event should be understood. Traditionally it was taken to mean that the dead body of Jesus was reanimated in the tomb and Jesus thereupon entered into a new and glorious existence. If the resurrection occurred in this way, then the tomb of Jesus would, as all the gospels attest, have been found empty after resurrection. But modern scholars tend to be sceptical about the empty tomb and to interpret the resurrection so that it is in no way dependent on the truth of this story. However, there would be little point in discussing here the question of how the resurrection should be understood. Indeed I am not at all certain that this is a genuine issue, since the resurrection appears to be understood in different ways by different authors even within the New Testament itself. The question I am concerned with rather is whether there is sufficient reason for believing that something miraculous happened to Jesus after his death. This question, unlike the previous one, is historical in character and the answer to be given to it must be based on the historical evidence.

There are two kinds of historical data that could be adduced in support of the belief that Jesus miraculously rose from the dead. The first consists of the empty tomb story, the second of the stories of the post-mortem appearances of Jesus to his disciples. The two are logically independent of each other. There is no inconsistency in accepting either one as historically reliable, but rejecting the other. But if one rejects both, then while one may continue to believe that Jesus was raised in the sense that he 'rose into the final judgment of God'[28] or that he was 'taken into the eschatological future'[29]— whatever these expressions may mean — one has no longer any reason for treating the resurrection as a miraculous event.

---

28   Ulrich Wilckens, 'The Tradition of the Resurrection' in *The Significance of the Message of the Resurrection for Faith in Jesus Christ*, ed CFD Moule, London 1968, p 76.

29   Thomas Sheehan, *The Second Coming*, New York 1986, p 258.

But does belief in a miraculous resurrection require that both sets of historical data be accepted as authentic? I think the answer to this question must be 'Yes'. Consider first what happens if one accepts the stories of the empty tomb, but rejects the stories of the appearances. Even if the tomb was found to be empty, this could scarcely be regarded as significant evidence for the occurrence of a miracle, since there are a number of ways in which the occurrence could be explained in a non-miraculous way. Perhaps Mary Magdalene unwittingly visited the wrong tomb or perhaps the body of Jesus had already been removed by his disciples. It might be thought however that these explanations are highly implausible, for if Mary Magdalene had visited the wrong tomb, her claim to have found the tomb empty would certainly have been checked and found to be false and if the disciples had removed the body, they would have known that Mary Magdalene's story was of no significance. But it must be remembered that St Paul makes no mention of an empty tomb and the earliest version of the empty tomb story states that the women 'said nothing to anyone, for they were afraid' (*Mark*, 16:8). If the story of the empty tomb did not emerge until some considerable time after the death of Jesus, then it might have been no longer possible to check its accuracy, since the precise location of the tomb could have been forgotten.

Consider now what happens if we treat the stories of the post-mortem appearances as authentic, but reject the empty tomb stories. We now have no reason for thinking that the body of Jesus did not remain in the tomb and corrupt in the usual way. But if it did, then the appearances must have been illusory, since the disciples were seeing someone who wasn't really there; and there is obviously nothing miraculous about being subject to an illusion or hallucination.

One might try to avoid this conclusion by arguing that what happened was that the soul or spirit of Jesus manifested itself to his disciples. This explanation is based on the supposition that the soul or spirit in human beings is something separate from the body — a notion that is difficult to justify philosophically. However, I do not propose to dwell on its limitations here, since even if we overlook them, it is still not possible to reconcile this interpretation with the claim that the resurrection was miraculous. If the soul is a separate entity from the body, there is nothing at all miraculous about the soul of Jesus surviving his death, since that is presumably what happens in the case of every human being. In any event, if the disciples thought that they saw the embodied figure of Jesus when his body was really in the tomb, then they were obviously the victims of an illusion and such illusory experiences provide no grounds for thinking that they were in contact with the soul or spirit of Jesus. Even if one were to argue that though the post-mortem appearances of Jesus were illusory, they were nonetheless miraculous, since they were brought about by divine intervention, one is still faced with the difficulty that if they were illusory, then they are easily susceptible of a natural explanation and it would be irrational to explain some phenomenon in supernatural terms if a satisfactory natural explanation is available.

Could it not be argued however that though the stories of the discovery of the empty tomb are probably not true, still this does not go any distance towards showing that the tomb was not in fact empty? And if it was empty, then the post-mortem appearances of Jesus need not have been illusory. But clearly this will not do. If the empty tomb stories are probably not true, then there is little or no evidence that the tomb was empty, still less any significant evidence that it was miraculously emptied. We have seen how strong the historical evidence must be for it to be rational to believe that a miracle has occurred. Here we are being asked to believe in the miraculous emptying of the tomb even though it is being assumed that the historical evidence in support of this claim is almost non-existent. And if it is unreasonable to believe that the body of Jesus was not in the tomb at the time of the post-mortem appearances, then it is unreasonable to believe that these appearances were anything other than illusions.

But suppose that in the post-mortem appearances what happened was not that the disciples saw the embodied figure of Jesus, but that they simply experienced his presence. Such experiences need not have been illusory. However, if that is all that was involved, there would be no reason for treating the resurrection as miraculous. It is not uncommon for people to experience the presence of a dead parent or spouse or for the members of a revolutionary movement to feel that their dead leader is still present amongst them. (One medical practitioner has estimated that forty five per cent of his patients who had lost their spouses had post-mortem experiences of their presence.[30]) But there is obviously no need to explain such experiences in supernatural terms.

It would appear then that if one is to defend the miraculous character of the resurrection, one must accept the authenticity not only of the stories of Jesus' post-mortem appearances, but also of the stories of the empty tomb. Let us now consider each set of stories in turn to see how much historical credibility can be attached to them.

All four gospels relate that the tomb of Jesus was found to be empty on the Sunday morning after his death. This establishes that by 70 AD or thereabouts stories of the empty tomb were circulating amongst his followers. But were these stories there from the first Easter or were they developed later as apologetical devices to counter anti-Christian propaganda and to provide evidential support for the authenticity of the post-mortem appearances of Jesus? The only evidence we have concerning Christian belief in the resurrection during the period between the death of Jesus and the writing of St Mark's gospel comes from St Paul's epistles. Paul lays great stress, as we have seen, on the importance of the resurrection for Christian belief, but he says nothing about the empty tomb. It is curious, to say the least, that someone who could tell the followers of Jesus at Corinth that 'if Christ has not been raised, then our preaching is in vain and your faith vain' (*I Cor*, 15:14) should make no mention of the empty tomb story if he was aware of it and believed it to be true. Paul had ample reason to cite the evidence of the empty tomb in his attempt to dispel the doubts of the Corinthians concerning the resurrection of the body. His failure to do so suggests that he knew nothing about it.

But is the silence of St Paul not outweighed by the testimony of all four evangelists that the tomb was indeed found to be empty? Unfortunately that testimony is highly unsatisfactory, for if we compare the four accounts, we will find that they

---

30 This phenomenon is discussed at length in Timothy Beardsworth, *A Sense of Presence*, The Religious Experience Unit, Oxford 1977.

contain at least six straightforward discrepancies, two apparent discrepancies and a number of implausible claims. Let us consider the straightforward discrepancies first. These may be summarised in terms of a series of questions followed by the different answers to these questions found in the gospels.

1. Who first discovered the empty tomb? Mary Magdelene on her own according to *John*; Mary Magdalene and the other Mary according to *Mark*; Mary Magdalene, Mary, the mother of James, and Salome according to *Matthew*; Mary Magdalene and Joanna and Mary the mother of James and other women according to *Luke*.

2. When? Before dawn according to *Matthew* and *John*, but after the sun had risen according to *Mark*.

3. Why did she/they visit the tomb? To anoint the body of Jesus according to *Mark* and *Luke*, but according to *John* the body had already been anointed on Good Friday by Nicodemus with a mixture of myrrh and aloes amounting to a hundred pounds in weight.

4. How many angels were there? One according to *Matthew*, two according to *Luke* and none according to *John*. (*Mark* speaks of a young man in a white robe rather than an angel.)

5. Was the news of the resurrection revealed to those who found the tomb empty? It was according to *Matthew*, *Mark* and *Luke*, but according to *John* it was not.

6. Did the women tell the news to the other disciples? They did according to *Matthew*, *Luke* and *John*, but according to *Mark* they remained silent.

The two apparent discrepancies in the gospel accounts are as follows:

1. *Mark*, *Luke* and *John* tell us that when the women arrived at the tomb, the stone was already rolled back, but *Matthew* implies that they saw the angel rolling back the stone.

2. *Matthew* also states that a guard was placed on the tomb at the behest of the chief priests to prevent the disciples removing the body, but the other evangelists say nothing about this.

If this incident had actually occurred, the silence of the other three gospels concerning it would be very difficult to explain. It is now almost universally accepted by scholars that this detail was inserted into *Matthew* for apologetical reasons.

Finally, there are a number of implausible details in the gospel accounts:

1. The women set out to anoint the body of Jesus without ensuring that they were accompanied by someone capable of rolling back the stone. According to *Mark* they had watched the burial and would therefore have been aware of the problem.

2. They waited to anoint the body until Sunday morning even though it was likely that by then decomposition would have already begun. The anointing could have been carried out before sunset on Friday evening — according to *John* this is what actually happened — or after sunset on Saturday. There is the further difficulty that anointing a dead body appears not to have been in accordance with contemporary Jewish custom.[31]

3. All four gospels claim that the body of Jesus was placed in a tomb provided by Joseph of Arimathea — 'a new tomb where no one had ever been laid'. But this claim is open to question on three grounds. The first is that the bodies of executed criminals were normally buried in a common grave.[32] The second is that the *Acts of the Apostles* (13:27-29) quotes St Paul as saying that Jesus was buried not by his disciples, but by his enemies — 'those who live in Jerusalem and their rulers'. The third is that this story, like the story of the soldier piercing the side of Jesus with a spear and the story of guards being placed on the tomb, fits in so well with the apologetical concerns of the evangelists as to arouse suspicion about its authenticity.

---

31  This point is discussed in RH Fuller, *The Formation of the Resurrection Narratives*, New York and London 1971, pp 51-2.

32  Thomas Sheehan has pointed out (*The First Coming*, New York 1986, p 254) that the Jewish legal document, The Mishnah, states that outside the walls of Jerusalem there were two common graves for executed criminals. The Mishnah was assembled about 200 AD by the Galilean Rabbi, Judah the Prince, but it contains information about Jewish traditions going back to the first century AD.

4. The final implausible detail is that two of the gospels introduce angels into their account — scarcely an indication that what we are dealing with here are matters of objective historical fact.

Is it surprising, in the light of all this, that the distinguished Biblical scholar, Rudolf Bultmann, dismissed the empty tomb stories as legends?[33] But not all scholars are as sceptical as Bultmann. Some play down the inconsistencies and improbabilities in the gospel accounts and claim that what matters is that all the gospels agree that Mary Magdelene and perhaps some other women visited the tomb on Easter Sunday morning and found it empty. Indeed some scholars make a virtue of necessity and argue that the inconsistencies give even greater significance to the points on which the gospel accounts are agreed. But this seems to involve a considerable degree of wishful thinking. If Mary Magdalene visited the tomb of Jesus on the first Easter Sunday, found it to have been miraculously emptied and reported this to the disciples later the same day, it would be almost impossible to understand how the gospel accounts of such an extraordinary event should be so garbled. It seems much more likely, particularly when account is taken of St Paul's silence on the matter and St Mark's claim that the women said nothing to anyone out of fear, that the empty tomb stories did not begin to circulate until some considerable time after the death of Jesus. If so, they would be of little historical value.

Even if we do not dismiss the empty tomb stories as legends, it is clear that the sort of evidence they provide falls very far short of what is required to warrant the belief that something miraculous occurred. There are few things better established inductively than that people, once dead, do not come back to life. The antecedent improbability of someone rising from the dead is therefore enormous, but there would be nothing very improbable about the entire empty tomb tradition being spurious. Mary Magdelene may have simply invented the whole incident, for example, or she may have unwittingly visited the wrong tomb, or she may have been frightened into running

33 See R Bultmann, *Theology of the New Testament*, vol 1 (trans by K Grobel), New York 1951, p 45.

away when attempting to find the tomb by someone who told her that the body of Jesus was elsewhere.

The empty tomb story is found in all four gospels, but stories of the post-mortem appearances of Jesus are found only in three. *Mark* merely relates the young man's promise that the disciples would see Jesus in Galilee. (The last twelve verses in *Mark*, where other appearances are mentioned, is now regarded by scholars as a second century addition.) But these appearances are also vouched for by St Paul, so that again there are four different accounts. However, the discrepancies between these accounts are just as marked as in the empty tomb stories. These may be summarised as follows:

1. According to *Mark* the appearances were all in Galilee, but according to *Matthew*, *Luke* and *John* there was at least one appearance in Jerusalem.

2. According to *Luke* and perhaps *John* the appearances were all in Jerusalem, but according to *Matthew* and *Mark* there was at least one appearance in Galilee. (The Galilee appearance described in *John* is in chapter 21 which is now generally regarded as a later addition to the gospel.)

3. Jesus first appeared on Sunday morning near the empty tomb according to *Matthew* and *John*, but according to *Mark* and *Luke* his first appearance was later and elsewhere.

4. According to *Luke* Jesus on Easter Sunday evening made a lengthy appearance to two disciples on the road to Emmaus and according to *Luke* and *John* he later that day appeared to a larger group of disciples. This appears to be in direct contradiction with the accounts given by *Mark* and *Matthew*.

5. According to St Paul Jesus was seen 'by more than five hundred brethren at one time' (*I Cor*, 15:30). This would have been by far the best attested of the post-mortem appearances, so that it is very difficult to understand why, if it really happened, it is not mentioned by any of the four evangelists.

6. According to *Luke* (24:50) the appearances ended on Easter Sunday evening when Jesus led his disciples out to Bethany and ascended into Heaven. (The same author in *Acts* describes

the ascension as taking place from Mount Olivet forty days later.) But according to *Matthew*, *Mark* and *John* the appearances continued for some time after Easter; these three authors, however, make no mention of an 'ascension'.

It is noteworthy too how much more 'physical' the appearances become in the later accounts. *Mark* and Paul speak only of Jesus appearing to or being seen by the disciples, whereas in *Luke* and *John* Jesus asks to be touched by the disciples and also makes a point of eating something. These details would appear to have been added to counter charges that the disciples had been the victims of an hallucination.

If we take it that chapter 21 of *John* is a later addition, then St Paul is the only New Testament writer who claims to have had a personal experience of the risen Jesus — 'Last of all, as to one untimely born, he appeared also to me' (*I Cor*, 15:8). His encounter with Jesus is described three times in *The Acts of the Apostles* (9:1-30, 22:3-21 and 26:9-23). Though there are odd discrepancies between the three accounts, all affirm that Paul, on his way to Damascus to persecute the Christians, experienced a sudden flash of light, fell to the ground and then heard the voice of Jesus speaking to him. There is no indication that he saw Jesus. Paul was blind for a short period afterwards. This episode has been the subject of much discussion by psychologists and medical experts. Perhaps the only thing one can say about it with any degree of certainty is that the evidence for thinking that anything miraculous occurred is far too tenuous to be taken seriously. One of the three accounts in *Acts* claims that Paul alone heard the mysterious voice. Another account says that it was heard also by his companions, and the third account is non-committal. But if everyone present heard the voice, it seems unlikely that this would not be affirmed in all three accounts, since it would constitute important evidence for the veridical character of the experience. Perhaps the most plausible explanation of what happened is that, in falling to the ground, Paul received a severe blow to the head which caused an occipetal lobe lesion. This would account for his temporary blindness. But obviously there would be nothing very unusual about someone who had received a severe blow to the head being the subject of an hallucinatory experience.

The empty tomb stories, despite their differences, contained at least one detail that was common to all the accounts — the role of Mary Magdelene in the discovery of the empty tomb on Easter Sunday morning. But the stories of the post-mortem appearances are hopelessly discordant. There is no core fact, affirmed by all, to which discrepancies of detail might subsequently have been attached. It is difficult therefore to avoid the conclusion that the account of the appearances given in *Matthew*, *Mark* and *Luke* are legends that were developed some considerable time after the death of Jesus. St Paul's claim that Jesus had appeared to the disciples on a number of occasions can be explained by the fact that the disciples came to believe that Jesus was somehow still alive and present amongst them. This is a not uncommon phenomenon when a charismatic leader dies suddenly and unexpectedly. After the death of Parnell many Irish people refused to believe that he had really died. The message 'Che lives' was seen everywhere, and no doubt believed by some, after the death of Che Guevara and a high proportion of Elvis Presley fans believe that the singer is still alive. The disciples's faith in Jesus as the Messiah who would restore the kingdom of Israel would have almost impelled them to believe that his death on the cross cannot have been the end.

However one explains the origin of the belief in the resurrection, there is no avoiding the conclusion that the stories of the post-mortem appearances are of little historical value. They are second-hand and very discordant accounts, written long after the death of Jesus by individuals who were Christian propagandists rather than historians. The evidence they provide for the resurrection is hopelessly outweighed by the antecedent improbability of such an event. To appreciate this point one need only consider what would happen to-day if it were to be claimed that someone had recently come back to life after having been clinically dead for three days. To merit even the most cursory consideration this claim would need to be supported by very much stronger evidence than the evidence for the resurrection. To merit acceptance it would need to be supported by evidence that is scientifically watertight.

## VI  Twentieth Century Miracles

A number of twentieth century miracle reports appear to be
supported by more convincing historical testimony than any
miracle report from the New Testament. I shall here consider
the most impressive of these — the reports of the 'miracle of
the sun' at Fatima and of remarkable healings at Lourdes. The
'miracle of the sun' took place on 23 October 1917 before a
crowd of between fifty and seventy thousand people.[34] Only a
section of the crowd perceived the supposed miracle, but it is
impossible to offer a reliable estimate of their number. It
appears, however, to have been large enough to provide very
strong historical evidence in support of the miracle. The eldest
of the three visionaries, Lucia, had said a month earlier that
the Virgin had promised that a miracle would take place that
day, but had given no indication of what form it would take.
Shortly after midday Lucia said 'Look at the sun' and those in
the crowd who were nearest the visionaries then saw it tremble
or dance in the sky and finally plunge towards earth. The
whole affair does not seem to have lasted longer than a couple
of minutes.

The incident at Fatima fulfils at least some of the requirements for a miracle, since Lucia correctly predicted when and
where it would occur and though she did not describe it in
advance, she directed the attention of the crowd towards the
sun. But was it a strictly anomalous event? If it happened as
described by the onlookers, then it almost certainly was. The
laws of motion are very well established scientific principles
and it seems highly unlikely that any reformulation of them
that would predict or explain the strange movements of the
sun at Fatima would not also give rise to false predictions. But
did these movements actually occur? It seems abundantly clear
that they did not, since otherwise they would have been
observed in many places outside of Fatima. It makes no sense
to say that though these movements actually happened, they
were visible only in Fatima; and it is wholly implausible to
claim that though visible elsewhere, they were seen only in
Fatima. One cannot avoid the conclusion therefore that those
who saw the movements were the victims of an illusion.

---

34  For information about the events at Fatima I am indebted to Geoffrey
Ashe, *Miracles*, London 1978, pp 116-20.

Although there are certain aspects of the affair that may not be easy to explain, there is clearly nothing very remarkable about a section of a large crowd that is eagerly expecting a miracle succumbing briefly to an illusion. We have no good reason then for thinking that the event at Fatima is not susceptible of a natural explanation.

The Lourdes miracle reports are more difficult to assess, since not only are they very numerous, but they extend over a long period of time — from 1848 to the present. It would obviously be impossible to offer an assessment of all these reports here. Instead I shall rely on the judgment of a well known defender of the miraculous, Rev Louis Monden, SJ, who in his book, *Signs and Wonders*, picks out eleven of the Lourdes miracle reports as particularly convincing.[35] However, none of the events cited by Monden conforms to the definition of a miracle that I have given above. There is no thaumaturge or wonder-worker involved in the happenings at Lourdes and no one therefore who, while claiming to act under divine influence, correctly predicted or deliberately brought about an anomalous event. Moreover, a very large number of seriously ill people come to Lourdes every year in the hope of being cured. It would not be unexpected in these circumstances if there were occasional cases of unusual remission of symptoms.

Could it not be argued however that if the cures selected by Monden turn out to be strictly anomalous events, there would have to be an explanation why so many such events occur at Lourdes? The coincidence could scarcely be brought about by chance simply, for if strictly anomalous events are highly unusual, the probability of a considerable number of them occurring in one place would be so low as to be scarcely worth considering. And any other natural explanation seems to be ruled out as a matter of principle by the fact that a strictly anomalous event is one that, by definition, cannot be explained scientifically. The only plausible explanation therefore is the supernatural one. Thus even if the cures at Lourdes are not miracles, as I have defined the term, they may still provide good evidence of a supernatural intervention in human affairs.

But should the cures selected by Monden be regarded as

---

35   L Monden, *Signs and Wonders*, New York 1966, pp 210-31.

strictly anomalous events? Two of them do not qualify for consideration here, since in both cases the patient had never visited Lourdes. Their only connection with the shrine is that water from it had been administered to them during their illness. Even if it turned out that these two cases involved strictly anomalous events, this would go no distance towards showing that an improbable number of such events had occurred at Lourdes. Fortunately the other nine cases cited by Monden form a sufficient basis for assessment. They comprise two cases of tuberculosis (Charles McDonald and Jeanne Fretel), three cases of malignancy (Rose Martin, Elizabeth Delot and Evasio Ganora), one case of severe ulceration of the legs (Abbé Fiamma), one case of epilepsy (John Traynor), one case of Addison's disease (Edeltraud Fulda) and one case of optic atrophy (Marie Biré).

All these cases were declared medically inexplicable by the Lourdes Medical Bureau. The procedures of that body and the scientific data supplied by it have frequently been criticised, but even if we accept its judgment in these nine cases, it would not follow that they were strictly anomalous events. To say that medical science cannot at present explain why something happened is obviously somewhat different from saying that the event was in breach of a well established scientific principle and that any attempt to reformulate that principle so as to take account of this occurrence will lead to false predictions. Being scientifically inexplicable is a necessary condition for an event to be strictly anomalous; it is not a sufficient condition.

But could not a case be made for treating these nine cures as strictly anomalous? The difficulty with this however is that it is not at all clear to which scientific principles the events reported by Monden are supposed to be counter-instances. There is no scientific principle to the effect that a spontaneous remission of symptoms never occurs in the case of patients suffering from malignancy, tuberculosis or any of the other ailments mentioned in Monden's dossier with the exception of optic atrophy. On the contrary, spontaneous remission was a frequent occurrence in patients suffering from tuberculosis in the period before an effective therapy had been developed. Even in cases of malignancy spontaneous remission, though rare, is not absolutely unknown. In 1988 *The Times* reported two cases of spontaneous remission in patients who had been treated in English hospitals; one case involved cancer of the pancreas, the other cancer of the stomach and liver.[36] But precise figures are difficult to come by in this context, since the phenomenon of spontaneous remission does not appear to have been closely studied. However, in a survey of 150 cases of acute leukemia occurring between 1926 and 1948, six patients were found to have experienced complete remission and four of these could be classified as spontaneous since the patient had received only supportive therapy.[37] In all these cases the remission was only temporary. But the same study points out that other similar cases have been reported in which the remission was permanent.[38] The mere occurrence of a cure in eight of the cases reported by Monden is not therefore a sufficient basis for the claim that a well established scientific principle had been breached.

However, it could be argued that what is miraculous about these events is not the mere occurrence of cures, but the rapidity with which they occurred. There is nothing remarkable about a patient recovering spontaneously from tuberculosis, but if the symptoms were to disappear within a very short period of time, then it could be argued that this is incompatible with a well established scientific principle. But there are two serious difficulties with this way of interpreting the miraculous character of the events at Lourdes — one a difficulty of principle, the other a difficulty of fact. The difficulty of principle is that it does not seem possible, at least in the present state of human knowledge, to formulate comprehensive and well established scientific principles relating to the rapidity of the healing process. No doubt it is possible to formulate *some* well established principles relating to it. There would, for instance, be little hesitation in describing the instantaneous healing of a deep lesion as something that is in breach of a well established principle. But at what stage does rapid healing become an unusual rather than an anomalous event? One cannot draw a

---

36  Cited in John Cornwell, *Powers of Darkness, Powers of Light*, London 1992, p 246.

37  See CM Southam, MD and others, 'A Study of the Natural History of Acute Leukaemia with Special Reference to the Duration of the Disease and the Occurrence of Remissions, *Journal of Cancer*, vol 4 (1951), p 10.

38  *Ibid*, pp 7-8.

sharp line between the two categories with any degree of assurance, particularly when account is taken of the influence of psychological factors on the healing process. Thus unless healing is very rapid indeed, we would scarcely be justified in describing it as contrary to a well established scientific principle.

The difficulty of fact is that in all of the nine cases cited by Monden there was a significant interval between the last thorough medical examination of the patient before the cure took place and the first medical examination after that event. Thus, of the two patients who were apparently cured of tuberculosis one, Charles McDonald, was last X-rayed three years before he visited Lourdes. The second, Jeanne Fretel, was last X-rayed almost two years before going there. Her case is further complicated by the fact that, in the absence of laboratory tests, there can be no certainty that she was correctly diagnosed as having tuberculosis peritonitis. In his study of the Fretel case Dr DJ West offers five other diagnoses which, he believes, are equally compatible with her medical history and which would make her speedy recovery easier to explain.[39] The rapid disappearance of external symptoms in these two cases was certainly unusual, but it is well known that the external symptoms of tuberculosis and of other internal ailments can persist for a considerable time after the healing process has begun. In the circumstances there is little justification for describing the disappearance of the symptoms as contrary to any well established scientific principle.

That the patient's recovery occurred a significant time after the last medical examination may be of less significance for the three cases of malignancy cited by Monden, since here there is less likelihood of spontaneous remission. But in all three cases the claim that the cure was incompatible with some well established scientific principle is seriously weakened by doubts about the correctness of the diagnosis. Two of these patients were never made the subject of laboratory tests, the diagnosis being arrived at simply on the basis of clinical observation. Moreover, one of them, Rose Martin, had previously been operated on — apparently successfully — for cancer and when she returned for treatment, it was assumed that the

---

39   DJ West, *Eleven Lourdes Miracles,* London 1957, pp 90-91.

cancer had recurred. But the medical data suggest that the later symptoms were the result of a continuing infection.[40] If so, the interval between the last medical investigation and the cure would assume considerable significance. The second patient, Elizabeth Delot, was found to have inoperable cancer of the abdomen when operated on in 1925. The surgeon reported that he had performed a gastro-enterostomy to give her temporary relief. Inexplicably, however, when X-rays were taken on three subsequent occasions, they failed to reveal any trace of the gastro-enterostomy. This raises serious doubt about the value of the medical testimony and therefore of the accuracy of the diagnosis — something that is recognised even by protagonists of the Lourdes miracles.[41]

The third case of malignancy is that of Evasio Ganora, who in January 1950 was judged, on the basis of an histological examination, to be suffering from Hodgkin's disease. A few months later he visited Lourdes where he made what appeared to be a remarkable recovery. It is noteworthy however that one of the three specialists who conducted the biopsy came to no firm conclusion. Moreover a specialist in this area to whom I submitted the medical data has informed me that Ganora's reaction to medical treatment renders the diagnosis highly suspect. He was given mustard derivatives and subjected to radio-therapy, but showed no response. This would be extremely unusual in a patient suffering from Hodgkin's disease. Ganora's symptoms seem more characteristic of brucellosis or toxoplasmosis and as a farmer he would have been exposed to both infections through his contact with animals. If he was in fact suffering from either of these ailments, his recovery at Lourdes would not be in any way remarkable.

There is a similar question-mark about the diagnosis in the case of Edeltraud Fulda, who was judged to have Addison's disease and made a rapid recovery after visiting Lourdes in August 1950. The medical data contain no record of her being the subject of any biochemical test and without this the diagnosis must remain uncertain. Furthermore, her case, as DJ West has pointed out, 'is capable of interpretation in terms

40  See *Ibid*, pp 51-2.
41  See an untitled article on Lourdes by DR Leroy in *New Problems in Medical Ethics*, ed Dom Peter Flood, OSB, Cork 1953, pp 223-4.

of a functional starvation with secondary deficiency anaemia, a condition which might well respond to a dramatic change in attitude and habits'.[42]

The most dramatic of the cures cited by Monden is that of Marie Biré, who in 1908 became completely blind from what was judged to be optic atrophy. Five months later, during a visit to Lourdes, she suddenly recovered her sight. When examined by doctors the same evening, her eyes had a white nacreous appearance, so that organically speaking she should still have been incapable of seeing. One month later her eyes had recovered their normal colouring. If Madame Biré had really been suffering from optic atrophy, her cure would certainly involve the violation of a well established scientific principle, for all the evidence indicates that optic atrophy is irreversible. However, a neurologist who has examined the medical data has told me that the case is susceptible of a perfectly ordinary explanation. He points out that optic atrophy should normally produce gradual loss of vision whereas in Marie Biré's case the onset of blindness was immediate. However, just before becoming blind she suffered a severe haemorrhage which could have lowered the haemoglobin level of her blood to such a degree as to cause temporary loss of vision. It would also explain the white nacreous appearance of her eyes. By the time she visited Lourdes her haemoglobin level might well have risen sufficiently to enable her to recover her sight.

There are two further cures in Monden's dossier. The first is that of John Traynor, who was wounded during the First World War and subsequently suffered from paralysis of one arm and frequent attacks of what was judged to be epilepsy. He visited Lourdes in 1923 and made a complete and immediate recovery. Taylor's compulsive fits are described as so violent as to cause him frequently to fall out of bed. When bathed in the pool at Lourdes, his leg movements caused most of the water to be kicked out of the pool. But this sort of behaviour is not at all characteristic of patients suffering from epilepsy. In the typical epileptic attack the patient first loses consciousness and becomes rigid and then becomes subject to spasms or short

---

42  West, *op cit*, p 95.

jerks.[43] Taylor's behaviour is however strongly suggestive of hysteria.[44] In the absence of brain scans or EEG tests it seems more plausible to conclude that, like many soldiers during the First World War, he developed hysterical symptoms as a result of his traumatic battle experiences. The rapid disappearance of symptoms induced by hysteria would of course be not at all unusual.

The final case is that of Abbé Fiamma, who had suffered for many years from ulcerations of both legs. He visited Lourdes in 1908 and, after bathing in the grotto, found that the ulcers had cleared up. The only unusual feature in this case — since the healing of external ulcers would be in no way remarkable if it occurred over a period of time — is the apparent rapidity of the cure. But how rapid was it? We are told that the Abbé underwent a medical examination before going to Lourdes, but there is no indication as to when precisely this took place. There is also no data on the Abbé's psychological state. This omission is of some consequence, since external ulcers are sometimes self-induced.It may be significant that the Abbé's recovery, like John Traynor's, was not declared miraculous by the ecclesiastical authorities. In any event, the evidence in his case is too sketchy to enable one to draw any firm conclusion.

There are therefore serious doubts affecting each of the nine miracle-reports from Lourdes. The historical evidence is deficient in all of them either because of uncertainty about the diagnosis or uncertainty about the rapidity of the cure or uncertainty about both. The scientific evidence is deficient in eight of the cases because of uncertainty about the precise content of the scientific principle that is supposed to have been breached. The inevitable conclusion is that in none of these cases does the evidence measure up to the standard required. *A fortiori* we have found no good reason for thinking that an improbable number of strictly anomalous events have occurred at Lourdes.

Admittedly this conclusion is based on merely a sample of the Lourdes miracle-reports. But there are two reasons for

43  See Sir Stanley Davidson, *The Principles and Practice of Medicine*, London and Edinburgh 1963, pp 974-5.

44  See *Ibid*, pp 1072-5.

thinking that even if all of them had been examined, the conclusion would not have been any different. The first is that the sample was chosen by an authority on the subject who is himself a staunch believer in Lourdes miracles. It is unlikely that he would have omitted from the sample any miracle-report that is supported by significantly stronger evidence. The second reason is the general character of the Lourdes miracle-reports. Unlike the miracle-reports found in the gospels, they exhibit no incontrovertible example of a strictly anomalous event. There is, for example, no instance of a lost eye or of an amputated limb being restored or of a mentally retarded individual being granted a normal intellectual life. The great majority of the cures are remarkable only because of the rapidity with which they apparently took place. The presumption must be therefore that none of the other cures would be free from the sort of doubts that surround the nine cases that have been examined.

## VII Conclusion

In 1731 a Parisian lawyer, Maître Barbier, wrote in his diary that 'it is always by miracles and strange events that religions have won favour in all ages and in every land ... The more one penetrates into religious matters, the more one realises how uncertain are the miracles accepted by the Church'.[45] We have found no reason for rejecting his opinion. Miracles can look impressive at a distance, but when one examines them closely, it seems invariably to turn out that either what was supposed to have happened probably did not happen or that what happened is susceptible of a natural explanation.

This conclusion is of course open to refutation. There may well be miracle-reports which are supported by much stronger evidence than any of the reports that I have examined. But the burden of proof lies with those who claim that this is so. If this claim cannot be substantiated, then we are justified in concluding that though miracles cannot be excluded in principle, there is no sound reason for believing that one has ever occurred.

45   Quoted in Norman Hampson, *The Enlightenment*, London 1980, p 151.

# 10  Evil and the Existence of God

## I  The Problem of Evil

T he word 'evil' is normally used nowadays in a moral sense. To refer to individuals or actions as evil is to condemn them morally in a particularly emphatic way. But 'evil' is also used occasionally in a wider fashion to refer to any sort of harm that could befall sentient beings. Thus an evil day is not necessarily a day on which some morally evil action was performed; it could also be a day on which a natural disaster, such as a storm or earthquake, occurred. Likewise when we speak of the evils that have befallen someone, we may be thinking of things such as diseases and accidents that are not necessarily the responsibility of anyone. We may distinguish then between two different kinds of evil. Moral evils are the consequences of morally bad decisions taken by human beings, such as wars, crimes and self-destructive vices. Natural or physical evils are evils brought about by natural processes that are independent of human control, such as disease, death, mental retardation and the destructive effects of storms, earthquakes and other natural disasters. These two categories, while conceptually distinct, overlap in various ways. Death and disease may, in certain instances, be moral evils rather than physical ones. Moreover some evils may belong to both categories at once. Thus a famine might be the result both of natural factors, such as drought and crop failure, and of human indifference, negligence and greed.

The two sorts of evil, whether taken separately or together, constitute a serious problem for the believer in a theistic or Christian God. In the great theistic religions God is conceived of as both omnipotent and morally perfect. But how could such a being allow evil to exist? As David Hume put it:

Is God willing to prevent evil, but not able? then he is impotent. Is he able, but not willing? then he is malevolent. Is he both willing and able? Whence then evil?[1]

St Augustine, though much more optimistic than Hume about providing a satisfactory answer to the problem, formulated it in a very similar way:

Either God cannot abolish evil or he will not. If he cannot, he is not all-powerful; if he will not, he is not all-good.[2]

What both these arguments are in effect asserting is that the following triad of propositions cannot all be true.

1  God is omnipotent
2  God is morally perfect.
3  Evil exists.

Now since proposition 3 can scarcely be rejected without falling into absurdity, it seems we have no alternative but to reject either proposition 1 or proposition 2. It follows — if omnipotence and perfect goodness are understood, as they are in the theistic tradition, to be essential attributes of God — that theism is false.

This version of the argument from evil may seem unanswerable at first glance, but as it stands it is unsuccessful or, if not unsuccessful, at least incomplete. I shall try to establish this point by first considering God as a morally perfect being and then by considering him as both morally perfect and omnipotent. In the first place, the presence of evil in the universe is not enough to show that it cannot have been brought into existence by a morally perfect creator. This is clear from the fact that human beings frequently perform actions that produce evil without being morally blameworthy. When a surgeon performs an operation, for example, he almost invariably inflicts

---

1  David Hume, *Dialogues concerning Natural Religion*, ed N Kemp Smith, Edinburgh 1947, p 98.
2  St Augustine, *Confessions*, Book 7, Chapter 5.

on the patient a certain amount of pain, anxiety, disability and danger to life, but he is not for this reason morally blameworthy provided the operation is a necessary means to a good that outweighs these evils. An action that produces evil may be morally justified therefore if it is a necessary means to an overriding good. It should be noted however that an action is not necessarily justified by fulfilling this condition. We would not normally be regarded as justified, for example, in killing someone in order to provide transplant organs for five others even if their lives could not be saved without these transplants and there is no other means of obtaining the organs. But this point has no bearing on the present discussion, for what is required to be established here is not that an action *must* be morally justified if it is a necessary means to an overriding good, but that it *may* be so justified. So long as we are prepared to concede that surgeons, dentists, policemen, judges, prison warders, academic examiners and the like can carry out their duties without being morally blameworthy, then we have no good grounds for arguing that the presence of evil in the universe is enough to show that it cannot have been brought into existence by a morally perfect creator.

But can this position be maintained if God is understood to be not only morally perfect, but also omnipotent? The usual reason why human beings must sometimes cause or permit evil so as to produce good is that their powers are limited. A surgeon must operate to heal the patient because he does not have the power to heal him otherwise. But an omnipotent being could achieve the same effect by a simple act of will. Could God be rightly called omnipotent if he did not possess the power to produce every conceivable good without permitting evil? If not, then the presence of evil in the world is enough to show that it cannot have been created by a being that is both omnipotent and morally perfect.

There is however a significant point to be made here about omnipotence. The old schoolboy conundrums: 'Can God create a stone so big that he cannot lift it?' or 'Can God create a being so powerful that he cannot control it?' raise an important philosophical point. What these questions bring out is that the claim that God is omnipotent cannot be understood to mean that God has the power to do any action that can be described in words, since this leads to contradictions. If the notion of omnipotence is to be rendered intelligible, it must be understood not as the power to do anything whatever, but rather as the power to do anything that is not excluded by considerations of logic. An omnipotent God would, in other words, be subject to logical constraints. He could not bring it about that, for instance, 5 should be the square root of forty nine, nor could he create such things as married bachelors, round squares or four-sided triangles.

Philosophers are not in agreement concerning the precise character of the logical constraints to which an omnipotent being would be subject. It obviously will not do to say simply that an omnipotent being can do everything that is logically possible, for there is nothing logically impossible about creating a stone so big that one cannot lift it or creating a being so powerful that one cannot control it. Nor is it logically impossible to bring about one's own destruction, even though this is something that God, when conceived as essentially eternal, cannot do. In my opinion the correct amount of omnipotence must run along these lines: God is omnipotent if he can do everything that is not either logically impossible or logically incompatible with his essential attributes. This formula may perhaps need further qualification if it is to be fully acceptable.[3] But we need not pursue that point here, for all that is required for our present purpose is that it be accepted that there are *some* logical constraints to which an omnipotent being is subject; and this cannot be denied without making the concept of omnipotence unintelligible.

Nonetheless it may seem paradoxical, if not downright self-contradictory, to say that there are certain constraints on the power of an omnipotent being. It must be remembered however that the concept of omnipotence, like the concept of infinity in mathematics, is an extraordinary one and we should not be unduly surprised therefore if it has paradoxical aspects. A paradox becomes intolerable only if it involves a contradiction. But the notion of an omnipotent God being subject to constraints would be self-contradictory only if these constraints constituted

---

3    Useful discussions of the difficulties surrounding the concept of omnipotence may be found in A Kenny, *The God of the Philosophers*, Oxford 1979, pp 91-9 and R Swinburne, *The Coherence of Theism*, Oxford 1977, pp 149-61.

genuine limitations on his power and this does not appear to be true of the logical constraints to which God is subject. To say that an individual's power is limited is equivalent to saying that it is logically possible for someone else to be more powerful. And it is clearly not logically possible to be more powerful than God if the sole restrictions on his power are that he cannot perform tasks that are logically impossible or logically incompatible with his essential attributes.

Once it is realised that the power of an omnipotent being would be subject to logical constraints, the flaw in the version of the argument from evil formulated by Hume and St Augustine becomes readily apparent. If the evil that exists in the world is a logically necessary means to some good or a logically necessary consequence of such a means, then not even an omnipotent being could bring about this good without permitting evil to occur. And if the good is overriding, that is, if it outweighs the evil involved, then an omnipotent being would not be morally blameworthy for not preventing this evil. Thus the mere existence of evil is not enough to show that the world cannot have been created by a being that is omnipotent and morally perfect.

It is perhaps worth pausing here for a moment to see what precisely has been established. I have not shown that the evil that exists is compatible with the existence of an omnipotent, morally perfect God, nor have I provided any kind of explanation for evil. All that I have done is to point out that it is not impossible that there is an explanation for evil that is compatible with the existence of an omnipotent, morally perfect creator. To provide a complete explanation for evil the theist must show that all the evil that exists is either a logically necessary means to some overriding good or a logically necessary consequence of such a means. This would be to solve the problem of evil. But the theist does not have to solve the problem to rebut the argument from evil. What the argument must do, if it is to be successful, is to show that there is at least some evil in the world that is *superfluous*, ie that is not a logically necessary means to an overriding good nor a logically necessary consequence of such a means. If the argument cannot do this, then it fails even if no plausible explanation for evil that is compatible with theism can be given.

It seems clear then that if the argument from evil is to be successful, it must be based not on the mere presence of evil in the world, but on the presence there of at least one evil that is superfluous. How are we to know if an evil is superfluous? It is frequently not at all easy to decide whether or not something is a logically necessary means to, or consequence of, something else. But it must be remembered that if some evil is not a means to some good, then *a fortiori* it is not a logically necessary means to it and if it is not a consequence of something, then *a fortiori* it is not a logically necessary consequence of it. It follows that if there is some phenomenon whose disappearance would result in the elimination of more evil than good, then it must be a superfluous evil. We can formulate this criterion in a slightly different, but perhaps more workable, way by saying that an evil is superfluous if its elimination would leave the world a better place than before, that is, would increase the proportion of good to evil in the world. This formulation needs to be qualified slightly, for there is one set of circumstances in which the disappearance of a superfluous evil would not necessarily increase the proportion of good to evil in the world, namely, if the world already contains more evil than good. Thus if we suppose that the world contains fifty units of evil and twenty units of good and that the elimination of some superfluous evil reduces the amount of evil in the world by ten units and the amount of good by five, this will result in the proportion of evil to good being increased, so that the world can scarcely be said to have become a better place. But in practice this qualification may be ignored, for if the world contains more evil than good, then at least one superfluous evil exists, since the world is itself a superfluous evil.

Are there evils in existence whose extermination would leave the world a better place than before? On the face of it there are many such evils. Would not the world be a better place if, for example, we could exterminate mental retardation or chronic depression or Alzheimer's disease or multiple sclerosis or motor neurone disease or epilepsy or Parkinson's disease or any one of the various forms of cancer that affect human beings? No doubt the consequences of these ailments are not wholly evil; they may evoke patience and courage on the part of the victim or kindness and sympathy on the part of others. But it appears impossible to defend the view that these benefits outweigh the evils that are involved. This would imply that the world would be a better place if these ailments were even more widespread than they are at present and that the human race is fundamentally misguided in trying to eradicate them.

There are, it is true, some caveats to be entered with reference to this line of reasoning. We must be careful, first of all, not to identify human welfare with the welfare of the world as a whole. A change which may be for the benefit of human beings may not benefit other sentient beings and may not leave the universe a better place. Secondly, human beings may well be mistaken in their judgments on what is conducive to their welfare. For example, the development of technology, which was for long regarded as an unqualified good, is now seen as something that may eventually make the Earth uninhabitable. Television, which was first seen as a marvellous advance in the art of communication, may in the end leave the human race semi-literate.

But it is difficult to accept that these two points constitute an effective defence against the argument from evil. It seems preposterous to suggest that painful, disabling and, in many instances, ultimately fatal diseases could in some mysterious fashion bring about more good than harm. If someone were to advocate that the human race should abandon the attempt to find a means of curing or preventing such ailments, he would, I believe, be widely, perhaps even universally, regarded as mentally unbalanced. Besides even if it turned out that any such disease produced more good than harm — suppose, say, it served to keep the human population within certain limits, thereby enabling other living species to survive — it would be very difficult to accept that an omnipotent being could not devise a means of bringing about the same good without allowing so much evil to occur. In short, there appears to be no possibility of reconciling the manifest evils that are present in the world with the existence of an omnipotent and morally perfect creator.

What can the theist say in reply to this? There are, it seems to me, three possible strategies that may be employed to counter the argument from evil. First the theist can argue that the problem of evil is a pseudo-problem and that consequently the argument from evil is misconceived. The task of the religious believer, according to this strategy, is not to solve the problem, but to dissolve it, to show that there is a false assumption built into its formulation; and once this has been exposed as false, the problem disappears. The second strategy is to meet the problem head-on and argue that it can be solved by providing a satisfactory explanation for all the evil that exists. An explanation for evil that is compatible with God's omnipotence and moral perfection is usually known as a theodicy. To provide an explanation for evil is in effect to admit that there is a genuine problem of evil, for an explanation is an answer to that problem. The second strategy is therefore incompatible with the first. In contrast the third strategy, which is something of a half-way house between the first two, is compatible with both. It is based on the claim that even if there is a genuine problem of evil, one does not need to solve this problem in order to show that the argument from evil is unsuccessful. This strategy leaves the problem of evil untouched, but tries to show that there are serious objections to all the different versions of the argument from evil, so that the problem of evil is not a genuine obstacle to belief in God. I shall now examine each of these strategies in turn.

## II  Attempts to Dissolve the Problem

Since there are three elements in the problem of evil — the doctrine that God is omnipotent, the doctrine that he is morally perfect and the fact of evil — it would be natural to suppose that there are just three ways of attempting to dissolve the problem, each one involving the rejection of one of these elements. Historically three different ways of dissolving the problem have indeed been employed by philosophers, but they are not so symmetrically aligned with the three constituents of the problem as one might perhaps have expected them to be. The first involves the denial of the reality of evil, the second the denial of the claim that moral terms are applicable to God so that the question of his moral perfection does not arise, and the third the denial that God is both omnipotent and morally perfect.

The first attempt to dissolve the problem may appear by far the least plausible of the three, but it has had two notable defenders — the philosopher, Benedict de Spinoza, and Mrs Baker Eddy, the founder of Christian Science. For Spinoza good and evil are not objective realities, but are qualities imposed on reality by the mind. Men regard something as good when it serves to achieve their purposes and regard it as evil when it serves to frustrate them, but in themselves things are neither good or bad. 'All things are necessarily what they are, and in Nature there is no good and no evil'.[4]

Spinoza's views on good and evil are derived from an elaborate system of metaphysics. Mrs Baker Eddy could scarcely be called a metaphysician, but her views on good and evil sound at times very similar to Spinoza's: 'Evil has no reality. It is neither person, place, nor thing, but is simply a belief, an illusion of material sense'.[5] However, she differs from Spinoza in one important respect. Spinoza does not reject the objective reality of the things we regard as evil — pain, mental suffering, disease and the like — but he denies that they are objectively evil. Mrs Baker Eddy on the other hand thinks that pain and suffering are simply illusions: 'When a sufferer is convinced that there is no reality in his belief in pain — because matter has no sensation, hence pain in matter is a false belief — how can be suffer longer?'[6]

It is difficult however to take either attempt to dissolve the problem of evil very seriously. Even if Spinoza is right in thinking that good and evil are not inherent in things, but are simply projected on to things by the mind, this does not make pain, mental suffering, disease and death any more acceptable or less dreadful. It therefore leaves untouched the problem why an omnipotent and morally perfect creator should allow his creatures to suffer as they do. Mrs Baker Eddy's denial of the reality of pain and suffering, on the other hand, is plainly confused. She believes that pain is both real and unreal, that as soon as one realises that pain is an illusion, one will cease to suffer. But even if she had confined herself to the simple assertion that pain is an illusion, her position would have little

---

4 Benedict Spinoza, *Short Treatise on God, Man and His Well-Being*, trans A Wolf, London 1910, p 75.

5 Mrs Baker Eddy, *Science and Health with Key to the Scriptures*, Authorised Edition, 1934, p 71.

6 *Ibid*, p 346.

to recommend it. There is so much suffering in the world and it is such an inescapable element in all our lives, that it seems wholly perverse to treat it as an illusion. In any event, pain cannot logically be merely an illusion any more than error or change can. If people believe that there is change, then they are at least subject to changing illusions, so that change is real. If people believe that they sometimes err, then their belief is either true or false and in either case they are subject to error. Pain too cannot be merely an illusion, for an illusion of pain would be a painful illusion, so that pain would still be a reality. This point was wittily made in a well known Limerick:

> There was a young fellow from Deal
> Who said 'Although pain is not real,
> When I sit on a pin
> And it punctures my skin,
> I dislike what I fancy I feel.'

The second attempt to dissolve the problem of evil involves rejecting the doctrine that God is morally perfect, but what it asserts about God is not that he is morally less than perfect, but rather that moral terms are not properly applicable to him, so that the question of the precise degree of his moral goodness does not arise. One contemporary philosopher who has adopted this approach is Brian Davies, OP, in his book, *Philosophy of Religion*. Davies argues that classical theism can quite properly treat the problem of evil as a pseudo-problem if it is not committed to the view that God is a moral agent; and he offers three reasons for thinking that it is not so committed. The first is that classical theism thinks of God as the source of all beings.

> But if God is the source of all beings, something has to be done to distinguish him from all beings, and the obvious thing to do is to deny that God is a being. Yet moral agents, whether bad or good, are obviously beings.[7]

The second reason is that duties and obligations arise only in social contexts and God is not a social being. The third is that

---

7   Brian Davies, *An Introduction to the Philosophy of Religion*, Oxford 1982, p 23.

a moral agent is one who can in some sense succeed or fail and it makes no sense to speak of the God of theism succeeding or failing, for there is no standard against which his performance can be measured.

None of these reasons seem to me to be at all convincing. The first seems to be little more than a play upon words. Since 'God is not a being' would in normal parlance be understood to mean that God is not real, that there is no God, the theist who claims that God is not a being must be using the term 'being' in a special sense to mean perhaps 'a limited reality' or 'something dependent for its existence on something else'. Now when Davies concludes that God is not a moral being, is he using the term 'being' in the ordinary sense or in this special sense? I do not see how he can answer this question either way without undermining his whole point. If he says he is using 'being' in its ordinary sense, then his position is incoherent, for he is asserting that God is not only the source of all being, but also non-existent. But if he says he is using 'being' in the special sense, then his conclusion that God is not a moral agent is a *non sequitur*, for from the supposition that God is not a moral being in the special sense of 'being' it does not follow that he is not a moral being in the ordinary sense.

Davies's second reason for claiming that God is not a moral agent is scarcely more persuasive than his first. No doubt it may be argued that the God of theism, as traditionally conceived, is not a social being. But does he not acquire responsibility for his creatures through the act of creation? And if he makes promises to his creatures and communicates with them, does he not have a duty to keep his promises and to assert nothing that is untrue? Theism is surely committed to the doctrine that God is faithful to his promises and that his word is true. But what guarantee can there be of this if he is not morally obliged to keep his promises and to avoid asserting what is false?

The third reason offered by Davies is that a moral agent is one who can in some sense either succeed or fail and it makes no sense to talk of the God of theism as succeeding or failing, since there is no standard against which his performance can be measured.

A man can be judged to have succeeded as a writer in the light of the history of writing. A watch-maker can be judged to have failed as a watch-maker against the background of the history of watchmaking. But what is the background for judging the Creator *ex nihilo*? There cannot be any, in which case the God of classical theism cannot be said to be even capable of succeeding or failing. And in that case he cannot be a moral agent.[8]

But success and failure can also be judged not in the light of history, but in the light of what the agent set out to achieve? The Frenchman, Joseph Niepce, succeeded in taking photographs even though photography had no previous history. The Russian, Alexander Popov, succeeded in communicating by means of radio waves even though he was the first to attempt to do so. There seems to be no conceptual difficulty therefore in saying that God succeeded in creating the universe or succeeded in creating a certain type of universe, even if no other universe has ever existed.

It might be thought that even though Davies's arguments are unconvincing, his conclusion may still be correct, for it is not implausible to suggest that the problem of evil appears a problem to us only because of our limited and anthropomorphic understanding of the divine nature. If we could see God not through a glass darkly, but face to face, then perhaps the problem would disappear, for we would realise that it makes no sense to speak of God as being subject to moral obligations. But I do not think that this position is defensible. Even if Davies had established that classical theism is not committed to the view that God is a moral being, this would not be enough to dissolve the problem of evil, for classical theism would still be committed to the doctrine that God is benevolent. Since an animal can be benevolent or malevolent, even though animals are not moral agents, it is clear that one does not have to be a moral agent to possess these characteristics. And if God is not benevolent, he is not the God of theism, for it would be futile to pray to him or worship him or expect him to fulfil his promises. This is enough to show that one cannot hope to dissolve the problem of evil by appealing to the limited and anthropomorphic

---

8  *Ibid*, p 24.

character of our conception of God, for theism requires that God be benevolent in a sense that is closely analogous to the sense in which human beings are benevolent. And once it is admitted that God is benevolent in this sense, there is inevitably a problem as to how he could permit so much evil to exist.

The third attempt to dissolve the problem of evil is the most plausible of the three. This involves the scaling down of the traditional theistic conception of God by modifying one or other of the two divine attributes involved in the problem of evil. Thus one could say that God, though very powerful, is not omnipotent, or alternatively, that though very good, he is not morally perfect. Admittedly, many theists might be reluctant to adopt either position, for they might feel that God is not God unless he is perfect. But against this it can be urged first that classical theism is itself a modification of the understanding of God that is found in the Bible; and second that if classical theism renders the problem of evil insoluble, then it must be either modified or abandoned. The first of these two points admittedly raises difficult issues which would take us too far out of our way to discuss in any detail here. Instead I shall concentrate on the question: Is this third attempt to dissolve the problem of evil successful within its own terms?

Two well known philosophers have argued that it is — John Stuart Mill and the twentieth century Australian philosopher, John Mackie. Mill makes the point as follows:

> The only admissible moral theory of creation is that the Principle of Good *cannot at once* and altogether subdue the powers of evil.... Of all the religious explanations of the order of nature, this alone is neither contradictory to itself, nor to the facts for which it attempts to account.[9]

Mackie, unlike Mill, was not in any sense a religious believer, but he thought that as a matter of logic the problem of evil can be readily dissolved by abandoning either the doctrine that God is omnipotent or the doctrine that he is morally perfect.

It is plain, therefore, that the problem of evil can be easily solved if one gives up at least one of the propositions that

---

9    JS Mill, 'Three Essays on Religion', in *The Philosophy of John Stuart Mill*, ed Marshall Cohen, The Modern Library, New York 1961, p 469.

constitute it. Someone who holds that there is in some sense a god, but one who is not wholly good, or though powerful, not quite omnipotent, will not be embarrassed by the difficulty.[10]

But this method of dissolving the problem, though it may appear convincing at first glance, is not in fact satisfactory. Even if we regard God as very powerful rather than omnipotent or, alternatively, as good in a limited sense rather than morally perfect, there is still a problem of evil. Consider first what happens when God is regarded as omnipotent, but limited in goodness. This supposition makes it possible to argue that superfluous evils exist because God is not as concerned with eradicating or preventing them as he would have been if his goodness were unlimited. But the difficulty with this hypothesis is that a God who tolerated the sort of evils that actually exist simply because of his lack of concern for others would be much more than merely limited in goodness; he would be a moral monster. This point can be brought home by citing analogies with human behaviour. What would we think, for instance, of a surgeon who performed operations without the use of an anaesthetic not because there was no anaesthetic available, but because he was not prepared to take the trouble to see that it was administered? Or how would we look on a doctor who could cure his patients' ailments, but was so indifferent to their welfare that he refused to do so? An omnipotent God who tolerated all the evils of the world because of lack of benevolence would be open to even greater condemnation than these two depraved characters — first because the amount of evil for which he is responsible is so much greater; second because an omnipotent being could eliminate evil by a simple act of will whereas the surgeon or doctor would have to exert themselves; and third because an omnipotent creator would be responsible not merely for not eliminating the evil, but, unlike the two depraved medics, responsible for not preventing its existence in the first instance. Such a being would be more akin to an evil demon than to a benevolent deity.

Consider now what happens when God is considered not as omnipotent, but as very powerful. It might be thought that on this supposition the existence of superfluous evils can be

---

10  JS Mackie, *The Miracle of Theism*, Oxford 1982, p 151.

explained by saying that while God does not want such evils to exist, he does not have sufficient power to prevent or eradicate them. But this too fails to get rid of the problem, for it is easy to point to evils that a very powerful God could have prevented or eliminated. We know that a very powerful God could have eliminated (and presumably also prevented) them because human beings have done so. The most obvious example of an evil that has been eliminated by human ingenuity is smallpox. During the nineteen seventies the smallpox virus, variola, which had ravaged mankind for more than a million years, was finally brought under control. As recently as 1974 it had, within the space of a single month, been responsible for the death of ten thousand Bihari Indians. But it now exists only in laboratories — one of the greatest, if still unsung, human achievements. And it seems probable that many more diseases will be eliminated in the future. But if mankind can get rid of these evils, why could God have not done likewise? To say that he is unable to do so is to reduce his power to such an extent that it is difficult to see how he could any longer be regarded as divine. Certainly a being which lacks the power to do something that man is capable of doing could scarcely be a proper object of worship. The discovery that such a being exists would appear to have no more significance for religious belief than the discovery that there are intelligent beings in some other part of the physical universe.

Even if we go further and scale down both God's omnipotence and his moral perfection, we are still no better placed to dissolve the problem of evil. For if a being who is infinite in goodness but incapable of eliminating any of the superfluous evils of the world is deemed unworthy to be an object of worship, he is clearly even less worthy if he is conceived to be limited in goodness as well as in power.[11]

---

11  For further discussions of this third attempt to dissolve the problem of evil see the following articles from *Analysis*: PJ McGrath, 'Evil and the Existence of a Finite God', vol 46, no 1, pp 63-4; R Crisp, 'The Avoidance of the Problem of Evil: A Reply to McGrath', vol 46, no 3, p 160; MB Burke, 'Theodicy with a God of Limited Power: A Reply to McGrath', vol 47, no 1, pp 57-8; PJ McGrath, 'Children of a Lesser God? A Reply to Burke and Crisp', vol 47, no 4, pp 236-8.

### III  Three Theodicies

The first strategy then does not work. The problem of evil is a genuine problem which cannot be just dissolved. The second strategy is to try to solve the problem by means of a theodicy whose function is to explain why God allows so much evil to exist. There are three principal theodicies in the theistic tradition and I shall now consider each in turn.

The first is the traditional Catholic theodicy, often called nowadays, in honour of its creator, the Augustinian theodicy. St Augustine was converted at different times to Neo-Platonism and to Christianity and there are elements from both systems in his thinking about evil. From Neo-Platonism he acquired the doctrine of evil as essentially negative. Nothing that exists, according to this, can be wholly evil, for if it were, it would be simply a *non-ens* or nothing. Being and goodness are equivalent. Everything that exists, insofar as it possesses reality, is good. Evil must be understood therefore as *privatio boni* — the privation, corruption or malfunctioning of something good. It is not however the mere absence of good; rather it is the absence of some good which ought to be present.

The second element that the Augustinian theodicy owes to Neo-Platonism is the principle of plenitude. This principle goes back to Plato and Aristotle, but Augustine found it in the *Enneads* of his philosophical mentor, Plotinus. It has been extraordinarily influential during the entire history of Western thought and has even been appealed to in the twentieth century by physicists endeavouring to provide an explanation for some of the extraordinary coincidences that occur in the basic forces in nature.[12] According to this principle the entire universe should be seen as the Great Chain of Being, that is to say, as a perfect continuum in which there are no gaps, no dislocations and no unrealised possibilities. If anything is logically possible, then it is actual. Reality, on this conception, is an immense hierarchy and every creature, however low it may be in the scale of being, is good and glorifies its creator. A universe

---

12  There is a fine account of the history of the principle of plenitude in Arthur C Lovejoy, *The Great Chain of Being*, New York 1860. For an example of the employment of the principle by modern physicists see CB Collins and SW Hawking, 'The Anisotropy of the Universe', *Astrophysical Journal* (1973), pp 317-26.

devoid of unrealised potentialities is better and more pleasing to God than any other type of universe. This explains why he has created beings, like man, who are capable of doing great evil and beings which appear to us to be repulsive or even malignant, such as tapeworms, crocodiles and viruses.

These Neo-Platonic themes are united in Augustine's theodicy with the Christian doctrine of the fall. God created man and indeed all other living beings in a state of perfect felicity in the Garden of Eden. But when Adam and Eve sinned, unhappiness, suffering, disease and death entered the world, affecting not only Adam and Eve and their descendants, but also the entire animal kingdom. For Augustine natural evils are the divinely preordained punishment for the fall of man. Thus since sin is the sole cause of all the evil that exists, there is really only moral evil in the world; what we call natural evil is merely a sub-class of this. As Augustine puts it in his commentary on the Book of Genesis: 'Everything that is regarded as evil is either sin or the punishment for sin'.[13]

Although Augustine's theodicy has exerted enormous influence on Christian thinking about evil, it is difficult to see it now as anything more than a museum-piece. Let us consider first its Neo-Platonic elements — the understanding of evil as essentially negative and the principle of plenitude. Neither of these doctrines seem to me to be of any help in resolving the problem of evil — the first because it is, depending on how one interprets it, either irrelevant or wholly implausible, the second because it is false.

The doctrine of evil as essentially negative, as John Hick has pointed out, was not intended by Augustine as an account of the empirical reality of evil; he is not claiming that we always experience evil as the loss or absence of goodness.[14] Instead the doctrine is an inference from the Christian understanding of God and creation. If the universe owes its existence to an omnipotent and morally perfect creator, then it follows, according to Augustine, that evil cannot be anything positive, but must be simply the privation of good. To suppose that evil is something positive, he thinks, would be to make

13  St Augustine, *De Genesi Ad Litteram*, i, 3.
14  See J Hick, *Evil and the God of Love*, London 1966, pp 60-2 and pp 185-8.

inevitable some form of dualism — the theory that the world was brought into being by two creatures, one good, the other evil. This reasoning seems to me to be unsound. A theistic God could cause or permit evil to exist provided it is a logically necessary means to an overriding good or a logical consequence of such a means. The question whether evil is a positive reality or merely the privation of good has no bearing on this point. Thus even if evil were a positive reality, an omnipotent and morally perfect creator could bring about non-superfluous evils, whereas even if evil is essentially negative, he could not cause superfluous evils to exist. In any event, even if we were to concede that from the ontological point of view evil is simply the privation of good, this would not lessen the problem of evil, for the problem arises primarily at the experiential level. It is the problem of explaining why a morally perfect and omnipotent creator allows so much pain, suffering and distress to be present in the universe. Nothing that one says about the ontological status of evil can therefore help to make this problem less acute.

However, the claim that evil is essentially negative could also be interpreted as meaning that evil is equivalent to nothingness or non-being, so that to treat it as real is to be subject to an illusion. This is a very different sort of interpretation, for if evil is a privation of goodness, it is a real privation and therefore not just nothingness. Thus the first interpretation implies that there is a real problem of evil, since evil is a genuine, though negative, reality that needs to be explained, whereas the second implies that there is no problem, since evil has no reality. But while this second interpretation makes the doctrine much more important, it also makes it wholly unacceptable, for the claim that an evil such as pain is unreal is, as we have seen already in connection with Mrs Baker Eddy's views, not merely at total variance with our experience of pain, but is also an incoherent supposition.

The principle of plenitude is likewise unacceptable, for there is no evidence in its favour and there is even good reason for thinking it to be necessarily false. The idea that there are no unrealised possibilities in the universe is a metaphysical extravagance that not merely lacks argumentative support, but also leads to absurd conclusions. No one endowed with what Bertrand Russell calls 'a robust sense of reality' believes in the existence of such things as dragons, unicorns, centaurs, elves, sprites, fairies, leprechauns, mermaids or Martians. And if even one such species is mythical rather than real and thus represents an unrealised possibility, the principle of plenitude is unsound.

In any event, there is good reason for treating the principle as something that is false not just as a matter of contingent fact, but as a matter of necessity, for it appears logically impossible for all logically possible species to be exemplified. This may sound paradoxical, but it becomes obvious once it is realised that the existence of one species may be logically incompatible with the existence of another. For example, the existence of an uncreated universe is logically incompatible with the existence of the God of theism and therefore logically incompatible with the existence of universes created by the theistic God. But there appears to be no good reason for thinking that either created or uncreated universes are logically impossible entities. The Great Chain of Being must therefore be regarded as an incoherent conception of reality, for not all the links in the chain are logically compatible with each other.

The Christian elements in Augustine's theodicy are no more helpful in explaining evil than the Neo-Platonic ones. There are two fatal flaws in the supposition that pain, disease and death came into the world as a consequence of the original sin of Adam and Eve. The first is that it runs completely counter to the scientific account of the history of life on earth. Science tells us that the human race came into existence between two and three million years ago. However, animal life has existed on earth for much longer, perhaps for as long as five hundred million years, and animals endowed with consciousness have existed for more than one hundred million years. All the evidence suggests that conscious life was from the beginning bedevilled by the same evils that afflict it to-day. Indeed the mechanism of evolution requires that this be so, for it involves survival of the fittest, which in turn requires that the majority of living beings be subject to premature death with all its attendant evils. The story of a Garden of Eden that was destroyed by the folly of our first parents has thus no factual basis and therefore cannot properly be used to explain anything.

But even if the story of the fall was factually correct, it still would not provide a satisfactory explanation for evil, since it fails to explain why a good God would have attached such dreadful consequences to the sin of Adam and Eve. For punishment to be just it must be in proportion to the seriousness of the crime and must be administered only to those who are guilty. The punishment imposed by God for the sin of Adam and Eve, according to Augustine's account, is in spectacular breach of both these conditions, for it was not only extraordinarily severe, but was imposed on every member of the human race and even on the animal kingdom. Thus the Augustinian theodicy, instead of explaining why a benevolent creator could allow so much evil to exist, unwittingly depicts God as a tyrant.

The second theodicy is now usually known as the Irenaean theodicy after the early Christian writer, St Irenaeus of Lyons. Its best known modern exponent is John Hick in his book, *Evil and the God of Love*. Instead of seeing evil as God's punishment for sin, the Irenaean theodicy sees it as a necessary means to a greater good. As a consequence it does not need to appeal to the doctrine that mankind originally inhabited a Garden of Paradise from which it was expelled as a result of the Fall. Evil exists, according to this theodicy, not because man has fallen from grace, but because the world is, in the famous phrase of John Keats, 'a vale of soul-making', that is, an environment in which human beings may exercise their freedom fully and thereby develop their higher moral and spiritual potentialities. This requires that there be sufferings to be endured, temptations to be overcome and dangers to be faced, for without these there would be few, if any, occasions for significant moral choice. In a world devoid of pain and distress and failure, the argument goes, there would be no room for virtues such as kindness, sympathy and heroism. Moreover in a world in which moral development is possible, there is bound to be moral failure and therefore moral evil. If God were to intervene to prevent human beings behaving badly or to eliminate the consequences of bad behaviour, human responsibility would be eroded. Men must take responsibility for the consequences of their actions and for the working out of their own destiny; otherwise human freedom would be little more than a charade. But even though the world, when conceived as a vale of soul-making, requires physical evil and inevitably produces moral evil, still a world in which there is evil, but also moral growth is better than a world in which there is neither.

Hick is aware that this value judgment may appear very implausible when seen in a purely terrestrial context. But he believes that belief in an after-life is crucial for theodicy.

> If there is any eventual resolution of the interplay between good and evil, any decisive bringing of good out of evil, it must lie beyond this world and beyond the enigma of death.... The Christian claim is that the ultimate life of man — after what further scenes of 'soul-making' we do not know — lies in that Kingdom of God which is depicted in the teaching of Jesus as a state of exultant and blissful happiness, symbolized as a joyous banquet in which all and sundry, having accepted God's gracious invitation, rejoice together. And Christian theodicy must point forward to that final blessedness, and claim that this infinite future good will render worth while all the pain and travail and wickedness that has occurred on the way to it.[15]

It will be seen that the Irenaean theodicy is based on two related value judgments. The first of these has been formulated in the following way by Hick: 'One who has attained to goodness by meeting and eventually mastering temptations, and thus by rightly making choices in concrete situations, is good in a richer and more valuable sense than someone created *ab initio* in a state of innocence or of virtue.[16] The second value judgment is that a world in which people are exposed to evil and to temptation is better — at least when the after-life is taken into account — than a world in which they are not. The validity of the second of these judgments is clearly not ensured by the validity of the first, for there is no guarantee that those exposed to temptations do not succumb to them. It will be necessary therefore to consider each judgment separately.

Hick, surprisingly, does not offer any argument in support of either judgement. He appears to think that one has only to understand them to appreciate that they are intuitively obvious.

15　*Ibid*, pp 375-6.
16　*Ibid*, p 291.

In fact both are open to serious objection. The principal difficulty with the first is that theism is committed to the view that God, though not subject to trial or temptation, is morally perfect. It does not seem possible therefore for a theist to argue without inconsistency that goodness that has been achieved through conquering temptation is richer and more valuable than goodness that is effortless.

Perhaps it might be said in reply that as moral development is logically impossible for God, this value judgment is true only of creatures. But this scarcely removes the appearance of inconsistency, for it does not explain how this value judgment can be true of creatures when it is not true of God. If God can be supremely good without passing through a period of soul-making, then why must creatures be exposed to pain and suffering and temptation to reach a much lower grade of goodness?

A second difficulty with this value judgment is that it envisages moral development simply in terms of 'meeting and eventually mastering temptations'. But if that is all that is required for moral development, then the Irenaean theodicy is in no position to explain why God allows physical evils to exist, for it seems clear that moral development would still be possible in a world devoid of physical evil. There is a variety of temptations that one could be subject to even if one were immune from pain and suffering — for example, the temptation to disobey divine commands or deal unjustly with others or be unfaithful to one's spouse or utter untruths or break one's promises. Thus the second value judgment appears to leave the Irenaean theodicy in a position where it cannot explain not merely why the world contains so much physical evil, but why it contains any physical evil at all.

The only way in which an Irenaean theodicist could counter this objection is by arguing that in a world containing physical evil there would be a wider range of temptation and as a result opportunity for a greater degree of moral development. Thus it is only in a world containing physical evil that one could be exposed to the temptation to torture, injure or kill one's fellow man. But this would be a very dangerous strategy for an Irenaean theodicist to adopt, for it is difficult to accept that a benevolent God would subject his creatures to pain and suffering for no other purpose than to ensure that they are subject to a wider range of temptations than would otherwise be the case. John Gaskin makes the point as follows:

> The notion of inflicting suffering in order to see how people react, what sort of character stamina they have is morally repulsive. If practised by a human agent it would be regarded as criminal or lunatic. If attributed to God I do not see how it could be regarded in a less reprehensible light.[17]

The first value judgment would appear then to be not only highly questionable, but also inadequate for the purpose for which it is used in the Irenaean theodicy. If it is unsound, then the second value judgment must be unsound also, for if there is no benefit to be gained from exposure to temptation, then, *ceteris paribus*, a world in which people are so exposed cannot be better than one in which they are not. However, let us suppose for the sake of argument that the first judgment is valid and let us suppose further that the presence of physical evil is a necessary, or at least a highly desirable, ingredient in a world of soul-making. Even granted these suppositions, the second judgment is still open to serious objection. The problem is that physical evil and temptation provide an opportunity for the practice of vice as well as of virtue, so there can be no guarantee that a world in which people are exposed to physical evil and temptation is better than one in which they are not. Another's distress can evoke sympathy, kindness and courage, but it can also give rise to selfishness, indifference and cowardice. One's own pain and suffering can degrade and embitter as well as ennoble. Here is how W Somerset Maugham, who qualified as a doctor before becoming a writer, described what he saw in hospitals:

> At that time ... there was a school of writers who enlarged upon the moral value of suffering. They claimed that it was salutary. They claimed that it increased sympathy and enhanced the sensibilities. They claimed that it opened to the spirit new avenues of beauty and enabled it to get in touch with the mystical kingdom of God.... I set down in my notebooks, not once or twice, but in a dozen places the facts I had seen. I knew that suffering did not ennoble; it degraded.

---

17  JCA Gaskin, *The Quest for Eternity*, London 1984, p 122.

It made men selfish, mean petty and suspicious. It absorbed them in small things. It did not make them more than men; it made them less than men.[18]

It is not however the reaction of people to physical evil that creates the greatest difficulty for the second value judgment, but rather the appalling sufferings inflicted on mankind by fellow men. There is abundant testimony to man's extraordinary inhumanity to man throughout the pages of history, though it is of course in the twentieth century that this inhumanity is displayed at its most horrific. Is it possible to contemplate the mass slaughter of the First World War, the Nazi extermination camps, the Stalinist tyranny in the Soviet Union, the destruction of Dresden, Hiroshima and Nagasaki and the Cambodia of Pol Pot without feeling that no amount of opportunity for moral development could compensate for such horrors?

But will this second value judgment not appear much more plausible if account is taken of the Christian doctrine of an after-life when, according to the Scriptures,

God shall wipe all tears from their eyes; and there shall be no more death, neither sorrow, nor crying, neither shall there be any more pain; for the former things are passed away?[19]

Belief in an after-life may indeed make the sufferings of this life easier to bear, but it would not be easy to argue that it makes a significant contribution towards solving the problem of evil. The principal objection to any argument of this type is that if it can be established that there are superfluous evils (or even one superfluous evil) in the world, then nothing that happens in the next life can obliterate that fact or make it compatible with the existence of a theistic God. The most that one can say is that God will make recompense to us in heaven for the sufferings that have been unnecessarily visited on us in this life. But this leaves the problem of evil untouched, for an omnipotent and morally perfect creator would not have allowed us to be afflicted with unnecessary evils in the first place.

It might still be contended however that the significance of belief in an after-life for the problem of evil is that it enables us to see how evils that appear superfluous from a purely terres-

---

18  W Somerset Maugham, *The Summing Up*, London 1948, p 62.
19  *Apocalypse*, 21, 4.

trial perspective may cease to appear superfluous once the after-life is taken into account. But this is based on the supposition that all the evils that are superfluous from a purely terrestrial perspective are logically necessary means to overriding goods in the after-life or logically necessary consequences of such means. And is this really credible? How, for example, could smallpox lead to enough good in the after-life to outweigh the miseries that it has caused here on earth? Since there is no reason for thinking that it could have any significant consequences during a post-terrestrial existence, the supposition that it has the required logically necessary relationship with some overriding post-terrestrial good seems wildly improbable.

Perhaps it might be said in reply that its connection with the after-life lies in the opportunities that it provides for moral development. But this seems very unconvincing, for the world still contains ample opportunities for moral development even though smallpox has been eliminated. In any event the virtues that might have been attained through exposure to smallpox or indeed to any physical evil — courage, patience, resignation and so on — would appear to have no role to play in the sort of existence envisaged by the Christian doctrine of heaven.

The difficulties attaching to the Irenaean theodicy are not confined to these two value judgments, for there are at least two other types of evil for which it appears incapable of offering any explanation. The first is animal suffering. Since animals are not moral agents, they are not susceptible of moral development. Even if one were to counter this difficulty by adopting the extremely implausible view that animal suffering is justified by the opportunities it provides for moral development for humans, one is still faced with the awkward fact that animals existed on earth for many millions of years before man appeared, so that the suffering they endured during this long period is still unaccounted for.

The Irenaean theodicy is also incapable of explaining why some of the evils that exist not merely do not provide an opportunity for moral development, but actually prevent or inhibit it. Infant mortality, for example, excludes the possibility of moral development. This may seem a comparatively minor consideration to-day, but it must be remembered that until about one hundred years ago the majority of human offspring died in infancy and even at present there is an infant mortality rate of about ten per cent in the world as a whole. Moreover many psychological conditions, such as severe mental retardation, schizophrenia, autism and various forms of psychosis, either seriously inhibit moral development or exclude it altogether. No doubt it can be argued that these evils provide opportunities for moral development not for the victims, but for those who look after them. The parents of a mentally handicapped child, for example, have many opportunities for exercising kindness, sympathy and patience. But if moral development is as important as the Irenaean theodicy makes it out to be, it seems impossible to understand why so many individuals are deprived of all opportunity for development in order to increase the opportunities for others.

The third theodicy is usually called Natural Law theodicy. It was first put forward, in a very concise form, by the third century Alexandrian theologian, Origen, in his defence of Christianity against the pagan writer, Celsus.

We affirm that God did not make evils, but that they arose incidentally, just as a carpenter's work produces shavings and sawdust.[20]

It was later formulated at greater length by Leibniz in his work *Theodicy* and it has had several notable twentieth century defenders including the Cambridge theologian, FD Maurice. Natural Law theodicy, like the Irenaean theodicy, is based on two related value judgments. The first is that a world that contains individuals endowed with free will is, *ceteris paribus*, better than a world that does not. It goes on to argue that the exercise of free will requires a relatively stable and predictable natural order. It requires, in other words, a world governed by natural law. Without natural law there would be no way of knowing what the effects of our actions would be and consequently free will would be pointless. The capacity of freely choosing to do x rather than y would be of no significance if we could not differentiate in advance between the consequences of doing x and doing y, which is what would be the case if the consequences of x and y were wholly unpredictable.

---

20  Origen, *Contra Celsum*, 6.55.

Now a world containing sentient beings and governed by natural law is one in which there would have to be a certain amount of natural evil. If, for example, there is a law of gravity, then some individuals will inevitably be killed or injured by falling to earth or being struck by falling objects. If there are laws of motion, then some individuals will be killed or injured by colliding with solid objects or being struck by solid objects in motion. Furthermore, if there are beings endowed with free will, then inevitably some will make morally wrong choices, thereby inflicting evil on themselves or on their fellow creatures. An omnipotent God could of course intervene to prevent such things happening, but if he did, man would no longer be responsible for the consequences of their actions. Human decision making would be little better than play-acting and the benefits to be derived from possession of free choice would be undermined.

The second value judgement involved in natural law theodicy may be formulated in a variety of ways. The strongest formulation is that the world that actually exists is the best of all possible worlds in the sense that it is better than any universe endowed with a different set of general laws. This is the formulation proposed by Leibniz in his *Theodicy*, but it was so effectively lampooned by Voltaire in *Candide* that few advocates of natural law theodicy are prepared to defend it to-day. Instead they argue that the natural law theodicy does not require that the universe be the best of all possible worlds. A theistic God, in creating the world, is not morally obliged to maximise goodness, for he would not be doing an injustice to anyone by creating a world that is somewhat less than the best. There is not however general agreement among natural law theodicists as to how far the world may fall short of being the best possible world and still be compatible with divine goodness. To simplify matters I shall formulate a minimalist version of this second value judgment — one to which all natural law theodicists would, I believe, subscribe, though many would claim that there are other conditions that the universe must satisfy before it could be said to be compatible with the existence of a theistic God. This minimalist version is that the world contains more good than evil and does not contain any superfluous evils. If this judgment turns out to be unsound, then any stronger version of it will also be unacceptable.

It is clear however that this second value judgment, even when it is formulated in this minimalist sense, leaves natural law theodicy open to serious objection. The first value judgment is not of course entirely free from difficulty. Not everyone believes in the reality of free will or believes that the possession of free will is a matter of great significance. But since in our ordinary way of thinking we do place a very high value on freedom, it is plausible to suppose that a world that contains individuals endowed with free will is, *ceteris paribus*, better than a world that does not. It is also not unreasonable to conclude that the exercise of free will by individuals possessing bodies requires that the world be subject to natural law. What is more questionable however is the claim that the existence of natural laws in a world in which there are sentient beings necessarily involves physical evil. It is perhaps not implausible to suggest that the operation of any conceivable set of natural laws would cause death and injury to sentient beings as they are actually constituted. But there does not seem to be any logical requirement that prevents them from being constituted in such a way as to be immune from such evils.

In any event, even if we waive the difficulties relating to the first value judgment, natural law theodicy still seems to be undermined by the problems surrounding the second. One serious difficulty with it is that it presupposes a solution to the problem of evil rather than helps to provide one. If the universe is indeed devoid of superfluous evils, then the problem of evil is resolved, but this second value judgment merely *asserts* that there are no superfluous evils. It offers no reason for thinking that evils which are to all outward appearances superfluous are not so in fact.

A second and even more serious difficulty with it is that the extent and the character of the physical evils that exist make it impossible to accept that they are all logically necessary consequences of the world being governed by a set of general laws. If this were so, then these evils, or their equivalent, would be present in every conceivable universe that is subject to natural law; and this seems wholly incredible. Could anyone seriously suggest that, for example, every possible universe that is subject to natural law would have to contain natural disasters, such as earthquakes, volcanoes and violent storms? Or that in every possible universe subject to natural law and containing sentient beings, these sentient beings must be exposed to all the physical and mental ailments, or their equivalent, that exist on earth. This second suggestion has in fact been refuted by the elimination of smallpox, since this shows that the existence of the smallpox virus is not a necessary consequence of the world being subject to natural law.

Why, to take the matter further, do viruses exist? Unlike bacteria, they do nothing but harm. Two well known scientists, Peter and Jean Medawar, have described a virus as 'simply a piece of bad news wrapped up in protein'.[21] Thus the world would have been a significantly better place if viruses had never come into existence. But it would be going beyond the bounds of credibility to suggest that it is logically impossible for viruses to be absent from any world that contains living beings and is subject to natural laws.

Again, why is it that many animal species can survive only by preying on other animal species? It would be extremely difficult to accept that in a world subject to general laws nature must, as a matter of logical necessity, be red in tooth and claw. Even if one were to concede — and this would be to concede a great deal — that, as a matter of logical necessity, certain animal species must be carnivorous, one would still be left with the problem why certain species prey on other species in such a repulsive way. The ichneumon fly, for instance, deposits its larvae in or on the body of another insect — usually a caterpillar — which then dies a slow and, to all appearances, extremely painful death by parasitic ingestion. This might be passed off as a strange aberration in nature were it not for the fact that the Ichneumonoidea is not a single species, but a group that includes more species than all the vertebrates combined.[22] There seems to be no good reason for thinking that it would be logically impossible for nature to have devised a less ferocious means of either preventing their existence or ensuring their survival.

---

21  PB Medawar, *The Life Science*, London 1978, pp 8-9.

22  My information concerning the Ichneumonoidea comes from a paper by Stephen Jay Gould entitled 'Nonmoral Nature', *Natural History*, vol 19, no 2; reprinted in Martin Gardner (ed), *The Sacred Beetle*, Oxford 1985, pp 32-45.

## IV   Is the Argument from Evil Defective?

It is clear that the explanations for evil provided by the classical theodicies are all seriously inadequate. Other theodicies may of course be devised, but it is difficult to hold out much hope for their success in view of the pronounced failure of the classical theories. However, there is one final strategy left to the theist. He can argue that though the problem of evil has not been resolved, still the argument from evil is unsuccessful and consequently evil is not an obstacle to belief in God. This approach is particularly associated with the distinguished contemporary American philosopher, Alvin Plantinga, and it has tended to dominate discussion of the problem of evil in recent years. Before discussing it in detail it should be pointed out that even if this strategy is successful in showing that the argument from evil is defective, this is not enough to show that evil does not constitute a serious problem for theism. So long as the problem of evil remains unresolved, there is no guarantee that it can be resolved and no guarantee therefore that evil is reconcilable with the existence of a theistic God. Thus even if all the existing versions of the argument from evil are shown to be defective, this does not imply that their conclusion is false nor does it provide sufficient reason for thinking that the argument from evil cannot be formulated in a way that is free from defect. The theist may indeed claim that the burden of proof lies with the antitheist, but the antitheist can reply that the burden of explaining why so much evil exists in a world created by an omnipotent and perfectly good God rests with the theist; and if neither burden is discharged, then the whole issue is left unresolved.

The only way that an exponent of this third strategy could avoid this conclusion is by showing that there is something about the argument from evil that renders it irremediably defective. Now this is precisely what Plantinga claims to have done. He distinguishes between two different versions of the argument — the deductive argument and the probabalistic argument — and contends that neither version has any probative force.[23] The first version, he argues, is demonstrably

---

23   Plantinga has discussed the problem of evil in his books *God and Other Minds*, Ithaca, NY 1974, pp 115-30, *God, Freedom and Evil*, London 1974, pp 7-73; *The Nature of Necessity*, Oxford 1974, pp 164-95 and in a lengthy article

unsound and there is no good reason for thinking that the second can be formulated in a way that renders it remotely effective as an argument. The difference between the two versions may be explained as follows: The deductive version sets out to show that the evil that exists is logically incompatible with the existence of a theistic God, so that one who asserts that all this evil exists and that theism is true is implicitly contradicting himself; the probabilistic version has the rather more modest aim of showing that the evil that exists renders the existence of a theistic God highly improbable.

The aim of the deductive argument, according to Plantinga, is to show that the following triad of propositions is inconsistent:

1  God is omnipotent.
2  God is wholly good.
3  Evil exists.

Plantinga points out that this triad is clearly not explicitly contradictory, for none of its members is the denial or negation of another member. But presumably what exponents of the deductive argument believe is that it is implicitly contradictory — that, in other words, an explicit contradiction may be deduced from it when it is supplemented by the addition of a necessary truth. But what is this necessary truth? Plantinga considers various possibilities, but rejects them all on the grounds that they are either not necessary or that their addition to the original triad does not generate a contradiction.

He then goes further and argues that it can be shown that this triad of propositions is not in fact inconsistent. His argument makes use of a recognised procedure in logic for proving the consistency of a set of propositions. Take any set of propositions, a, b and c. If there is a fourth proposition, d, which is possibly true and is consistent with a and b and if a, b and d together entail c, then a, b and c are consistent. Plantinga now puts forward for consideration the following proposition:

d.  All the evil in the world is the result of the choices of free moral agents and it was not within the power of God to create a world containing a better balance of good over evil.

'The Probabilistic Argument from Evil', *Philosophical Studies* (USA), 35(1979) pp1-53.

What d implies is that all the evil in the world is really moral evil, since what we call natural or physical evil is the work of non-human free agents — presumably fallen angels or demons. It should be noted that Plantinga is not committed to the truth of d. All that his argument requires is that it be possibly true, that in other words it is not necessarily false. Now d, he contends, is consistent with

a  God is omnipotent; and
b  God is wholly good

and a, b and d together entail that the universe contains as much evil as it does. It follows a, b and c are consistent.

This argument seems to me to be successful within its own terms, but it has only limited effectiveness as a rebuttal of the argument from evil. The problem with it is that it applies to only one form of the argument, namely that proposed by Hume and St Augustine and, as we have seen already, that form of the argument collapses once account is taken of the fact that even an omnipotent being would be subject to logical constraints. There is no contradiction in asserting both that God is omnipotent and perfectly good and that evil exists, since the evil that exists may be a logically necessary means to an overriding good or a logically necessary consequence of such a means. Where the contradiction arises is in asserting that God is omnipotent and perfectly good and that at least one superfluous evil exists, since any free agent would be morally blameworthy if he was knowingly responsible for the existence of a superfluous evil and a theistic God would be knowingly responsible for any superfluous evils that are present in the world.

Plantinga may have confused the issue somewhat by distinguishing so sharply between the deductive and the probabilistic argument from evil. Historically the distinction is perhaps justified, for the argument from evil has sometimes been formulated as a deductive argument and sometimes as a probabilistic one. But the distinction suggests that every version of the argument from evil is either wholly deductive in character or wholly probabilistic and this is incorrect. The strongest version of the argument contains, in my view, both a probabilistic element and a deductive one. What this version of the

argument sets out to do is to establish in a probabilistic fashion
that some of the evils that exist are superfluous and then
establish deductively that the existence of even one superfluous
evil is logically incompatible with the existence of an omnipotent
and perfectly good God. But since the conclusion of the argument
is a judgment of probability — that it is improbable that all the
evil that exists is compatible with the existence of a theistic
God — the argument as a whole may be deemed to be probabilistic rather than deductive. Let us now consider whether
Plantinga's criticism of the probabilistic argument is sufficient
to undermine it.

His criticism consists of two logically independent objections.
The first is that even if we allow that the evil that exists makes
it improbable that theism is true, it doesn't follow that we
should regard theism as false, for it may be that theism is
probable with respect to something else that we know. There is
good reason for rejecting theism only if the evidence in its
favour is outweighed by the evidence against it, that is, only if
theism is improbable with respect to the relevant body of total
evidence. The probabilistic argument for evil can be successful
therefore only if it is supplemented by a further argument to
the effect that the evidence in favour of theism is outweighed
by the evidence from evil against it. This supplementary
argument would involve an examination of all the arguments
for God's existence and, as Plantinga points out, this 'would be
a substantial and difficult project – one no atheologian has
undertaken so far'.[24]

The logical point that Plantinga is making here is undoubtedly
correct. The probabilistic argument cannot, on its own, hope to
establish anything more than that the existence of a theistic
God is improbable with respect to the evil that exists. But I
believe that Plantinga exaggerates the difficulty of estimating
whether or not the evidence from evil against theism is
outweighed by the evidence in its favour. This task would
involve considering not all the arguments for God's existence,
but only those which, if sound, provide evidence for the view
that a benevolent God exists. And, as we shall see shortly, very
few of the arguments for God's existence fall into that category.

---

24  Plantinga, 'The Probabilistic Argument from Evil', p 3.

However, it might be said in reply that any argument that provides evidence for the existence of a divine being makes the truth of theism more probable and should therefore be taken into account when considering the probability of theism with respect to the relevant body of total evidence. Thus if there is an argument for God's existence that provides evidence for the view that, say, an omnipotent and omniscient being exists and a second argument that provides evidence for the view that an omnipotent and benevolent being exists, then considerations of economy would suggest that it is the same being that is in question in each case, so that both these arguments should be regarded as forming part of the evidence for theism.

This reasoning would indeed be acceptable if the evidence for the existence of a benevolent God outweighs the evidence from evil. But if it is outweighed by the evidence from evil, then arguments that provide some reason for thinking that God exists, but provide no reason for regarding him as benevolent, should be treated as evidence for the existence of a deistic, rather than a theistic, God. They would not then have a bearing on the probabilistic argument from evil, since the conclusion of that argument is compatible with the existence of a God who is indifferent to, or malevolently disposed towards, human beings. Thus Plantinga's first objection can succeed only if a. there is evidence for the existence of a benevolent God; and b. this evidence outweighs the evidence from evil. If condition b is not fulfilled, then considerations of economy should lead us to conclude that either there is no God or that God is, at best, indifferent to the welfare of his creatures.

How many of the arguments for God's existence provide evidence for the view that a benevolent God exists? The cosmological and design arguments clearly do not, since there is no guarantee that a Necessary Being or a Great Designer would be well disposed towards man. The moral argument may appear more promising at first. But this impression is misleading, for even if it were established that what makes an action right is that it is commanded by God and that what makes an action wrong is that it is forbidden by him, it would not follow that God is benevolent. The fact that God issues commands to his creatures is no more a guarantee that he is benevolent than the fact that an earthly ruler issues commands to his subjects is a guarantee that he is not a tyrant.

Robert Adams has attempted to counter this difficulty by stipulating that moral rightness and wrongness are constituted by the commands and prohibitions of a *loving* God.[25] But this gets rid of one difficulty at the expense of creating another, for the commands of a loving God, unlike the commands of a malevolent or indifferent deity, could be largely known hypothetically. It would be possible, in other words, to have a pretty fair idea of what a loving God would command or forbid even if there is no such being. This means that Adams's approach to morality may be regarded as a version of the ideal observer theory and as a consequence it provides no good reason for believing that a loving God exists. Adams's attempt to extricate himself from this difficulty is unconvincing.[26]

The argument from miracles seems no better placed than the moral argument to provide evidence for the existence of a benevolent God. It is true that the miracles that are invoked as evidence for God's existence usually involve acts of benevolence, such as healing the sick or raising the dead. But rescuing a small number from death when one could just as easily have rescued a multitude or healing a few victims of a disease when one could as easily have eliminated the disease itself would not normally be regarded as expressions of benevolence or moral goodness. In any event, the good that is brought about through supposedly miraculous events is insignificant compared to the amount of evil in the world.

The argument from religious experience on the other hand would appear to provide evidence for the existence of a benevolent God, since those who claim to have experienced the presence of God often describe it as an encounter with ineffable goodness and love. But it is not easy to assess the evidential value that should be ascribed to a direct impression of someone's goodness. In human contexts we would be inclined to say that the way in which people behave provides much stronger

---

25  See Robert Adams, 'Moral Arguments for Theistic Belief', in *Rationality and Religious Belief*, ed CF Delaney, South Bend, Indiana 1979, pp 116-40.

26  For a fuller discussion of Adams's reformulation of the moral argument see PJ McGrath, 'Plantinga and the Probabilistic Argument from Evil', *Philosophical Studies* (Ireland), Vol XXXIII (1992), pp 115-7. The entire article (*Philosophical Studies*, pp 113-39) provides a more detailed account and analysis of Plantinga's views on evil.

evidence of their benevolence than does a direct impression of their goodness. This point would appear to be a *fortiori* valid of religious experience, since a very powerful or omnipotent being could readily produce a convincing illusion of goodness. The evidence from religious experience would therefore appear to provide only a flimsy defence against the probabilistic argument from evil.

The only argument for God's existence which, if sound, provides unequivocal support for the existence of a benevolent God is the ontological argument. A God who is lacking in benevolence could not be a maximally perfect being or be 'that than which nothing greater can be conceived'. Moreover, the ontological argument, if sound, establishes that it is a necessary truth that a maximally perfect being exists and therefore the evidence it provides is the strongest possible — evidence that must outweigh any evidence to the contrary that is derived from the existence of evil. But the ontological argument, as we have already seen (chapter 7), is almost certainly irremediably flawed and consequently it cannot be taken seriously as an argument for theism.

Plantinga's first objection then is lacking in substance. The evidence for the existence of a benevolent God appears very slight compared to the evidence against his existence provided by the evil that is present in the world. If theism is improbable with respect to the latter, then it seems safe to conclude that it is improbable with respect to the relevant body of total evidence. But is theism improbable with respect to the evil that exists? This brings us to Plantinga's second objection which is, in essence, that there is no reason for thinking that evil counts as evidence against theism. Plantinga's reasoning here is based on the claim that

the relationship between a pair of propositions A and B when B is evidence for or against A is a relationship that conforms to the calculus of probabilities or is based on a relationship that so conforms.[27]

There are three standard interpretations of the calculus of probabilities — the personalist interpretation, the logical

---

27  Plantinga, 'The Probabilistic Argument from Evil', pp 10-11.

interpretation and the frequentist interpretation — and Plantinga finds that on none of them is it at all plausible to argue that the evil that exists renders the truth of theism improbable.

The reasoning employed by Plantinga to arrive at this conclusion is complex, but we need not examine it in detail here, since his second objection is based on an assumption which is to all appearances false. There is no good reason for thinking that every valid probability claim must conform to the calculus of probabilities and there are ample grounds for rejecting this supposition. If it were correct, then all valid inductive arguments would have to conform to the calculus of probabilities and this seems excluded for two reasons. The first is that the laws of probability are logical laws and are therefore independent of the special character of the world, whereas induction can be usefully employed as a form of inference only if the world fulfils certain conditions which need not be fulfilled in every possible world. The second is that the calculus of probabilities would have no practical significance if it were not possible to establish that certain outcomes are equiprobable. If the outcome of games of chance and the like were readily influenced by, say, prayers or by acts of will, then the calculus of probabilities would be no more than a theoretical construct. How then do we know that certain outcomes are equiprobable? The answer obviously is that in the past the results obtained from tossing coins, rolling dice and so on conformed sufficiently closely to the laws of probability to indicate that the different possible outcomes were approximately equiprobable. This however is equivalent to saying that our knowledge that certain outcomes are approximately equiprobable derives not from the laws of probability, but from evidence supplied by induction; and this in turn implies that inductive inference cannot be explained in terms of the calculus of probabilities. I conclude that Plantinga's attempt to show that the argument from evil is defective ends in failure.

## V  Conclusion

However, a theist could still argue that the argument contains a serious flaw even though Plantinga hasn't quite put his finger on it. This flaw, it might be claimed, is to be found in the probabilistic section of the argument where the conclusion is drawn that one or more of the evils that exist are superfluous. But what is the basis for this conclusion? The only evidence that can be put forward in its support is the negative point that we do not know of any overriding good to which the evil in question is either a logically necessary means or a logical necessary consequence of such a means. And this is scarcely sufficient, since there is no guarantee that if there is such an overriding good, we would have some knowledge of its existence.

This objection raises an issue of some importance, but I think it is incorrect in claiming that the reasoning in the probabilistic section of the argument from evil is based wholly on ignorance. The argument does not say: 'Since nothing is known of an overriding good to which this evil has the required logical relationship, it is probable that there is no such good'. Rather what it says is: 'Since the consequences of this evil are a, b and c and none of these remotely qualify as an overriding good, it is highly improbable that there is an overriding good to which this evil has the required logical relationship'. Consider once again the example of smallpox. Everything we know about smallpox suggests that its only significant consequences are the familiar evils associated with it — illness, death, disfigurement and so on. Since all the evidence indicates then that smallpox is not a means of any kind, never mind a logically necessary means, to an overriding good, nor any kind of consequence of such a means, one may conclude that it is highly probable that smallpox is a superfluous evil.

No doubt it might be suggested that this conclusion is premature in view of the limitations of human knowledge. Perhaps smallpox has consequences of which we know nothing. But few would be tempted to accept this suggestion if the consequences of smallpox or any similar disease were being discussed in a different context. Suppose someone were to offer us an effective means of eliminating some disease roughly comparable to smallpox in terms of its capacity for causing evil — leukaemia, say. Would we hesitate even for a moment to employ it? And if we refused to do so, would we not be universally regarded as either mentally unbalanced or grossly malevolent? Yet these reactions would be quite irrational if there were good reason for doubting that smallpox, leukaemia or any comparable disease is a superfluous evil.

Even if there were some grounds for thinking that smallpox has, after all, a logically necessary causal connection with some overriding good, theism would still be in serious difficulties concerning it or concerning any apparently superfluous evil that has been eliminated by human endeavour. For if smallpox is not a superfluous evil, then its elimination, *ceteris paribus*, left the world a worse place than it was before, since it involved the elimination of an overriding good. This in turn means that the world would be a better place if smallpox were to return. But if this is so, then the absence of smallpox is a superfluous evil. It follows that either smallpox or its absence is a superfluous evil, so that a superfluous evil either has existed or now exists. And either eventuality is incompatible with the existence of a benevolent God.

There is however one loophole in this argument. If the evil consequences of smallpox were exactly balanced by its good consequences,then the world would, *ceteris paribus*, be rendered neither better nor worse than it was before through the elimination or the return of smallpox. If this were the case, then neither smallpox nor its absence would be a superfluous evil. But it must be doubtful if this loophole is of any great help in the defence of theism. The supposition that the good consequences of smallpox are exactly balanced by its evil consequences is extremely improbable granted the enormous number of consequences produced by smallpox since it first appeared over one million years ago. Furthermore if, as seems likely, other apparently superfluous evils are eliminated through human endeavour, the defence of theism requires that the good consequences of all these evils are exactly balanced by their evil consequences. And this supposition is so improbable as to be unworthy of serious consideration.

Some theists might respond to this by accepting that there are superfluous evils, but denying that this has any implications for religious belief on the grounds that belief in a theistic God is based on faith rather than on evidence and is consequently not open to refutation by rational argument. This would be to abandon any hope of reconciling belief in a theistic God with the existence of evil in an attempt to ensure that one's religious belief is beyond the scope of rational criticism. But any such attempt seems certain to fail for the following reason. The claim that one's belief in God is based on faith rather than on reason may be interpreted in one or other of two ways. According to the first interpretation what it means is that one's belief in God, though not supported by reason, is not contrary to it. But the claim that it is not contrary to reason is open to refutation by rational argument, since otherwise it would be meaningless. Thus on the first interpretation the claim that belief in God is based on faith rather than reason does nothing to lessen the significance of the argument from evil. The second interpretation is that belief in a theistic God is simply contrary to reason. But this is the conclusion of the argument from evil. To admit that belief in God is based on faith in this sense is to concede everything that the argument from evil sets out to prove. The argument from evil cannot therefore be regarded as irrelevant to theism. And if theists are unable to show that the argument is defective, they appear to have no option but to accept its conclusion.

# Index